WOMEN OF FAITH IN VICTORIAN CULTURE

Also by Anne Hogan

RESEARCHING CHILDREN'S LITERATURE: A Coming of Age?
(co-editor with N. Broadbent, J. Inkson and M. Miller)

Also by Andrew Bradstock

SAINTS AND SANDINISTAS

RADICAL RELIGION AND POLITICS IN THE ENGLISH
REVOLUTION

FAITH IN THE REVOLUTION

First published in Great Britain 1998 by
MACMILLAN PRESS LTD
Houndmills, Basingstoke, Hampshire RG21 6XS and London
Companies and representatives throughout the world

A catalogue record for this book is available from the British Library.

ISBN 0–333–69455–4

First published in the United States of America 1998 by
ST. MARTIN'S PRESS, INC.,
Scholarly and Reference Division,
175 Fifth Avenue, New York, N.Y. 10010

ISBN 0–312–21217–8

Library of Congress Cataloging-in-Publication Data
Women of faith in Victorian culture : reassessing the angel in the
house / edited by Anne Hogan and Andrew Bradstock.
    p. cm.
Includes bibliographical references and index.
ISBN 0–312–21217–8
  1. English literature—19th century—History and criticism.
2. Christianity and literature—Great Britain—History—19th
century. 3. Women and literature—Great Britain—History—19th
century. 4. Women and religion—Great Britain—History—19th
century. 5. Christian literature, English—History and criticism.
6. Great Britain—History—Victoria, 1837–1901. 7. Angels in
literature. I. Hogan, Anne. II. Bradstock, Andrew.
PR468.R44W6   1997
820.9'352042—dc21   97–38361
                                                                CIP

Selection, editorial matter and Introduction © Anne Hogan and Andrew Bradstock 1998
Chapter 6 © Anne Hogan 1998
Chapters 1–5, 7–14 © Macmillan Press Ltd 1998

This book is printed on paper suitable for recycling and made from fully managed and
sustained forest sources.

10   9   8   7   6   5   4   3   2   1
07   06   05   04   03   02   01   00   99   98

Printed and bound in Great Britain by
Antony Rowe Ltd, Chippenham, Wiltshire

Women of Faith in Victorian Culture

Reassessing the Angel in the House

Edited by

Anne Hogan
Department of English
University of Southampton New College

and

Andrew Bradstock
Department of Theology
University of Southampton New College

For
Caitlin

Contents

viii   *Contents*

Acknowledgements

We would like to thank a number of friends and colleagues who have helped in various ways with the production of this book. The original setting for most of these essays was a symposium held at LSU College (now University of Southampton New College) in June 1995 under the title of 'The Angel in the House', and we would like to thank all those who contributed to its success, particularly our co-organizer Mary Read, our colleagues Peter Barry, Mary Grey, Claire Jowitt and Nicola King, and all who gave papers or attended the sessions. It is as a consequence of their enthusiasm and interest that this book has come to be. We would also like to thank our respective Heads of Department, Andrée Heaton (Theology) and Bernard Tucker (English), for all their help and support while we have been editing the texts; Mary Grey for writing the Preface; Sarah Boss for reading and commenting on a part of the text in draft; and Tim Forsyth for invaluable help and advice on word processing. We also acknowledge our debt to Ruth Willats for her enormous help at the copy editing stage, and to Charmian Hearne, our editor at Macmillan, for all her enthusiasm for the project, sound advice and patient understanding of the pressures of academic life.

We wish to include a special word of thanks to Mary Read, who not only worked tirelessly with us in organizing the original Angel symposium while completing her studies at the college, but also gave invaluable help at an early stage with the preparation and selection of chapters for this volume. We are sorry that she was not able to see the project through to its conclusion, but hope she approves of the way it has turned out.

Finally, Anne would like to thank Peter for his support and interest in the book, and Andrew would like to thank Heather.

Notes on the Contributors

Andrew Bradstock is Senior Lecturer in the Department of Theology, University of Southampton New College, where he teaches church history – including the Victorian period – and political theology. His publications include *Saints and Sandinistas* (1987) and *Faith in the Revolution* (1997).

Susan P. Casteras, who served for nearly 20 years as Curator of Paintings at the Yale Center for British Art, recently moved to Seattle where she now teaches at the University of Washington. The recipient of numerous awards and fellowships, she is the author of more than 50 books, essays and articles on Victorian art, including *Images of Victorian Womanhood in English Art*, *Pre-Raphaelitism in its European Contexts*, *A Struggle for Fame: Victorian Women Artists and Authors*, *The Grosvenor Gallery: A Palace of Art in Victorian England* and *English Pre-Raphaelitism and its Reception in Nineteenth-Century America*. She has also lectured extensively throughout America and England, for example, at the National Gallery of Washington, the Metropolitan Museum of Art and the Tate Gallery.

Carol Marie Engelhardt is a Visiting Assistant Professor of History at Clarion University, Clarion, Pennsylvania. She received her doctorate in 1997 from Indiana University for a thesis on textual representations of the Virgin Mary in Victorian England. She was book review editor for the journal *Victorian Studies*.

Sean Gill is Senior Lecturer and Head of the Department of Theology and Religious Studies in the University of Bristol. His recent publications include *A History of Women and the Church of England from the Eighteenth Century to the Present* (1994) and the edited volume *Religion in Europe: Contemporary Perspectives* (1994).

William Gray is Senior Lecturer in the School of English at University College, Chichester, where he also teaches in the School of Religion and Theology. He has published articles on George MacDonald and C.S. Lewis, which interpret their work in a psychoanalytic perspective, and a book on Lewis for the 'Writers and Their Work' series (1998).

Mary Grey, from 1993 to 1997 Professor of Contemporary Theology at LSU College, Southampton, and formerly Professor of Feminism and Christendom at the Catholic University of Nijmegen, The Netherlands, is scholar-in-residence at Sarum College, Salisbury. Her many publications include *Redeeming the Dream* (1989), *The Wisdom of Fools?* (1993), *Beyond the Dark Night – a Way Forward for the Church* (1997) and *Prophecy and Mysticism: the Heart of the Post-modern Church* (1997). She is co-founder of the charity 'Wells for India'.

Anne Hogan is Senior Lecturer in the Department of English at University of Southampton New College, where she teaches the nineteenth-century novel. She is joint editor of the journal *Primary English* and a co-editor of *Researching Children's Literature: a Coming of Age?* (1994).

Siv Jansson teaches English at several universities in London, including Imperial College, the University of North London, Royal Holloway College and Roehampton Institute. She has completed a doctoral thesis on representations of mothering in the nineteenth-century novel and is currently researching children's literature, fantasy literature and images of Jewish women in nineteenth- and twentieth-century fiction.

Peter Merchant is Senior Lecturer in English at Canterbury Christ Church College, and has research interests that reach back to the eighteenth century. He has written on Paltock's *Peter Wilkins* for *Eighteenth-Century Fiction* (1996), De Tabley's 'Jael' for *Victorian Poetry* (1998) and Dickens's *Great Expectations* for *Dickens Quarterly* and *The Dickensian*.

Sue Morgan is Lecturer in History at University College, Chichester. Her publications include 'Feminist Approaches to the Study of Religion', in P. Connolly (ed.), *Approaches to the Study of Religion* (1998), '"Knights of God": Ellice Hopkins and the White Cross Army, 1883–95', in R.N. Swanson (ed.), *Gender and the Christian Religion, Studies in Church History*, 34 (1998) and entries for Jane Ellice Hopkins and Sarah Robinson in the *New Dictionary of National Biography*.

Terry Phillips lectures in English at Liverpool Hope University College. Her major research interests are in the nineteenth- and twentieth-century novel, and particularly in the relationship of women to modernism. She has recently contributed an article on May Sinclair to *Image and Power*, edited by Sarah Sceats and Gail Cunningham.

Frederick S. Roden has completed a PhD dissertation in the Department of English, New York University on gender and spirituality in Victorian literature. He has published an essay on Catholicism in Wilde, in *Reading Wilde, Querying Spaces* (1995), a chapter on Rossetti's prose theology in *Women's Theology in Nineteenth-Century Britain* (1998) and a comparative study of Rossetti and Hildegard in *Hildegard of Bingen: a Book of Essays* (1998).

Henrietta Twycross-Martin lectured in the English Department of Goldsmith's College, London University from 1973 to 1996, teaching medieval studies and latterly nineteenth-century literature and eighteenth- and nineteenth-century women's writing. Her published work includes 'Woman Supportive or Woman Manipulative? The "Mrs Ellis" Woman', in Clarissa Campbell Orr (ed.), *Wollstonecraft's Daughters: Womanhood in England and France 1780–1920* (1996). She has compiled the CBEL and NDNB entries on Sarah Stickney Ellis and the CBEL entry on Mary Sewell.

J.R. Watson is Professor of English at the University of Durham. He is author of several books on the Romantic and Victorian periods, including *Wordsworth's Vital Soul* (1982), *English Poetry of the Romantic Period 1789–1830* (2nd edition 1992) and *The Poetry of Gerard Manley Hopkins* (1988). He is the editor of *Everyman's Book of Victorian Verse* (1982) and (with Kenneth Trickett) of *A Companion to Hymns and Psalms* (1988), and recently published *The English Hymn* (1997).

Joss West-Burnham is Subject Leader in Cultural Studies at the Manchester Metropolitan University. Her published works include (with C. King, A. Robinson and M. Atkinson) *Through the Glass Ceiling: Effective Management Development for Women* (1993); '"Twinned Pairs of Opposite Extremes": Vita Sackville West's *All Passion Spent* and *Pepita*', in G. Griffin (ed.), *Difference in View: Women and Modernism* (1994); '*The Lady Magazine* 1885 to the Present Day', in S.G. Riley (ed.), *Consumer Magazines of the British Isles* (1993); and short works on George Eliot, Adrienne Rich and other women writers. Her research interests include the relationship between religion, gender and issues of selfhood in the work of nineteenth-century women writers.

Preface

Mary Grey

The Angel in the House as literary motif has exercised its fascination ever since Virginia Woolf singled it out as the reason why women found it impossible to succeed with serious writing: 'It was she who used to come between me and my paper when I was writing reviews. It was she who bothered me and wasted my time and so tormented me that at last I killed her ... She was immensely charming. She was utterly unselfish ... She sacrificed herself daily. If there was chicken, she took the leg; if there was a draught, she sat in it ... above all – I need not say it – *she was pure* ... In those days – the last of Queen Victoria – every house had its angel.'[1]

The uniqueness of this book is that the writers have taken this *leitmotiv* as a challenge to understand the lives of women of faith in Victorian times across a variety of approaches: they explore the Angel in the House across the disciplines of history, literature, religion and cultural studies and show just how difficult it was for women to write against the grain of the cultural stereotypes of purity and obedience. The book originated as a day conference at La Sainte Union College when the excitement of this cross-disciplinary approach was very tangible: the book certainly keeps this energy alive and I believe it makes an important contribution to the understanding of the struggles of Victorian women in the spheres of both religion and literary achievement.

NOTE

1.   Virginia Woolf, 'Professions for Women', a Paper read to The Women's Service League, in Harriet Scott Cheesman (ed.), *Literary Angels* (New York: Ballantine Books, 1994), pp. 136–7.

Introduction

Anne Hogan and Andrew Bradstock

The Victorian feminine ideal of angelic virtue, used originally by Coventry Patmore in his domestic epic *The Angel in the House* (1845–62), embodied sexual purity and a strong sense of Christian morality, placing women in a secondary role to men. Woman's appropriate sphere of influence was seen as domestic, and with this a clear line was drawn between the 'female' values expressed in the well-run Victorian Christian middle-class home and the 'male' public values of a fast-expanding capitalist economy. Yet, while the angelic image remained a defining idea throughout the nineteenth century, Patmore's angel – with its emphasis on women's moral and spiritual superiority – was always a more complex figure than she at first seemed. While in many a Victorian household she undoubtedly was held up, in Virginia Woolf's phrase, as 'the woman that men wished women to be', others found her image a challenging, even emancipating, one; it is this complexity which informs the discussion in this book.

The power of the image – the Angel in the House – is reflected in the great deal of critical attention she continues to attract; has she not by now been done to death, we may ask, and if so, why another book on the theme? Is there still more to be said? Is the angel to be resurrected once again to face a further trial by the critics? Well, yes, since for all the words expended on her, little has been said about the angel's impact on *religious* women – on women of faith, women struggling with faith and women challenged to communicate their faith, whether at home or abroad. What became of the angel when she moved from the home to the pew, the convent or the mission field? What power did she hold over novelists, artists and writers wrestling with issues of women's spirituality in a nineteenth-century setting? How emancipatory, how restricting was her image when seen within the context of Victorian religious life? These are the concerns of this book, which in its 14 distinct but complementary chapters offers a reconsideration of the influence of the angelic imagery on religious heroines as revealed in fictional and non-fictional writings of the Victorian period.

Our study begins with an examination of the responses to the Victorian angelic ideal made by the writers Sarah Stickney Ellis and Anne Brontë. Ellis was the author of several celebrated conduct-books in the 1840s, including *The Women of England* and *The Wives of England*, and is generally cited as a firm supporter of the philosophy of 'separate spheres' for men and women. Henrietta Twycross-Martin, however, shows Ellis's approach to the role and status of the middle-class wife to be rather more problematic; Ellis had a low opinion of most men, and seems to have based her support for separate spheres partly upon the belief that it would give women an independent power-base and help to secure them a status within marriage. Siv Jansson then looks at the way that Anne Brontë in *The Tenant of Wildfell Hall* (1848) and Elizabeth Gaskell in *Ruth* (1853) both replicate and deconstruct the notion of the angel. Jansson focuses on the ways in which these novels portray less than entirely conventional religious heroines as central characters, and shows how such representations can be seen to provide both a reinforcement of aspects of the angelic stereotype and also a critique of Victorian patriarchy.

Anna Kingsford is a less well-known writer from the Victorian period, although she was eventually to become an important figure in the study of comparative religion and especially spiritualism. Peter Merchant explores her novel *Beatrice* (1863) in the light of previous martyrological narratives, and looks, *inter alia*, at how the image of the female martyr was constructed in the middle of the nineteenth century. The theme of Christina Rossetti's novella *Maude* (composed 1849–50 and published posthumously in 1887) is the spiritual crisis of a religious woman writer in the mid-nineteenth century, and Frederick Roden considers the implications of this crisis, which sees Maude torn between feminine duty and spiritual devotion, between the call to be a part of a mundane community and her desire to realize her poetic art. The subject of Joss West-Burnham's chapter, George Eliot's *The Spanish Gypsy* (1868), provides an opportunity to observe something of the response to the Angel in the House of this major Victorian writer and acknowledged agnostic and intellectual.

Two more contrasting responses to the angel are provided in the essays by Anne Hogan and Terry Phillips. Hogan looks at Mrs Humphry Ward, an influential and popular novelist whose work often dealt with religious issues of the day. In discussing her novel *Helbeck of Bannisdale* (1898), in which the sceptical heroine

Laura Fountain is in love with a devout Catholic, Hogan shows how Mrs Ward, a conservative Anglican, reached a position, at the end of the nineteenth century, of cautious admiration for the Roman Catholic position on women, which continued to hold fast to the angelic ideal. The chapter also contrasts the work of Ward with George Moore, who, in his novel *Evelyn Innes* (also 1898), presents the reader with a Catholic heroine who eventually renounces her lover and operatic career for the sake of her faith. Phillips' chapter looks at May Sinclair, another late Victorian writer, and in particular her novels, *The Three Sisters* (1914) *Mary Olivier* (1919) and *A Life and Death of Harriett Frean* (1922). Technically, Sinclair's work falls outside the Victorian period since her major fiction was written between 1914 and 1922; however, as Phillips points out, the central characters of the three novels discussed are fictional representations of products of a Victorian upbringing shared by Sinclair herself. According to Phillips, Sinclair's attitude to the Angel in the House theme contrasts markedly with that of Ward and Moore, since, when taken together, these novels challenge and rewrite the Victorian ideal of womanhood as exemplified by that ideal. Two of the novels recount the Victorian upbringing of the central character and her training for the role of angel, and in *Mary Olivier*, a largely autobiographical novel, the eponymous heroine rejects her conventional religious upbringing and develops her own spiritual insights, aided by her study of philosophy.

William Gray's psychoanalytical reading of George MacDonald's *Lilith* (1895) could be said to explore a male literary response to the Angel in the House. This chapter examines the representation of the female (and specifically the maternal) in George MacDonald's fantasy writing, and the central concern of the novel is shown to be the dilemma of taking leave of the mother or angel in order to achieve an individual identity.

Since we have set out to take an interdisciplinary approach to our theme the scope of this volume is wider than the purely literary, and several contributors explore the lives of Victorian women of faith as portrayed in biographies, obituaries and missionary narratives of the time. J.R. Watson's chapter shows how, with perhaps only one notable exception, women made no serious contribution to popular English hymnody until the nineteenth century, when the work of Cecil Frances Alexander, Charlotte Elliott, Frances Ridley Havergal and others began to sell in edition after edition. Watson argues, however, that their work often reinforced stereotyped ideas about the roles of women (and for that matter children); their hymns extolled the values of submission and meekness, and not infrequently employed such terms as 'Master' to speak of Christ. Linda Wilson next undertakes a close study of selected nonconformist obituaries as they appeared in denominational magazines of the nineteenth century, and discovers that, for some women, their faith was sufficiently strong to challenge contemporary ideas of womanhood, such as the Angel in the House, and might occasionally manifest itself in 'unconventional' behaviour. Wilson also offers a critical evaluation of the usefulness of obituaries as a source of women's religious history.

In her study of nineteenth-century Anglican representations of the Virgin Mary, Carol Marie Engelhardt explores what these representations might tell us about how those who constructed them – Anglican clergymen – and, by extension, the Church of England, understood women in the Victorian period. Engelhardt argues that in an age when women's role as wives, mothers and moral guides was emphasized, the Virgin Mary's maternal role was consistently restricted by Anglicans, even by members of the Oxford Movement. Sean Gill's essay takes us beyond the shores of Britain and examines the women missionaries who went abroad in increasing numbers in the nineteenth century, often undertaking teaching and nursing work under the supervision of denominational committees or Christian charitable organizations in England. Gill explores the image and reality of these missionaries, drawing on biography and popular fiction of the period, and argues that for many women part of the appeal of the mission field lay in the opportunities it afforded them to use their abilities freed from some of the crushing limitations of Victorian society.

Our study ends with two further critical reflections on the power of the angel as the nineteenth century drew to a close. Susan Casteras's chapter reveals how, from the late 1860s through to the early 1880s, the Aesthetic Movement, and one of its key icons, the aesthetic female, posed a unique and revealing threat to the cult of domesticity so prevalent in examples of Victorian art. With her languid pose, intense absorption with art and the beautiful, and disdain for worldly matters (including domestic responsibilities to home and family), the aesthetic female emerged as a potent foe to the Angel in the House. And, in conclusion, Sue Morgan focuses on the movement for social purity which emerged as a real sexual-political force during the last quarter of the nineteenth century, and examines the work of arguably its most influential protagonist, Ellice Hopkins. Morgan reveals how the social purity campaign provides us with an ideal backdrop against which to examine the distinctive character of late nineteenth-century women's religious discourse, particularly with regard to the connection of sexuality and spirituality.

If each individual chapter leaves us with much to ponder, two conclusions in particular might be drawn from the book as a whole. First, that the Angel in the House (or in the church, chapel, convent, mission field or street), rather than simply defining a singular restrictive role and status for women, evoked a variety of responses – some critical and some affirming – which suggests she possessed a complexity which has not always been acknowledged. And second, that if the angel herself is dead, she still continues to haunt us, as she did our Victorian forebears, challenging us to consider again her usefulness for understanding the place, importance and contribution of women of faith in the age which gave her birth.

1

The Drunkard, the Brute and the Paterfamilias: the Temperance Fiction of the Early Victorian Writer Sarah Stickney Ellis

Henrietta Twycross-Martin

With gratitude we ought to acknowledge our belief, that morally and spiritually there is perfect equality between men and women; yet in the character of a noble, enlightened, and truly good man, there is a power and a sublimity so nearly approaching what we believe to be the capacity of angels, that as no feeling can exceed, so no language can describe, the degree of admiration such a character must excite ... if all men were of this description, these pages might be given to the winds. We must suppose, however, for the sake of meeting every case, and especially the most difficult, that there are men occasionally found who are not, strictly speaking, noble, nor highly enlightened, nor altogether good ...

(*The Wives of England*, Sarah Stickney Ellis, 1843)

This opening quotation may come as something of a surprise to those who associate Sarah Stickney Ellis with writings promoting a domestic, supportive and above all subordinate role for women.[1] Male excellence is foregrounded and female excellence is not mentioned; but for the attentive reader the implication remains that if men and women are created morally equal, the man who is not 'altogether good' will be less good than a 'truly good man' *or* a truly good woman. This passage thus neatly exemplifies the complexities that underlie the interplay between 'separate spheres' ideology, gender and serious Christianity[2] in the writings of this early to mid-nineteenth-century writer, best known today for her four conduct-books: *The Women of England, The Daughters of England, The Wives of England* and *The Mothers of England* (published between 1839 and 1843).[3] However, in her own time Sarah Stickney Ellis was more generally known for her varied literary career, her support for total abstinence and as an educationalist who believed that middle-class girls needed training in household management rather than in accomplishments, in which she anticipated Isabella Beeton by more than a decade. As well as writing about the education of girls, Mrs Ellis also put her theories into practice at Rawdon House, a prestigious boarding-school for girls, which she opened in 1845 and which gained some notoriety through being satirized in the pages of *Punch*.[4]

Sarah Stickney was born in Holderness in Yorkshire in 1799 to a Quaker tenant farmer, and had a comfortable middle-class upbring-ing. When her father lost money in the agricultural depression of the 1820s, she used her Quaker connections to launch herself on a literary career, writing on moral topics intended to appeal to respectable Christian families who might normally have reservations about the propriety of reading fiction. Her family had been active in anti-slavery campaigning and her earliest substantial work, *The Negro Slave*,[5] was published in 1830. This led Mary Howitt[6] to put Sarah Stickney in touch with Thomas Pringle, Secretary of the Anti-Slavery Society, through whom she met Thomas Roscoe and Leitch Ritchie, to discuss her plans for publishing *Pictures of Private Life*, a further collection of moral tales, which appeared in 1833. Over the next few years Sarah Stickney established a name for herself as a didactic writer, publishing both poetry and domestic fiction before she married William Ellis, a Congregational clergyman and noted writer on missionary topics, in 1837.

Although Sarah Stickney left the Society of Friends and became a Congregationalist on her marriage to William Ellis, it seems likely that her moral agenda as a writer owed much to her Quaker back-ground: Quakers had always been active in both the anti-slavery and temperance movements, and, like other nonconformists, accepted that in matters of conscience women had autonomy to act on their beliefs. After her marriage, all her works that carry an author's name are attributed to 'Mrs Ellis', and she continued with an active career as a writer of moral and didactic works, both fiction and non-fiction. She also edited and contributed to a range of jour-nals, not all of them primarily didactic,[7] and acted as amanuensis to her husband, helping to prepare for publication accounts of his journeys to Madagascar. Both Mr and Mrs Ellis became staunch proponents of 'total abstinence' temperance,[8] in support of which Mrs Ellis wrote a number of didactic pieces, including *Family Secrets, Or Hints To Those Who Would Make Home Happy*,[9] a three-volume collection of short stories published in 1841 all dealing with the problem of drunkenness in middle-class families. Although, like Mrs Ellis's fiction in general, *Family Secrets* is much less well-known than her conduct-books, there is a very close relationship between *Family Secrets* and *The Wives of England* in particular. *Family Secrets* was written at roughly the same time as *The Wives of England* and, by highlighting women's experience in coping with men who are frequently very far from good, these stories dramatize issues of gender, dominance and submissive support within family life in ways that often relate closely to Mrs Ellis's discussion of gender-relations in that conduct-book.

Although she went on writing into the 1860s, Mrs Ellis's influence was at its height in the 1840s, very much the decade of the 'Woman Question',[10] to which her writings made a significant contribution. Her active literary career following her marriage, which involved a kind of self-marketing as expert on women's domestic role, inevitably meant that her activities were not limited to the domestic role she advocated for other women. Yet all Mrs Ellis's books assert that woman's role is to be found in the home, and, although there were sound commercial reasons for such an emphasis by a woman writer of the 1840s, it seems she believed not only that most women would operate within the domestic sphere, but that most women ought to do so, and in this respect it is fair to consider her a conservative. In other respects, however, in keeping with her Quaker background,[11] Mrs Ellis was more of a liberal, and always, even as early as 1839, supported the idea that unmarried middle-class women ought to be able to work in the family business or outside the home if they needed to, without loss of caste.[12] Nevertheless, in her conduct-books Mrs Ellis is careful, ostensibly at least, to present women as 'relative creatures' existing in and for their menfolk. At the same time she is emphatic that it is the woman's function, particularly the mother's function, to keep a family together and keep it securely Christian: the moral health of the family is in the hands of the women of the family, which is why they must put the needs of their menfolk first, and sacrifice any claim of 'self'.

Yet the picture Mrs Ellis paints of the home is not a reassuring one: both her conduct-books and her fiction focus on the gap between the ideology of patriarchal authority and the lived experience of women coping with men as they actually are. It is this that makes her view of family dynamics both conservative and at the same time surprisingly disenchanted. In all her writings, Mrs Ellis explores the kinds of power women could legitimately obtain and utilize within existing social and legal structures. Hence, while it would be difficult to see her as a radical in any accepted sense, in her various writings she was undoubtedly attempting to define and enhance women's status: she advocated a married woman's domestic autonomy, giving her the 'separate sphere' of household management to run free of husbandly interference, insisted that a woman's moral influence might secure her family and herself, and in her didactic temperance stories provided graphic accounts of women coping, or failing to cope, with potentially disastrous domestic situations, which could include brutal male violence. Not surprisingly, much of her writing comes close to advocating a kind of subversive management of men by women, and these tendencies in her work brought some adverse comment at the time.[13]

When Mrs Ellis was forming her ideas on power-relations within the family, marriage was the only acceptable career for the majority of middle-class girls; but once an early nineteenth-century woman entered marriage she forfeited her independent legal existence. Although many families set up trusts, any property a wife had before marriage became her husband's, unless her family had arranged marriage settlements for her, and any money she inherited or earned during her marriage similarly became her husband's. Short of an Act of Parliament, divorce was impossible to obtain, and a separated woman's property remained her husband's.[14] Children were similarly considered the legal property of the husband, so that if a woman separated from her husband she had no automatic right of access to her children, although this changed in 1839 when the Infant Custody Bill was passed.[15] No wonder that 'slavery' and marriage could be equated; one result of the anti-slavery campaigns of the early part of the century seems to be that women were alerted to the similarities between the married and the enslaved woman, since both were under the legal authority of their 'lord and master'.

Notwithstanding the social and legal subordination of middle-class women within the family and marriage, the belief in the moral equality of the sexes could sanction a role beyond the domestic for women working for charitable causes, although such women often needed to employ a public rhetoric indicating unwillingness to step outside their 'proper sphere'. Rather, the domestic sphere was constantly redefined to include varieties of public or semi-public activities, and it seems that women's work within the anti-slavery campaign was of particular significance. Many women were involved in the anti-slavery campaigns of the early nineteenth century, some became involved in the temperance movement as well, and some also went on to campaign for women's legal and political rights.[16] It seems that for women interested in combining 'good causes' with a literary career, the topics of slavery and of temperance might offer similar advantages, and, like Mrs Ellis, at least some of those who had campaigned against slavery in the 1830s moved on to support temperance in the 1840s. The close conceptual relationship there could be between anti-slavery and temperance propaganda can be illustrated from the work of Clara Lucas Balfour, a noted anti-slavery campaigner who became a temperance activist, and who quoted Mrs Ellis with considerable approval in her own temperance compendium for children, first issued in 1843 as *The Juvenile Abstainer*. The work was revised and reissued in 1853 under the title *Morning Dew Drops*,[17] with an introduction specially commissioned from Harriet Beecher Stowe,[18] the last page of which has a facsimile of Beecher Stowe's signature on a scroll held aloft on the left by an elaborately well-dressed little white girl and on the right by a little negro boy in native costume of a baggy kilt made of skins. The implied 'white sister, black brother' message also suggests a certain middle-class orientation, since the little girl's clothes are emphatically expensive: it is respectable to campaign against slavery. Presumably, whoever commissioned Beecher Stowe's introduction hoped to suggest a similar respectability in teetotal campaigning, which did not command as much middle-class support as anti-slavery had done. In Chapter XVIII of *Morning Dew Drops*, headed 'The Testimony of the Studious', Balfour cites both Mr and Mrs Ellis as temperance supporters, but singles out Mrs Ellis's significance as a high-profile author, before quoting extensively from Mrs Ellis's temperance booklet, *A Voice From The Vintage, On The Force Of Example*:

> Mrs Ellis, the wife of a very valuable missionary, and the authoress of one of the most popular books [*The Women of England*]

that have been written by a lady in the present day, has been a pledged abstainer for many years …. the total abstinence cause is indebted to Mrs Ellis for some excellent writings from her eloquent, truth-telling pen.[19]

In *Family Secrets* Mrs Ellis sometimes associates the rhetoric of enslavement with addiction to alcoholism, and on one occasion gives an account of the speaker at a temperance meeting using such language to influence his audience, while a couple of references in *The Wives of England* also show that Mrs Ellis was well aware of the parallel that could be drawn between the status of wife and slave. In Chapter I, 'Thoughts Before Marriage',[20] she advises a woman to 'think very seriously before she binds herself for life to that worst of all slavery, the fear of a husband', and in Chapter IV, 'Behaviour To Husbands',[21] she distinguishes between a married woman's due rights, and slavery under a tyrant:

> On the other hand, those women who calmly and equitably maintain their rights, for rights all women have, who, acting upon the broad principle of yielding what is due from a wife to a husband, make a clear distinction betwixt that, and what would be expected by a tyrant from his slave … are on the whole to be preferred as companions.

In companionate marriage a woman has a certain status; but marriage to a domineering husband will be slavery. The anti-slavery campaign seems therefore to have supplied a conceptual framework that could be applied to analogous situations, whether enslavement to drink or, in extreme cases, to a husband.[22] Although Mrs Ellis uses such slavery images rarely, and never became a campaigner for women's legal and political rights in the way that some anti-slavery activists did, it is clear that her stress on separate spheres was a way of gaining an autonomous space for women. Her position, however, becomes more ambiguous when she discusses the exercise of a woman's moral autonomy within the family, especially in relation to male failings.

As the opening quotation illustrates, Mrs Ellis believed that men and women were created equal, both morally and spiritually, which implies that in individual cases a woman might well be the moral superior of her husband. As a committed Christian, Mrs Ellis also believed that the question of individual salvation was far more

important than the value system of law and custom which subordinated women. It is not therefore surprising that in her books the
childless Mrs Ellis elevated motherhood into an icon of female
power, for whatever authority the father of a family might have
under law and custom, motherhood, and the Christian and moral
influence of the mother in the domestic setting, was the one thing
that was woman's alone. It is also not surprising that if on one level
Mrs Ellis's conduct-books deal with the serious Christian woman's
moral duties in domestic life, her subtext deals with the covert
power of the woman whose influence might serve to secure her
from ill-treatment within an institution that kept her peculiarly protected but also peculiarly vulnerable to male abuse. For Mrs Ellis,
the devout Christian woman whose menfolk loved her, listened to
her and did not exploit their power was also the personally secure
woman; a woman's moral influence was her prime attribute, which
it was both her duty and her protection to exert in order that patriarchal power in the family might be used benevolently. Mrs Ellis is
also very aware that some men will prove resistant to such
influence; she emphasizes that a woman must think long and hard
about her choice of husband, not least because once married the
wife will still have the duty of uncomplaining service to fulfil, whatever her husband is like.

One result of this rather arid view of gender-relations is that in
many instances Mrs Ellis's writings come very close to promoting
covert manipulation of men, since covert manipulation avoids confrontation, preserves the appearance of womanly submission and
is, of course, for the good of all.[23] Thus an apparently conservative
moral argument about the gendered role of women as domestic
servers not only endowed women with physical space to control
and moral authority to wield, but also licensed a corresponding
acknowledgment of male shortcomings, since the more faulty men
were, the more necessary female influence over them, and the more
justifiable its exertion. Male shortcomings were of course strongly
foregrounded in both the anti-slavery and the temperance campaigns, although usually with a different class emphasis. The brutality of male slave-owners to their slaves is a recurrent theme of
anti-slavery campaigners, with women anti-slavery activists often
highlighting the sexual abuse and disruption of family life experienced by enslaved women and children.[24] The temperance movement also foregrounded male rather than female drunkenness as
leading to violence and family disruption, but while the anti-slavery

campaigns emphasized middle-class men's abuse of slaves, the temperance campaign usually emphasized the problem posed by working-class drinking. As a work of domestic fiction aimed at the religious middle classes in the early 1840s, *Family Secrets* seems to have been unusually graphic in dealing with *middle-class* violence and family disruption caused by alcoholism.

However, other such depictions may have circulated as temperance tracts: a number of temperance narratives were published by J. Wright of Bristol in 1838, under the title *The Temperance Annual, A Collection of Interesting Narratives, Adapted As A Present For The Young.* Of these short stories, one is excerpted from *The Pickwick Papers*, while the rest, with one further exception, are stated to be reprinted from American publications. The exception, *The Drunkard*, is abridged from Mary Russell Mitford's *Stories of American Life*, and this one narrative does deal with a clearly middle-class family: the narrator hideously abuses his wife and children, beating them, forcing drink upon them and finally killing his wife, after which he is incarcerated in a lunatic asylum. It is possible, given the different conditions of American society, that tracts depicting middle-class drunken violence were more common there than in England. The inclusion of such a tale in Mary Mitford's collection may show both her awareness of women's suffering within the apparently secure setting of a middle-class family and her prudential sense that such a topic was better included in stories located 'over there' rather than 'over here'.

Such American tracts, however, may have influenced English writers, and in any case by the late 1850s and the 1860s drunkenness within the middle-class family is a fairly staple theme in domestic fiction. Obvious examples are *Janet's Repentance*, in the collection *Scenes from Clerical Life* (1857), by George Eliot and *Danesbury House* (1860), by Mrs Henry Wood, for which its author won a prize offered by the Scottish Temperance League. What seems to make Mrs Ellis unusual as a writer of domestic fiction is her treatment of alcoholism and violence within the middle-class family as early as 1841. George Eliot had a strong interest in evangelical religion in her girlhood, and in a letter dated 27 October 1840 she discussed Louis Aimé-Martin's *L'éducation des mères de famille* in terms of 'Woman's Mission'.[25] It is possible therefore that *Janet's Repentance* owes something to Mrs Ellis's temperance fiction, since it is set in the 1830s, contains scenes of vicious physical violence and deals with the influence an evangelical minister has on the heroine, who has succumbed to drink because of her husband's habitual ill-treatment when drunk himself. Indeed, there may even be an in-joke to signal this indebtedness; during a discussion of the preaching abilities of rival dissenting ministers, the narrator of *Janet's Repentance* comments drily that 'the Rev. Mr Stickney's gift as a preacher was found to be less striking on a more extended acquaintance.'

Perhaps because Mrs Ellis wrote as a serious Christian, presented women as 'relative creatures' dedicated to their menfolk and never challenged the theoretical basis of patriarchal authority, she was better placed to illustrate abuses of patriarchal power from alcoholism within the middle-class family than other writers of domestic fiction in the early 1840s, who similarly aimed at high print-runs and a broadly conservative, religious audience. While the problems men may cause the women in their families are implicit rather than explicit in Mrs Ellis's conduct-books, such problems are dealt with much more graphically in her temperance fiction. In the latter particularly, textual strategies are often important in presenting potentially disruptive material as inoffensively as possible. There is frequent use of first-person narration by a female speaker, but when third-person narration is used, the narrative voice often suggests a female perspective on events, and constructs a putative female audience which is invited to think about women's moral strategies (loving self-sacrifice, moral influence and trust in God) for coping with problems that are usually caused by men. However, explicit moral censure of men, particularly fathers, is usually mild, while any female dereliction of duty is often strongly emphasized.

While Mrs Ellis's temperance fiction appears to be deliberately designed to warn women of the dangers they may encounter within family life, any overt challenge to the social status quo is tactfully avoided, and the narrative strategies of her texts thus reflect the moral strategies offered for women's guidance within the tales themselves. Nevertheless as a didactic writer Mrs Ellis takes the reader into darker corners of middle-class life and middle-class male psychology than has hitherto been appreciated,[26] in coping with which women have only their serious Christianity and independent moral consciences to aid them. But so armed, they are usually invincible in this world, and by implication invariably so in the next. What emerges most clearly from Mrs Ellis's temperance fiction is that a woman who lacks the fortress of faith and conscience in her

heart is powerless to defend herself and may be overwhelmed by
the consequences of male weakness to temptation. For Mrs Ellis a
woman's conscience provides her with an autonomous power-base
no husband or father can challenge: the paradox is that in her writings God the Father provides strength with which women may save
or resist the earthly paterfamilias in his most enslaved, brutal or
tyrannical manifestations as a drunkard. Mrs Ellis thus deploys the
moral arguments that licensed women's activities within the anti-
slavery or temperance movements within the middle-class family
itself, to the advantage of women as well as men. To an audience
accustomed to think of 'Woman's Mission' as partly at least concerned with a domestic extension into charity work directed to the
less fortunate, whether slaves, drunkards or the poor, the location
of the 'less fortunate' within the middle-class family may have
seemed a slightly surprising inversion, especially when the drunkard in question was identified as a father or a husband.

The title *Family Secrets* obviously implies that something normally
kept concealed within the family is being revealed to a wider circle,
albeit a circle interested in domestic affairs, and no other well-
known writer of the early 1840s seems to have located drunkenness
so firmly as a middle-class problem likely to impinge particularly
harshly on women, whether because they are dealing with men
who become alcoholics, or even become alcoholics themselves
because of male insensitivity or unkindness. In all these stories,
whether the drunkard is male or female, alcoholism is consistently
shown to be an illness brought on by moral weakness, which is
strategically useful since it does not suggest that either male or
female victims are unduly depraved.

It is significant that *Family Secrets* made quite a stir at the time of
publication; an obituary notice of Mrs Ellis published in a local
Hoddesdon paper on her death in 1872 commented: 'Many will
remember the talk occasioned by the publication of "Family
Secrets"', and this is confirmed by a *Sketch of the Literary Career of
Mrs Ellis*, which is prefaced to *The Mother's Mistake*, a novella by Mrs
Ellis probably dating from 1859. The *Sketch*, written in the third
person but undoubtedly by Mrs Ellis herself, says:

> Soon after the *Women of England* appeared, Mrs Ellis commenced
> a series of stories under the title of 'Family Secrets'. These were
> published in monthly numbers, and found a very extensive sale.
> They were written with the view of introducing the subject of

temperance, on which the author was much interested, to a class of readers which at that time the great question of total abstinence had scarcely reached; and for all the repugnance – and it was not a little – which attended both the writing and the first issue of these stories, the author was more than rewarded by the tokens of sympathy which attended their reception in various quarters, as well as by the incalculably large number of copies that were sold.[27]

This may be authorial aggrandizement, but there is a limit to how much a known moral writer can embroider facts, and support for the hint above that writing and publishing these stories brought Mrs Ellis a certain notoriety can be found in the pages of *Punch* for 1847, where Jerrold's series *Capsicum House* is a thinly disguised joke at the expense of Rawdon House School, which Mrs Ellis had opened at Hoddesdon in 1845. Rawdon House was a prestigious finishing-school for girls aged 16 or over, where practical domestic skills formed a prominent part of the curriculum.[28] *Capsicum House* makes great play with jokes about drink and Mrs Ellis: the school rebel provides a recipe for rum punch in which she advises the rum should be poured in blindfold, as 'one can't have too much', and the girls take it in turns to sit up until three in the morning, reading *The Wives of England* and practising how to receive a drunken husband when he returns home late, the proprietress, Miss Griffin, having hired a man specifically to come in pretending to be drunk. The point of this joke is that the girls are honing their skills in reproachful upbraiding, learning how to dominate and control an errant husband, and they even take the pledge among themselves never to have a tipsy husband. All this would be unintelligible to anyone unfamiliar with Mrs Ellis's status as proprietor of a school and noted author of both conduct-books and temperance fiction.

Punch was right to link Mrs Ellis's conduct-books and temperance fiction, since both focus on issues of gender and power, but in *The Wives of England* Mrs Ellis is far from advocating control of a drunken husband by reproof. Instead, in a passage that could have come straight out of *Family Secrets*, she shows male weakness, vulnerability and depravity contrasted with female fear, vulnerability and enduring duty. The passage opens with the wife, waiting for her husband's return:

[she] trims her fire again, and draws her husband's chair beside
the hearth, bethinking her with joyous recollection of some other
little acts of kindness by which she may possibly be able to make
his home look more attractive. But still he comes not; and that
strange sickness of the heart begins again, and creeps along her
frame, until her very fingers ache with anguish … . Another hour,
and still he comes not. Yet hark, it is his step – she flies to meet
him – Let us close a scene for which earth holds no parallel; for
here are mingled, horror, shame, repulsion, and contempt, with a
soft tenderness like that of some sad mother for her idiot child –
joy that the shrouding wings of love once more can shelter him –
bliss that no other eye but her's is there to see – kind yearning
thoughts of care to keep him in his helplessness from every touch
of harm – feelings so gentle, yet so powerful, of a strange glad-
ness to be near him in his degradation – to press the hand which
no one else in the wide world would hold – to kiss the brow
which has no trace of beauty left! And to do this night after night
– to live through all the changes of this scene, through months
and years, only with less of hope and more of anguish and
despair! Such is the picture not exaggerated, for that would be
impossible, of one short portion in the experience of how many
women. We cannot number them. They are to be met with in
society of every grade.[29]

This is a discourse of power, where male authority is dethroned and
female devotion elevated, fused with a Christian discourse of the
passive victim, suffering and serving in order to redeem. The essential context is the religious one, which provides the terms of reference and which at one level reinforces a wife's subservience; but at
the same time the wife is elevated above the husband, whose only
hope of support lies in her. No wonder Mr Punch took refuge in
laughter and in suggestions that girls were being taught a sharply
polarized view of relations between men and women, with the advantage very much to the women.

It is necessary to look in some detail at representative stories from
Family Secrets in order to show how ambivalent Mrs Ellis's gender
constructs are, and how, while lip-service is paid to male supremacy
in terms of family hierarchy and external status, this supremacy
is often construed as essentially theoretical, a paradigm that is kept
in place as much by the woman's determination that it should be

maintained as by any intrinsic male superiority. What often emerges is the paradox that the more flawed the man, the more admirable female adherence to submission, and the more dependent the man becomes on this submission for both status and support. In these stories, a number of Mrs Ellis's women end up with overt power: one message is that dutifully supportive women may gain quite tangible benefits in this world as well as, by implication, in the next. The obvious difficulty in discussing these texts lies in the lack of available reprints, and their consequent unfamiliarity; for this reason four narratives will be given in précis, the first two of which, *The Favourite Child*[30] and *Dangers of Dining Out*,[31] focus on the wife–husband relationship, while the last two, *Somerville Hall*[32] and *Fireside Recollections*,[33] deal with the daughter–father relationship.

On the whole it is fair to say of Mrs Ellis's portrayal of family relationships in *Family Secrets* that although physical brutality may be experienced at the hands of a father, husbands or lovers are more often psychologically cruel or thoughtlessly self-indulgent and insensitive. For example, in *The Favourite Child*, Isabel, used to alcohol for medicinal purposes before marriage, takes to drinking heavily after her marriage because her wealthy but miserly husband married her for her portion and, far from keeping her in the luxury to which her indulgent mother had accustomed her, insists on the bare minimum of household expenditure. Isabel's control of the household keys stands her in good stead, and she takes what she wants by stealth, but while the narrative voice deprecates her doing what she knows her husband would not like, the reader is also encouraged to make every allowance for her unhappy circumstances. Indeed, the narrative voice implies that Isabel's husband is a more than sufficient cause for her drinking, while his failure to treat her addiction as an illness rather than a crime merely adds to her problems. When her husband has a stroke and is reduced to a state of physical helplessness, Isabel is the only one in the family who knows from experience what that feels like, and she can be genuinely useful to him. In a symbolic reversal of roles he now relies on her supporting arm to get out into garden. Finally, she is given complete control over the household and has no desire to drink. The ostensible moral has to do with repentance, Christian development and submission to duty, but the covert one suggests that enslavement within an unhappy marriage may lead to enslavement to drink, whereas a woman who is well-treated, valued for her self and allowed to run her own home in her own way will not become an alcoholic.

Dangers of Dining Out charts the marriage of Frederick Bond, a promising young doctor, who marries Eleanor, a sheltered, well-to-do young woman of good background, who adores her husband, only to suffer a profound shock when he gives his first dinner-party at home and reverts to bachelor behaviour. Eleanor's 16-year-old sister is molested by one of the drunken guests: struggling to escape, the girl's dress is torn from top to bottom and her hair comes down; the dining-room furniture is overturned, the servants look on in contempt and that night, when all have gone home, Eleanor is left with her drunken husband:

> The guests may depart, the servants may retire, but the wife must bear the presence of her husband ... there he lay, inanimate and gross, and she, the subject of indignity and insult, had no-one to defend her – she, his once honoured wife, and mistress of his house, was left to be the plaything of rude men, and the object of pity to her own domestics![34]

So shocked and disillusioned is Eleanor that she cannot speak to her husband about it, and lacking the influence she might have exerted he begins the downward slide into drinking so heavily that his medical practice suffers. Ultimately, having been drunk when he should have operated on a patient, Lady Mornford, Frederick loses his partnership, and he and his family retire in poverty to a country cottage, where he drinks ever more heavily, believing himself responsible for his patient's death. Five years pass; Eleanor and the children undergo countless privations, such as making shirts and eating brown bread and milk out of wooden bowls for breakfast, to provide Frederick, weakened by drink, with the luxuries he needs. Finally, Eleanor decides to investigate the circumstances of Lady Mornford's death, and her discovery that this was not caused by her husband and the shock his family's sacrifices occasion him combine to bring about Frederick's redemption and the family's restoration to respectability, as he entrusts his future to God and to temperance. This tale is clearly intended to warn middle-class young women about a side of life they might know nothing of before marriage and might never have associated with a potential husband; presumably a covert warning about male sexual behaviour is also being conveyed, but tactfully displaced from the actual husband onto the drunken guest. The implication seems to be that, prior to marriage, young men and young women inhabit very different worlds, and once married it is the wife's duty to 'domesticate' her husband, even if this involves an uncomfortable recognition of male weaknesses: far from being protected, the wife may well have to guide and protect her spouse, as much for her sake as for his.

Somerville Hall is unique among these temperance tales in being narrated by a young man, Arthur, who falls in love with the local belle of Yorkshire society, Kate Somerville, a motherless and unconventional girl whose father, the proprietor of Somerville Hall, has taken to drink under the influence of a sinister Mr Fergusson, whom Kate openly loathes. Having been rejected by Kate, who feels she must stay with her father, Arthur goes to India for seven years and on return finds her thin and worn, with Somerville physically and mentally in thrall to Fergusson. When asked whether she has ever tackled her father over his drinking, Kate replies, 'I want the moral courage', pointing out that filial respect makes the topic difficult. Kate again rejects Arthur, knowing that her father has squandered her dowry, and Arthur later hears that Somerville has had a stroke and that Fergusson has decamped, leaving the old man bankrupt. In the moral dénouement, Kate's initial outspoken dislike of Fergusson, which meant her father dismissed her warnings as prejudice, coupled with her failure to confront her father over his drinking, are seen as grave moral faults on her part. Like so many of Mrs Ellis's moral judgements, this appears both arbitrary and severe, but a constant feature of her temperance fiction is the displacement of moral significance from a weak, vicious or unkind man onto the woman, who then has to cope with the consequences of his behaviour. While apparently a narrative device designed to draw attention to the importance of female adherence to duty, this ostentatious lack of censure directed at male weakness has the paradoxical effect of suggesting that family authority would collapse if the same moral standards were applied to men as are applied to women. In the current instance, Somerville survives to live out his life under Kate's care in a humble dwelling, supported by all that remains of their wealth, Kate's own money inherited from her mother's dowry. Roles are thus reversed, and Kate becomes 'a strict, an unflinching monitress', and 'as a parent guards a helpless child, so she watched over him in his weakness.'

In terms of text, subtext and subversion of the one by the other, *Somerville Hall* is a typical example of how Mrs Ellis's temperance fiction often seems to work. On the surface an outspoken and vigorously independent young woman learns to moderate her attitudes and comes to depend humbly upon God as her only support; the narrator, initially a callow, sneering and unpleasant youth, comes to understand and learn from this change in his beloved. However, the story is obviously riddled with paradox. The lack of censure given Somerville's dereliction of duty to Kate compared with that given Kate's failure to reprove him, might suggest to the alert between-the-lines reader that Kate's guilt is emphasized to suggest the serious consequences to *her* of not facing up to her father's drinking problem in time, since she ends up unmarried, supporting both herself and her father out of her own non-patriarchally derived income. Neither the narrator nor Somerville come out well from this story, let alone the villain Fergusson, but Kate emerges humble, chastened and *in loco parentis.*

Fireside Recollections is the last story in the three-volume collection, and here the narrator, this time a woman, similarly sacrifices a chance of marriage to remain and look after a drunken father, whose complete degradation is very explicitly described. The story is startling in the graphic account it gives of family disintegration caused by a mother's death, including a scene in which the father, by now a confirmed alcoholic due to bereavement, deliberately burns a pet dog so fearfully that his young son has to kill it at once to save it further suffering, and a later scene in which the same son is so violently struck by his father that he is permanently lamed and finally dies of his injuries. In spite of her father's brutality, his daughter devotes herself to looking after him, but although he would clearly have died of drink without her care, she is powerless to effect his cure. This narrative demonstrates the social prejudices against which the teetotal movement had to contend, since both the drunkard and his otherwise exemplary daughter regards it as degrading for any middle-class person to associate with teetotallers. However father and daughter finally overcome their prejudices and attend a temperance meeting at which they hear a reformed drunkard speak. The daughter says:

I had never heard anything like it before. I had never heard a human being, called as he had been out of darkness and degradation, inviting his fellow-creatures to break the bondage of custom, and to free themselves from the slavery of a cruel tyrant, who could rule them no longer than they chose to be slaves ...[35]

They both sign the pledge and commit themselves to total abstinence; the daughter looks after her father happily to the end of his days. In this story middle-class prejudice is overcome so that both middle and working classes unite to combat the evils of drink. The daughter saves her father in that her care buys him time, but she learns that her own strength does not suffice: what is needed is the example of others combined with the support of a mass movement, articulated through taking the pledge. In this text Mrs Ellis dramatizes one of the obstacles she faced as a middle-class author writing for a middle-class readership, since there was considerable middle-class prejudice against teetotalism, particularly in the south of England,[36] which *Family Secrets* was presumably intended to help counter.

Since *Family Secrets* is, as its subtitle makes clear, primarily intended to encourage rather than discourage women in the performance of their moral and domestic duties, it is not surprising that most stories end happily, but this is not invariably the case; in one instance a woman ends in an asylum, and in another, a husband proves resistant to his wife's entreaties so that worn down by neglect, she dies; after a penitent interval, he resumes drinking and dies destitute. Since Mrs Ellis was writing *The Wives of England* at roughly the same time as *Family Secrets*, it is not surprising that in the opening chapter of *The Wives of England*, when advising women to think hard before marriage, Mrs Ellis firmly advocates breaking off any engagement formed to a man who drinks heavily, since the wife who is constantly urging restraint on her husband is likely to lose his affections:

> It is one of the greatest misfortunes to which women are liable, that they cannot, consistently with female delicacy, cultivate, before an engagement is made, an acquaintance sufficiently intimate to lead to the discovery of certain facts which would at once decide the point ...[37]

When one looks at novels of the early 1840s, such graphic depictions of male drunkenness and violence within a middle-class family setting are hard to find: the obvious parallels are somewhat later, in *Wuthering Heights* (1847), which has drunkenness, violence and cruelty to a pet dog, and *The Tenant of Wildfell Hall* (1848), which similarly shows drunkenness, violation of family ties and abuse of children. Although there is no record of any of the Brontës reading Mrs Ellis's works, there is a strong argument to be made for Mrs Ellis's influence on these more famous Yorkshire women-writers. Mrs Ellis had a demonstrably high profile in the 1840s, as is shown not only by her conduct-books, but by the stir her temperance fiction made, by Thackeray's and Jerrold's satirical attacks on her in *Punch*, and also by Geraldine Jewsbury's dislike of her ideas,[38] which the latter attacked in her novel *The Half-Sisters*, published in 1848. Since Patrick Brontë co-founded a temperance society at Haworth in 1834,[39] it seems likely that Mrs Ellis might have been familiar reading in the Brontë circle, especially as Branwell was known to be a heavy drinker long before his final descent into incurable alcoholism after his dismissal from Thorpe Green in 1845. It is impossible to tell whether personal experience or literary example most influenced Emily and Anne's depictions of domestic drunkenness, but at the very least Mrs Ellis had opened the way for depictions of middle-class families in which heavy drinking was associated with sometimes extreme physical and psychological violence.[40] Possibly, a more significant debt to Mrs Ellis's writings may be the emphasis Charlotte and Anne place on the autonomous power of the female conscience to combat patriarchal oppression, which is such a feature of *Jane Eyre*, *Villette* and above all *The Tenant of Wildfell Hall*.

The latter novel comes closest to echoing the concerns of Mrs Ellis's temperance fiction, since not only does Helen Huntingdon marry a profligate man who becomes a hopeless alcoholic, but she is an evangelical who enlists God on her side, and claims her conscience as the one area over which her domineering husband has no authority. Having failed to influence Arthur Huntingdon, who in turn attempts to alienate and corrupt their son, Helen's conscience becomes a very powerful weapon in her struggle to emancipate both herself and her child from her husband's power, and since she has this weapon on her side, she is able to leave her husband, take her son and retain her moral status. The voice of conscience here overtly transcends both the law and social custom, as it implicitly, but only implicitly, does throughout Mrs Ellis's writings. At the end of the novel Huntingdon dies, and Helen marries Gilbert

Markham. With some skill the text makes plain that Helen, schooled by suffering, is spiritually superior to Gilbert, whose own mature account of his earlier self demonstrates that when he met Helen he was an egotistical and selfish young man, who yet possessed the redeeming feature that he admired not only Helen's beauty but also her moral qualities. Unlike Huntingdon, Gilbert is thus clearly capable of benefiting from female influence, and by having him relate the story retrospectively after many years of marriage to Helen, the text suggests he has indeed both received and profited from such influence.[41] Thus in many ways *The Tenant of Wildfell Hall* is an extension of lines of thought present in *Family Secrets*, as is perhaps suggested by a similarity in their respective prefaces: in the preface to *Family Secrets*, Mrs Ellis justifies her topic on the grounds of truth, saying:

> If the occupation of writing books were simply an amusement, how pleasant might the task be made, by dwelling only upon popular or pleasing themes – But when the office of the writer is undertaken as a duty, rather than a pleasure … . Human life must then be described, not as it might be, but as it is; in order that truth may be recognized under the garb of fiction; and that error of opinion may thus be traced out to its inevitable consequence – error of conduct.[42]

In the preface to the second edition of *The Tenant of Wildfell Hall*, Anne Brontë similarly justifies her choice of subject-matter, to which she says some readers have objected:

> My object in writing the following pages was not simply to amuse the Reader; neither was it to gratify my own taste, nor yet to ingratiate myself with the Press and the Public: I wished to tell the truth, for truth always conveys its own moral to those who are able to receive it.[43]

Later in the same preface, Anne Brontë's firm defence of her narrative might equally well apply to Mrs Ellis's temperance fiction:

> Oh, reader! If there were less of this delicate concealment of facts, – this whispering, 'Peace, peace, where there is no peace', there would be less of sin and misery to the young of both sexes who are left to wring their bitter knowledge from experience.[44]

In conclusion, then, Mrs Ellis's temperance fiction, as well as her conduct-books, should be looked at in the context of the Woman Question debates of the 1840s, which owed much to women's increasingly public profile in moral campaigning over such issues as slavery. However, it is probably more useful to redefine the debate, for what is being discussed is less a 'woman' question than a 'man and woman' question. Whether one looks at Mrs Ellis's temperance fiction or her conduct-books, the gender-gap becomes of prime importance, constructed as the gap between the gender that has overt power and the gender that does not have such power and usually may not claim it, lest patriarchal authority and the family be undermined. These issues are endemic to the fiction of the 1840s: *Dombey and Son, Jane Eyre, Shirley, The Half-Sisters, Vanity Fair, The Tenant of Wildfell Hall* all attest to this decade's fascination with analysing gender-roles, but in no other writer's works are the paradoxes so openly set out, and in no other writer of the decade, apart from Anne Brontë, is so apparent an agenda for woman-power so clearly expressed or given so firm a religious base. Hence Mrs Ellis's works add their own particular serious Christian perspective to the gender debates of the 1840s by highlighting the gap between the ideology of masculine superiority and female subservience, and the moral status of most men and most women, which in her writings usually allows the moral advantage to the woman. Her temperance fiction shows women negotiating not only the gap between masculine superiority and specific male failings, but also negotiating the gap between the Christian woman's duty to support or save her menfolk at need, and an ideology that insists on women's subservience to patriarchal authority. It is of course only in so far as they are committed Christians that Mrs Ellis's women are licensed to exert moral influence within the patriarchal family at all, but there is no doubt that if the text is evangelical duty towards male relatives, the subtext of her temperance fiction is that duty thus exerted will promote the security and comfort of the woman concerned, and that women have not only the duty but also the right to exert such influence.

NOTES

1. Coventry Patmore's poem 'The Angel In The House' has given its title to a generalized concept of 'woman as domestic angel', often

cited as the typical Victorian view of middle-class women. However, any attempt to apply this concept as it is usually interpreted to the writings of Mrs Ellis shows both how elusive and how reductive it can be, given her interest in women's moral power and consequent potential for the manipulation of men.

2. Although Sarah Stickney Ellis's didactic works always assume that profound Christian belief is the only basis for those wishing to live a good life, she was never narrowly denominational in her outlook and regarded all varieties of Christianity as worthy of respect. In a review of *Shirley*, which is probably by Mrs Ellis and which appeared in a journal edited by her, the treatment of religion in that novel is objected to as follows: 'Genuine religion, under whatever form it may be embraced, is as dear to one man as another' (see Vol. I, p. 37, in *The Morning Call. A Table Book of Literature and Art* Vols. I–V [London: J. Tallis and Son, 1850–2]. An obituary notice that appeared in a Hoddesdon paper on the death of Mrs Ellis noted that 'She began to write fiction at a time when most religious persons thought it a doubtful thing to read it.' The audience at which she aimed her didactic works seems to have been 'most religious persons'.

3. *The Women of England, Their Social Duties and Domestic Habits* (London: Fisher, Son and Co., 1839); *The Daughters of England, Their Position in Society, Character and Responsibilities* (London: Fisher, Son and Co., 1842); *The Wives of England, Their Relative Duties, Domestic Influence, and Social Obligations* (London: Fisher, Son and Co., 1843); *The Mothers of England, Their Influence and Responsibility* (London: Fisher, Son and Co., 1843). For Mrs Ellis's contribution to 'separate spheres' ideology, see L. Davidoff and C. Hall, *Family Fortunes* (London: Hutchinson, 1987), pp. 148–92; also C. Hall, *White, Male and Middle Class* (Cambridge and Oxford, Polity Press, 1992), pp. 75–93. For a view qualifying Hall and Davidoff's arguments, see A. Vickery, 'Historiographical Review: Golden Age to Separate Spheres? A Review of the Categories and Chronology of English Women's History', *The Historical Journal* 36:2 (1993), 383–414.

4. *Capsicum House*, started in *Punch*, Vol. 12, 87.

5. See Clare Midgley, *Women Against Slavery: The British Campaign 1780–1870* (London: Routledge, 1992), p. 94, for reference to a work by a 'female author', cited as *The Negro Slave. A Tale. Addressed to the Women of Great Britain* (London: Harvey and Dalton, 1830). As one of Sarah Stickney's earliest publications, *The Negro Slave* shows that there was a gendered element in her writing from the start of her career.

6. Mary Howitt was an eminent author from a Quaker background, to whom Sarah Stickney wrote for advice when starting her literary career, and from whom she received warm encouragement. It is clear that Quaker networks could provide useful support for women writers. See *The Home Life and Letters of Mrs Ellis edited by her nieces*, p. 49. As well as writing for journals and translating the works of the Swedish domestic novelist Fredricke Bremer, Mary Howitt carried on a literary partnership with her husband William Howitt, and her

career thus has close parallels with that of Mrs Ellis, for whom she may have provided something of a role-model.

7. For example, Mrs Ellis edited Fisher's *Juvenile Scrap Book* between 1840 and 1848.

8. Sarah Stickney may initially have been influenced by her Quaker background to write against the evils of drink in her early collection of moral fiction, *Pictures of Private Life*. One of these moral exempla, 'Marriage As It May Be', although not written as propaganda for total abstinence, does have a husband who becomes a drunkard and thus clearly warns against the dangers of excessive drinking. Although it is clear from *The Home Life and Letters of Mrs Ellis* that neither Sarah Stickney nor her Quaker father were teetotallers, she may have been a supporter of temperance rather than abstinence before her marriage, since the early nineteenth-century temperance movement was particularly active in the north of England, and was enthusiastically supported by many Quakers. After their marriage, both the Reverend and Mrs Ellis became committed to the total abstinence cause. For the distinction between the early nineteenth-century temperance movement that advocated moderation and the later nineteenth-century temperance or teetotal movement that advocated total abstinence, see chapter 1 of Lilian Lewis Shiman, *Crusade Against Drink In Victorian England* (London: Macmillan, 1988). Terminology is confusing, since 'temperance' could cover advocacy either of moderation or of total abstinence.

9. London: Fisher, Son and Co., 1842.

10. See E. Helsinger, R. Sheets and W.Veeder, eds, *The Woman Question: Society and Literature in Britain and America 1837–1883* (Manchester: Manchester University Press, 1983).

11. Quakers tended to support a range of liberal causes such as anti-slavery, temperance, the prevention of cruelty to animals, etc.

12. See *The Mothers Of England*, Chapter XI, 'On The Training of Girls', p. 357.

13. See particularly Geraldine Jewsbury's scathing review of Mrs Ellis's 'Chapters on Wives', in *The Athenaeum* 1707 (14 July 1860).

14. See L. Holcombe, *Wives and Property: Reform of the Married Women's Property Law in Nineteenth-Century England* (Oxford: Martin Robertson, 1983), for a detailed account of the legal position of women in this period.

15. Caroline Norton, granddaughter of the playwright Sheridan, made a notoriously unhappy marriage in 1827 to the Hon. George Chapple Norton, and after separating from him she campaigned for a change in the law to allow her custody of her children. The Infant Custody Bill was the result of her efforts and those who supported her. The Nortons' publicly tempestuous relationship helped draw attention to the legal plight of the unhappily married woman.

16. Midgley, pp. 156–77, points out the relationship there could be between women's work for the anti-slavery movement, for temperance, and in some cases for feminism. She concludes that 'there was an important connection between anti-slavery and feminism in Britain'.

17. *Morning Dew Drops* (London: W. & F.G. Cash, 1853).
18. According to *Home Life and Letters*, in 1856 Mrs Ellis was reading 'another slave story by Mrs Stowe', adding 'It is certainly inferior to "Uncle Tom's Cabin", but I have read it with a good deal of interest and some pleasure.'
19. *A Voice From The Vintage, On The Force Of Example, Addressed To Those Who Think and Feel, by the author of 'The Women of England'* (London: Fisher, Son and Co., 1843). Although most of Mrs Ellis's writings which promote total abstinence date from the 1840s, she returned to this theme in 1855, with the publication by Sampson, Low, and Son, of her short novel *My Brother, or The Man Of Many Friends*, attributed to 'An Old Author'. This had a frontispiece by Cruikshank, whose series of pictures on temperance themes, *The Bottle* and its sequel *The Drunkard's Children*, had appeared in 1847 and 1848. In Cruikshank's series, however, the family devastated by drink is clearly working-class. The sequence of events illustrated in *The Bottle* has close similarities to the plot of Mitford's American story *The Drunkard*, since both husbands kill their wives and end up in lunatic asylums, but the class positioning is different.
20. *The Wives of England*, p. 13. See also Mrs Ellis's article 'Frightened Wives', in *The Morning Call*, Vol. I, pp. 120–6 and 226–30. This article deals very circumspectly, although seriously, with the topic of oppressed wives, and draws specific illustration not from drunken abuse but from a husband's irritation over having the decorators in!
21. *The Wives of England*, pp. 93–4.
22. The association between marriage and slavery may have become current first among American feminists, since there was an early and close link between American abolitionist and feminist activists. Probably the most elaborate and famous nineteenth-century discussion of the relationship between the enslaved and the married state appeared as late as 1869, when John Stuart Mill published *The Subjection of Women*.
23. For an analysis of Mrs Ellis's 'moral manipulation' as an attempt to empower women, and the adverse reaction it provoked from *Punch* writers such as Thackeray, see my article 'Woman supportive or woman manipulative? The "Mrs Ellis" woman', in C. Campbell Orr, ed., *Wollstonecraft's Daughters, Womanhood in England and France 1780–1920* (Manchester: Manchester University Press, 1996).
24. See Midgley, pp. 93–118.
25. Sarah Lewis's *Woman's Mission* (London: J.W. Parker, 1839), was a part-translation and part-adaptation of Aimé-Martin's work. Although Mrs Ellis cannot have known of Sarah Lewis's book when writing *The Women of England*, she had read *Woman's Mission* by the time she wrote *The Mothers of England*. Since Eliot had read Aimé-Martin, it is more than possible that she also read Sarah Lewis and Mrs Ellis.
26. See Davidoff and Hall, pp. 180–5. Mrs Ellis's contribution to domestic ideology is discussed at length, but there is no reference to the way men are presented in her temperance fiction.

27. See 'Sketch of the Literary Career of Mrs Ellis' p. vii, in *The Mother's Mistake* (London: Adams and Gee, 1859).
28. See John Eimeo Ellis, *Life of William Ellis Missionary To The South Seas And To Madagascar* (London: John Murray, 1873), pp. 190–1, for an account of Rawdon House School. He says that the educational aims were 'moral training, the development of character, and some preparation for the domestic duties that would naturally fall to the lot of most girls in after life ...'
29. *The Wives of England*, chapter VII 'Trials of Married Life', pp. 194–5.
30. *Family Secrets* Vol. I (London: Fisher, Son and Co., 1842), pp. 330–431.
31. Ibid., pp. 7–130.
32. Ibid., pp. 192–268.
33. *Family Secrets* Vol. III (London: Fisher, Son and Co., 1842), pp. 281–398.
34. See 'Dangers of Dining Out' in *Family Secrets*, Vol. I, pp. 29–30.
35. See 'Fireside Recollections' in *Family Secrets*, Vol. III, p. 385.
36. L. Shiman, *Crusade against Drink in Victorian England* (London: Macmillan, 1988), pp. 18–29, for an account of the middle-class nature of the earlier 'moderation' temperance movement, compared to the more working-class nature of the teetotal movement launched in 1832. See also Brian Harrison's *Drink and the Victorians: The Temperance Question in England 1815–1872* (London: Faber, 1971) for a very useful account of the early temperance movements. John Eimeo Ellis, p. 179, comments defensively on Mr and Mrs Ellis's support for temperance as follows: 'Both were too clear-sighted and large-hearted to entertain what could justly be called extravagant or extreme opinions, or to sympathize in the illiberal denunciations and ill-judged schemes of many advocates of "Teetotalism"'. But he adds, 'They took an active part in the formation and working of a Temperance Association ...' and details their charitable work with alcoholics.
37. See chapter I of *The Wives of England*, p. 12.
38. See Mrs Alexander Ireland, ed., *Selections from the letters of Geraldine E. Jewsbury to Jane Welsh Carlyle* (London: Longmans, Green, and Co., 1892), pp. 348–9. See also J. Wilkes' introduction to her edition of *The Half-Sisters* (Oxford: Oxford University Press, 1994), p. xiv.
39. See Juliet Barker, *The Brontës* (London: Weidenfeld and Nicolson, 1994), p. 219, and Shiman, p. 48.
40. For the interesting suggestion that Mrs Ellis's name may have provided the first element in Emily Brontë's pseudonym, and for support for the view that Mrs Ellis's fiction writings may have influenced Anne Brontë, see Marianne Thormählen, 'The Brontë Pseudonyms', *English Studies, A Journal of English Language and Literature* 75:3 (1994). See also Thormählen's article 'The Villain of "Wildfell Hall": Aspects and Prospects of Arthur Huntingdon', in *The Modern Language Review* 88:4 (1993), 834–6, for Anne Brontë's possible indebtedness to medical authorities on alcoholism.
41. For a rather different interpretation of *The Tenant Of Wildfell Hall*, see Siv Jansson, 'The Tenant of Wildfell Hall: Rejecting the Angel's Influence', in this volume. Certainly Anne Brontë would have needed to look no further than Mrs Ellis to find a writer very well

aware of the possible consequences for women who married men
resistant to moral influence.

42. See Preface in *Family Secrets*, Vol. I, p. 5.

43. See Anne Brontë 'Preface to the Second Edition', *The Tenant of Wildfell Hall* (London: Thomas Newby, 2nd edn, 1848).

44. Ibid.

2

The Tenant of Wildfell Hall: Rejecting the Angel's Influence

Siv Jansson

The ideology of the Angel in the House is a part of the iconography of the nineteenth century. Coventry Patmore's phrase provided a name for the ideal, all-encompassing image of Victorian woman-hood which combined the perfection of purity, spirituality, love and beauty. The angel has, however, also come to represent submission, immobility and confinement: and, as Nina Auerbach has pointed out,[1] contains within its phraseology a conflicting and problematic schism between the real and the ideal. The cult of the angel was constructed and fortified from many sources: artistic representa-tions, pamphlets, articles, magazines, advice and conduct manuals, letters and autobiography. Fiction played a part in this process; the vast majority of fiction produced in the nineteenth century sup-ported, to a greater or lesser extent, the myth of the angel. Charlotte Yonge, for example, has a clearly didactic purpose in her work, which is primarily to maintain the status quo (although Yonge's work merits a deeper reading than this). However, other women novelists took a position, whether conscious or unconscious, with regard to the image of the angel: some in an elided or subterranean way, such as George Eliot; others, such as Elizabeth Gaskell and Anne Brontë, in a more directly confrontational and combative form.

In *Ruth* and *The Tenant Of Wildfell Hall*, for example, both writers engage with the image which was subsequently given the name the angel in the House; they employ a similar language, though with differing results, to explore the problematic conflicts at the centre of the image, and to take issue with the possibility of such an ideal woman's existence, or indeed with the right of society to expect

31

such an impossible standard. They use images of religious women as a ploy to write into their texts their own radical reassessments of the dominant culture, and, although retaining some ambivalence in their own position, both novels can be described as rebellious texts, which disclose and enclose a questioning subtext, whose purpose is to confront the ideals by which they themselves would have been judged.

Each novel centres on an extreme transgression against the angelic image: in *Ruth*, a seduction and the birth of an illegitimate child, in *Tenant*, Helen Huntingdon's abandonment of her husband. Both heroines re-enter society and are 'redeemed' for their 'sins' against it, and both operate as redeemers themselves: Ruth by becoming the saviour of her community, and Helen by her attempted, though unsuccessful, redemption of Arthur Huntingdon. However, there are differences of view and tone and variations of emphasis, within these basic similarities: Helen Huntingdon is a much harsher, more vengeful angel than Ruth Hilton, and this is supported by Anne Brontë's refusal of the martyr ending which Gaskell confers on Ruth. Brontë's novel is more intimately concerned with Helen's horrific marriage as the reason for her transgression, whereas Gaskell focuses more on Ruth's innocence and ignorance as the foundation of her fall. However, both writers employ the image and language of the Angel in the House as a methodology for questioning and undermining its veracity, and the shock with which both novels were received by a Victorian reading public suggests the penetration of such questioning.

One of the most crucial issues for Victorian women, and one which is confronted in different ways in these novels, is the question of 'influence'. Conduct-books and advice texts are riddled with references to 'woman's influence' and its centrality in giving the nation a high moral tone. The authors treat this issue in different ways, but both find methods of questioning the nature and effect of woman's influence: Anne Brontë by arguing that a woman has virtually no influence at all, beyond that which a husband or lover chooses to grant her, Elizabeth Gaskell by suggesting that the worth and power of female influence was not automatically connected to moral standing, as was assumed by Victorian society. Helen Huntingdon is a 'good' woman whose faith and virtue are power-less in the face of her husband's degeneracy, while Ruth Hilton is a 'bad' woman who becomes the most positive force for 'good' in her community. Both novels assess the question of 'influence'; Anne

Brontë apparently approves Helen's attempts at redeeming Arthur, although demonstrating their fruitlessness, while Gaskell allows Ruth to redeem herself in a thoroughly conventional and acceptable manner, while at the same time undermining the conventions of sin and redemption in Victorian morality. Both novels speak clearly in the language of redemption, and forgiveness of sin, but the question posed is, where – and with whom – does the real 'sin' lie?

Of the two novels, however, Anne Brontë's *The Tenant Of Wildfell Hall* is the most obviously subversive text. In her Preface, Brontë writes of her determination to deal with the 'truth' in her story, though what that truth is, is not specified, only emerging through the novel. In fact, several truths are inscribed in *Tenant*: the truth of the ignorance in which young girls are raised, and the inadequacy of the information upon which they base marriage choices; the truth of the power relations between the sexes; and, finally, the ineffectuality of 'woman's influence', that mysterious and nebulous power to which so much was ascribed and by which so little is achieved, at least in this novel.

Anne Brontë's own religious beliefs centred on a liberal doctrine of eternal love and the possibility of salvation for even the most unregenerate sinner.[2] Her novel is both a tribute to this possibility and an acknowledgement of its potential ineffectuality, particularly because of the social, moral and economic constraints surrounding the woman as saviour, which rendered her ultimately powerless to effect the redemption which was a part of her sacred duty and trust. The most immediately noticeable, and paradoxically revealing, aspect of *Tenant* is the 'concealed' form of its telling. Although Anne Brontë employs the same layered narrative technique as Emily Brontë in *Wuthering Heights*, her use of letters and journals is a method which conveys Helen's story as concealed, hidden from public narrative or hearing. Nelly Dean speaks the story of Catherine and Heathcliff: Gilbert Markham, as Helen's narrator, is reading it, or writing it. This is because Helen's is a story which *cannot* be spoken; it is a story of degradation, of failure, and Anne Brontë, keenly aware of the shocking nature of her subject-matter, was determined to convey to her readers both the injustice that Helen, as Arthur's wife, is implicated in his degradation, and the subversive notion that she is forced to fail him as an Angel in the House because he fails her as a husband. Why Markham chooses to communicate Helen's story to his friend Halford, who never

appears in the novel and about whom we know nothing, is unsatis-
factorily explained: the reference to Halford having told Markham
'a very particular and interesting account of the most remarkable
occurrences of your early life'[3] is hardly convincing. This is, first of
all, not Markham's story but Helen's, and she tells him through the
medium of her journal, because her story cannot be spoken.
Gilbert's action, therefore, is doubly suspect: this is a secret story,
not meant to be communicated, yet it is being communicated, not
only to Halford but to many other readers. This narrative form has a
very specific function, therefore: namely, to disclose the story and
make public its degrading nature, while utilising it as an example of
purity and piety.

The story proper is told in retrospect, beginning with Markham's
meeting with Helen Huntingdon, *née* Graham, the mysterious
'tenant', mother of a young son, a curious, bitter and angry woman
who, when she begins to understand the measure of Gilbert's feelings for her and to reciprocate them, gives him her journal as an
account of her life. The giving of the journal is a further indication
of the secrecy of the story, her inability to verbalize it and its shame-
ful nature:

> She did not speak, but flew to her desk, and snatching thence
> what seemed a thick album or manuscript volume, hastily tore
> away a few leaves from the end, and thrust the rest into my
> hand, saying, 'You needn't read it all; but take it home with you,'
> – and hurried from the room. But when I had left the house, and
> was proceeding down the walk, she opened the window and
> called me back. It was only to say, – 'Bring it back when you have
> read it; and don't breathe a word of what it tells you to any living
> being – I trust to your honour'.[4]

The wish to prohibit communication and the inability to communicate exist even when she is giving Markham the opportunity to
read her story. The haste and nervousness in her behaviour reveal
both a sense of shame and an eagerness to give: she 'flew' to her
desk, 'snatching' at her volume, 'hastily' tore out pages, 'thrust' the
rest at Markham and 'hurried' from the room. What were the pages
she tore out? We are never enlightened. The secretive nature of the
story is inscribed within these acts of concealment.

So what is the necessity behind this? We learn now how Helen
Graham is a motherless girl raised by her aunt and uncle. Wilful,

pious and with an unshakeable faith in her own judgement, she meets Arthur Huntingdon at a ball and is immediately attracted to and troubled by him. Helen's first impressions of Arthur indicate what, to the reader, becomes only too apparent, long before Helen establishes his character:

> There was a certain graceful ease and freedom about all he said and did ... There might be, it is true, a little too much careless boldness in his manner and address, but I was in so good a humour, and so grateful for my late deliverance from Mr Boarham, that it did not anger me.[5]

Brontë has foregrounded the meeting with Arthur in a conversation just prior to the ball, between Helen and her aunt, which is full of warnings and admonishment:

> 'I want to warn you, Helen ... and to exhort you to be watchful and circumspect from the very commencement of your career, and not to suffer your heart to be stolen from you by the first foolish or unprincipled person that covets the possession of it.'[6]

Not only her aunt's words, but the evidence of her own experience in the early stages of her relationship with Arthur, suggest to Helen that he is not what he seems. But it remains her conviction that the worth of her piety and good influence are what Arthur needs: indeed, that it is her 'mission' to be his 'angel'. Helen is consistently identified as an 'angel', both in the language of the text (her ability to quote the Bible at will is one example of this) and by Arthur himself, in phrases like 'sweet angel'[7] and 'I know she is an angel'.[8] Her aunt's words about Arthur, that he is 'a bit wildish', which she defines as 'destitute of principle, and prone to every vice that is common to youth',[9] fail in sufficiently warning Helen of the true nature of what she is undertaking; first, because she believes herself to be a good judge of character and therefore that she understands Arthur's faults, and second, and more significantly, because it reinforces her sense of her 'mission' as a reforming 'angel' in Arthur's life:

> 'Do you imagine your merry, thoughtless profligate would allow himself to be guided by a young girl like you?'
> 'No; I should not wish to guide him; but I think I might have influence sufficient to save him from some errors, and I should

think my life well spent in the effort to preserve so noble a nature from destruction ... sometimes he says that if he had me always by his side he should never do or say a wicked thing, and that a little daily talk with me would make him quite a saint. It may be partly jest and partly flattery, but still –'
'But still you think it may be truth?'[10]

This conversation is a crucial episode, establishing both the focus of the novel and Helen's absolute conviction that, whatever Arthur may be now, being confronted by her love and moral worth on a daily basis will 'influence' him to become a good man. The fact that Arthur is playing this role precisely for the purposes of seduction is apparent both to Helen's aunt and to the reader, and discloses the trap into which Helen is walking, but the language of redemption becomes stronger as the passage continues. Helen states, 'if I hate the sins, I love the sinner, and would do much for his salvation', and 'I shall consider my life well spent in saving him from the consequences of his early errors, and striving to recall him to the path of virtue – God grant me success![11] These are almost the words of a preacher, rather than a woman in love, yet Helen is, apparently, fulfilling her role as potential domestic angel to perfection. She is intending to utilize good intentions and virtuous love, not to 'guide' Arthur (which would suggest too much dominance) but to 'influence' him: she is placing his happiness before her own, is willing, at this time, to make any necessary sacrifices, forgive any sins already committed, and call on God to aid her in becoming his 'angel'. With such firm commitment to her correct role, and such eagerness and energy to carry it out, Helen must, surely, achieve some measure of success.

But Helen fails – dismally. Brontë's account of her marriage to Arthur is one of the most savage indictments of both the legal and economic constraints which supported Victorian marriage, and the mythical ideology which deceives Helen into it. Maria H. Frawley has analysed the way in which the language of 'angelicness' is used by Arthur to entrap Helen and convince her that she will act as his redeemer:

it is important to note his means of attracting her – his use of language that appeals to her desire to function as a saviour – and the power that he maintains over her because of this language.[12]

Brontë states, without equivocation, that the Angel in the House may exist, but her worth and influence are meaningless and succeed only in deceiving young women into marriage. Helen has been warned by her aunt: 'Oh, Helen, Helen! You little know the misery of uniting your fortunes to such a man!'[13] but Helen ties herself for life to a man who is a drunkard, a liar, immoral, cruel, violent and weak. There are some similarities between Helen's conversations with her aunt, and Nelly Dean's questioning of Catherine Earnshaw on why she wants to marry Edgar Linton: the older woman, with some knowledge of the actuality of Victorian marriage (even without, in Nelly's case, any experience of it) tries to disclose its power structure to the younger woman. Both try to awake their auditors to the fact that once the choice is made, it cannot be changed, that the reasons for the choice must be sound, not romanticized or mythologized, and that, although the woman may hold the balance of power during courtship, that changes once marriage has taken place:

'How so, my dear? is Mr. Huntingdon a good man?'
'He is a much better man than you think him.'
'That is nothing to the purpose. Is he a good man?'
'Yes – in some respects. He has a good disposition.'
'Is he a man of principle?'
'Perhaps not, exactly; but it is only for want of thought: if he had someone to advise him, and remind him of what is right –'[14]

'Why do you love him, Miss Cathy?'
'Nonsense, I do – that's sufficient.'
'By no means; you must say why.'
'Well, because he is handsome, and pleasant to be with.'
'Bad,' was my commentary.
'And because he is young and cheerful.'
'Bad, still.'
'And because he loves me.'
'Indifferent, coming there.'[15]

Nelly's later comment that Catherine will find Edgar 'not so pliable as you calculate upon'[16] is a more explicit warning of reality, upon which, as Nelly rightly guesses, Catherine has not calculated. Similarly, Helen's aunt queries her belief that she is able to become the reforming angel of Arthur's life, pointing out that Arthur is ten years older and asking Helen 'how is it that you are so beforehand in moral acquirements':[17] the subtext of her question is that Arthur, as male, older and more experienced, will be even more immune to her 'influence' and that she will have only so much power as he 'allows' her which is, as it turns out, no power at all.

The progressive deterioration of the marriage is an explicit demonstration of everything Helen has been warned about, and everything that Brontë intends to criticize. As Catherine Earnshaw's inability to restore her original relationship with Heathcliff is a disclosure of Edgar's authority, so Helen's eyes are gradually prised open to the reality of Arthur's power over her. She increasingly comes to know her husband, and her illusions about both him and herself are destroyed. Brontë manages the deterioration very well: through numerous revealing episodes Helen struggles to maintain, not only her image of Arthur, but, more crucially, her image of her role in his life. At the beginning of Chapter 23, Helen is newly married and already realizing the mistake she has made; but declares in her journal that 'my duty, now, is plainly to love him and to cleave to him'.[18] Brontë describes her continual attempts to communicate to her husband her disapproval of his behaviour, her desire that he should be better and the worth of her own good example; but never, at any time in their relationship, does she have more influence than Arthur permits her. Early in the marriage, he criticizes her for being too religious, stating that 'a woman's religion ought not to lessen her devotion to her earthly lord'[19] – a notion perfectly in keeping with Victorian ideology, which, for all its emphasis on female piety, was ambivalent about the notion of women placing faith before family and domestic duties. The angel must be religious, but not too religious; which parallels the notion that she can have influence, but not power.

As Brontë develops this theme, Arthur's behaviour worsens and Helen's actual and moral powerlessness become increasingly evident, culminating in Arthur's adulterous liaison with Lady Lowborough, which is conducted virtually under Helen's eyes, and his refusal to allow Helen to separate from him. Furthermore, he remains oblivious to all sense of guilt and still believes that Helen's outrage springs from jealousy, rather than from disgust. It is here that Brontë's careful construction of Helen's angelic image and determined redemptive posture has its greatest power: at the beginning of Chapter 34 she declares 'I HATE him!', and in Chapter 36 she states, 'he may drink himself dead, but it is NOT my fault!'[20]

Such forceful pronouncements are a refusal of the role of the Angel in the House, but what gives Brontë's novel its power and its radicalism is that Helen has tried to play the role absolutely correctly; and Brontë shows that, whatever her determination, she cannot redeem her husband, because he refuses to allow it. The angel may be perfect, but she has no influence; and Brontë argues that Helen's disgust with her husband is justified, rather than something to be condemned, because she has not failed him as a wife: he has failed her as a husband. This is an absolute subversion of the angelic image, which stated unequivocally that fulfilment of the angelic role would inevitably yield influence over a husband and make him better. If this didn't occur, it was specifically the failure of the wife, not the husband.

Brontë is a little more ambivalent when it comes to the question of Helen's implication, as Arthur's wife, in his degradation; although she allows Helen to leave him (which no doubt shocked Victorian readers more than any of Arthur's actions towards Helen) the concealed and secretive way in which Helen 'tells' her story suggests that she does have feelings of shame and failure over both her misguided decision to marry Arthur and her inability to have any effect on him. Although Helen declares that it is not her failure, nevertheless Brontë does not entirely deny Helen's implication in Arthur's degeneration, without necessarily ascribing any blame to her:

'Don't you know that you are a part of myself? And do you think you can injure and degrade yourself, and I not feel it?'[21]

The other way in which Brontë subverts the angelic image is by disclosing the opposition between Helen's role as good wife and her role as good mother. She aligns Helen decisively with conventional Victorian images of motherhood in a passage at the beginning of Chapter 28:

when I clasp my little darling to my breast ... one of two thoughts is ever at hand to check my swelling bliss; the one: 'He may be taken from me'; the other: 'He may live to curse his own existence.' In the first, I have this consolation: that the bud, though plucked, would not be withered, only transplanted to a fitter soil to ripen and blow beneath a brighter sun ... he would be snatched away from all the suffering and sins of earth ...[22]

This is a clever strategy, since Brontë is placing Helen beyond re-
proach as a Victorian parent to foreground her decision to leave
Arthur as the only method of protecting her son. This is crucial to
Brontë's intent, since never, at any point, does she question Helen's
status as an Angel in the House: she wants to show that the role
itself is inadequate, contradictory, founded on myth and subject to
conflicting moral imperatives. Brontë poses the question explicitly:
if Helen is a true angel, she will stay with her husband and continue her endeavours to effect his reform. Her duty is to remain by
his side, whatever his treatment of her. But if she does this, she will
be permitting Arthur to corrupt his son and mould him in his own
image. Young Arthur is very quickly under the influence of his
father, rather than his mother, and is encouraged to drink, gamble
and treat Helen with disrespect:

> My greatest source of uneasiness, in this time of trial, was my son,
> whom his father and his father's friends delighted to encourage
> in all the embryo vices a little child can show, and to instruct in all
> the evil habits he could acquire – in a word, to 'make a man of
> him' was one of their staple amusements ...[23]

Apart from the questions this passage provokes concerning
definitions of masculinity, it reminds us that one of the issues Anne
Brontë confronts in *The Tenant Of Wildfell Hall* is Victorian beliefs
about raising children. Marion Shaw has discussed the author's
attitudes on this subject,[24] but there is a further level at which
Brontë particularly targets the education of sons. She argues that, in
addition to women having no influence over husbands, they have
no influence on sons. Nineteenth-century advice manuals and
conduct-books are extremely ambivalent regarding the mothering
of sons: they necessarily have to assume an 'influence' on sons,
because a part of the angel's identity resides in her moral effect on
the male population, but also stress that this influence must not be
too profound, otherwise it threatens the development of 'normal'
masculinity. While no one would deny that mothers do have an
influence on sons (though not necessarily the influence that the
writers of conduct-books desired) Brontë wants to emphasize, as a
part of her general project, that young Arthur will inevitably cleave
more to his father than to his mother. As it becomes a part of
Helen's angelic duty to counteract this, her only option is to remove
young Arthur from his father's house, which is a rather equivocal

victory. Brontë stresses the rejection of feminine influence when young Arthur becomes increasingly attached to Gilbert Markham as the novel progresses, something which Helen feels she must ob- struct. This may seem like the normal need of a young boy for a father-figure, but because of the nature of his biological father, Helen's paranoia is extreme, and understandable.

Part of the imperative behind Helen's mothering is her knowledge that the elder Arthur's mother was hopelessly over-indulgent to her son, and it is to this she ascribes Arthur's defects. This implies a contradictory position, since it suggests that mothers do have a pro- found influence on sons, while Helen's experience is designed to suggest the opposite: but Helen's position and the author's position are what is contradictory. Helen seeks to find reasons for Arthur's behaviour that do not stem from his own weak character; blaming his parenting is therefore a way to divert blame from him, and hope that with good influence, he can be redeemed. Anne Brontë's atti- tude is very clearly that no such redemption can be effected, and that it is a part of the illusion of the Angel in the House.

Helen's return to nurse Arthur in his illness operates, however, as an act of redemption for her, for leaving him and thereby abandon- ing her role, whilst also allowing her to adopt the guise of avenging and self-righteous angel, instead of ineffectual and victimized one. Brontë is fully aware of the full significance of Helen's act in leaving her marriage, and her return to Arthur is both a reinforcement and reassessment of the angelic role she has transgressed. Helen does not make the ultimate sacrifice like Ruth Hilton, but she risks her son's welfare by returning to Arthur, even a physically weakened Arthur, because his rights as father and husband are not weakened. This is another clash between the angel as wife and the angel as mother, since it is perfectly appropriate for Helen to return to Arthur to save him, but questionable mothering since it exposes her son to Arthur's influence again. Arthur is weaker, both physically and mentally, and even has some spurious superstitious fears con- cerning his impending death and his fate after it, but it is significant that Brontë does not have Arthur repent. There are no death-bed recantations; Arthur is irredeemably bad and weak, and, like George Eliot's Hetty Sorrel, is only interested in heavenly assistance if it can save him from his fate. Helen's language has adopted an interesting tone in these scenes, as the submissive angel becomes the avenging angel, the *enforcer* of constriction and confinement, rather than the subject of them:

I watch and restrain him as well as I can, and often get bitterly abused for my rigid severity; and sometimes he contrives to elude my vigilance, and sometimes acts in open opposition to my will. But he is now so completely reconciled to my attendance in general that he is never satisfied when I am not by his side. I am obliged to be a little stiff with him sometimes, or he would make a complete slave of me; and I know it would be unpardonable weakness to give up all other interests for him. I have the servants to overlook and my little Arthur to attend to, – and my own health too, all of which would be entirely neglected were I to satisfy his exorbitant demands … my patient makes no scruple of calling me up at any hour when his wants or his fancies require my presence. But he is manifestly afraid of my displeasure; and if at one time he tries my patience by his unreasonable exactions, and fretful complaints and reproaches, he depresses me by his abject submission and deprecatory self-abasement when he fears he has gone too far.[25]

This passage suggests, first of all, that Helen's instinct for self-sacrifice remains intact, and that she is restrained from becoming Arthur's slave only because it would be 'unpardonable weakness'. But, crucially, it is Helen's *choice* not to be his slave, as it was her choice to leave him: she is empowered by her desertion of him, rather than weakened by it. Other concerns have a claim on her, concerns which conflict with Arthur's 'exorbitant demands' – such as her son. The schism between angelic wife and angelic mother is thus demonstrated here. Furthermore, Anne Brontë's revisionary reinterpretation allows Helen to occupy the higher moral ground because she has left her husband, rather than because she remained with him. Helen tells Arthur 'you may judge of what I will do – if it be not incompatible with the higher duty I owe to my son (higher, because he has never forfeited his claims, and because I hope to do more good to him than I can ever do to you)'.[26] Instead of supporting the received ideology by condemning Helen for her action, Brontë empowers her actually and spiritually by breaking the angelic mould, while still describing a truly angelic role in her nursing of Arthur and her attempts to redeem him. Brontë argues that Helen is a true 'angel' in putting the welfare of her son first, while simultaneously attempting to save her husband's soul, and that the demand of the conventional 'angel' role, that Helen should have stayed with Arthur, would have forced her to collude in the corruption of her son. By asserting her 'higher duty' to young Arthur, Anne Brontë demonstrates both the inherent divisions within the conventional angel image and offers an alternative which she defines as truly angelic. The character of the avenging angel is further clarified in the following exchange which Helen describes between herself and Arthur:

'I am willing to do anything I can to relieve you.'

'Yes, now, my immaculate angel; but when once you have secured your reward, and find yourself safe in heaven, and me howling in hell-fire, catch you lifting a finger to serve me then! – No, you'll look complacently on, and not so much as dip the tip of your finger in water to cool my tongue!'

'If so, it will be because of the great gulf over which I cannot pass; and if I could look complacently on in such a case, it would be only from the assurance that you were being purified from your sins, and fitted to enjoy the happiness I felt ...'[27]

The avenging angel does not lack compassion: when Arthur cries 'Helen, you must save me!'[28] it reduces Helen to tears, but Arthur's self-destruction is presented as entirely his fault, and not a result of Helen's 'failure'. The refusal to assert that she would rescue Arthur from hell is a categorical statement that, having brought himself to this condition, the road to redemption is finally his responsibility. Not only does Helen still occupy the higher moral ground, but she is not obliged to help Arthur – thereby re-emphasizing Helen's choice of the role of avenging angel. Anne Brontë's vision of the Angel in the House may be presented in recognizable and familiar language, the language of patriarchal Victorianism, but she empowers Helen within the confines of 'angelic' ideology. Helen is not a rebel, in that she attempts very conscientiously to become an 'angel', and remains identified with that image throughout the book; Brontë simply redefines the image. The novel is therefore radical on two levels: it demonstrates the problematic nature of the angel role, and also reassesses the requirements of 'angelicness', offering an alternative definition which rests on courage, integrity and piety rather than simple submission. The public construction of the Angel in the House insisted on these qualities as part of its requirements, but Brontë's re-vision suggests that it is the exhibition of these very qualities which may require the 'angel' to behave in an 'unangelic' way. Throughout the novel, Brontë has reiterated

Helen's sexual purity: she refuses the opportunity to escape with Hargrave, while forcing herself to tolerate her husband's infidelity, and therefore Helen's angelic image is never compromised by any act other than the leaving of Arthur.

It can be argued that by returning Helen to Arthur in the guise of nurse, Brontë is opting for a conventional ending by enabling her to redeem her 'sin' in deserting him, and allowing her to play perhaps the most angelic role of all. Michael Wheeler, quoting Elizabeth Stone's 'God's Acre', states that 'angels "do most especially minister" at a deathbed',[29] and the identification of nurses with angels is a familiar one. However, Brontë deliberately redeems Helen in this way to foreground the final statement of her ineffectuality. She transforms Helen from a metaphorical domestic angel into, almost literally, a 'heavenly' angel who heals, who quotes the scriptures, who fights for Arthur's soul and appears at his deathbed. As a part of this foregrounding, the author subtly alters the impact of Helen's 'influence'. Its purpose, and demonstration through biblical quotation, remains fundamentally unchanged: at the commencement of her relationship with Arthur she refers to the hope of reforming and improving him, and at the end of their marriage she is still trying to do the same. The change lies in Arthur's reaction to this: his amusement, tolerance and irritation become, in his illness, fear and peevishness. This is Brontë's ultimate assertion, however, that women's 'influence' is worthless, unless the target of it chooses to be influenced. Arthur's seeming susceptibility to Helen's words is rooted in his terror of the possibility of damnation, and he is only susceptible when he is feeling this fear. The fact that he dies unredeemed is Brontë's final word on the myth, and Arthur remains uninfluenced.

Brontë's view is therefore a curious combination of belief and pessimism, and she both redefines and reinforces the image of the Angel in the House, while displaying no faith in its effectiveness. The root of this doubt may lie in Brontë's apparent lack of belief in the ability of men to perceive women as anything other than angels or devils. Gilbert Markham's description of Helen at the novel's end as 'my darling angel'[30] has an ominous ring: the only other person who has referred explicitly to Helen as an angel is Arthur Huntingdon. The author tries to build images of hope and fruitfulness around the impending marriage to Gilbert: it takes place in spring, rather than winter, in contrast to her marriage to Arthur, and Brontë likens Helen to a 'Christmas rose' in her betrothal scene with Gilbert, suggesting growth and blooming in the midst of apparent barrenness. However, by imaging Helen in this way, Brontë associates her with both beauty and festivity, and winter and coldness, and these small hints and omens imply that the author's view of *this* relationship may also be full of doubt. We only have Gilbert's account of the perfection of their marriage; Helen's voice is quite absent from the closure of Gilbert's narrative, and this silence is as ominous an identification of the Angel in the House as Gilbert and Arthur's characterization of her. Perhaps the marriage is only perfect because Gilbert allows Helen's influence, but Brontë offers no description of it.

The Tenant Of Wildfell Hall occupies, therefore, an extremely significant position within the context of the construction of the Angel in the House. Anne Brontë demonstrates a clear awareness of the qualities of the ideal Victorian woman, and both critiques and reinscribes her through Helen Huntingdon. Helen enacts a truly angelic role, whilst at the same time committing the most unangelic act by leaving Arthur. Her motivation for doing this is to fulfil the maternal aspect of the angelic role, while necessarily having to abandon the wifely aspect. Anne Brontë thus shows the potentially insurmountable and irreconcilable problems at the heart of the Angel in the House, while also offering an exposure of the ineffectiveness of those who enact the role as fully as they can. Five years later, Elizabeth Gaskell will offer a further confrontation with the angelic role, by presenting, in *Ruth*, a sexually impure woman who functions impeccably as an Angel in the House, and who also nurses, appears at death-beds, is a wonderful mother and heals the man who has wronged her, in the process contracting his illness and dying from it, thereby enacting the ultimate sacrifice. *Ruth*, unlike *Tenant*, supports the notion of woman's influence: Ruth Hilton is the most morally and spiritually influential character in the novel. She is identified with images of spirituality and purity, and Gaskell uses this as a mechanism by which Ruth can redeem herself for her sexual sin. This seems a conventional strategy, but Gaskell's radicalism lies, first, in her assertion of the right of 'fallen women' to be given another chance, and second, and more significantly, in presenting a woman who is both angelic and sinful, who is the embodiment of the perfection of influence while lacking the sexual purity that the image demands.[31]

Gaskell, like Brontë, thus dramatizes the conflict and impossibility of such an ideal: both confront their readers with subversive images of women who abandon their angelic place yet retain their angelic role. In Brontë's novel, Helen's rejection of her marriage is a dangerous moment in nineteenth-century literature; it may lack the obvious dramatic impact of, for example, Ibsen's *Nora*, slamming the door on her marriage 40 years later, and her reasons for leaving Arthur may be more conservative. But the action, however, is no less important for all that. Both Elizabeth Gaskell and Anne Brontë pursue a radical project within these novels, and the impossible and restrictive representations of women disclosed through Helen and Ruth locate both texts as among the most radical and subversive re-readings of Victorian womanhood in nineteenth-century fiction.

NOTES

1. Nina Auerbach, *Woman & The Demon* (Cambridge, Mass: Harvard University Press, 1982), pp. 69–70.
2. For an exploration of Anne Brontë's religious beliefs, see, for example, Edward Chitham, *A Life of Anne Brontë* (Oxford: Blackwell, 1991); Elizabeth Langland, *Anne Brontë: The Other One* (Basingstoke: Macmillan, 1989); Winifred Gerin, *Anne Brontë* (Edinburgh and London: Thomas Nelson & Sons, 1959).
3. *The Tenant Of Wildfell Hall* (Penguin edition, 1979, edited by G.D. Hargreaves, introduced by Winifred Gerin), p. 33.
4. Ibid., p. 146.
5. Ibid., p. 153.
6. Ibid., p. 149.
7. Ibid., p. 163.
8. Ibid., p. 185.
9. Ibid., p. 153.
10. Ibid., pp. 165–6.
11. Ibid., pp. 166–7.
12. Maria H. Frawley, *The Female Saviour In The Tenant Of Wildfell Hall*, Brontë Society Transactions, 20, Pt 3, 1991, p. 135.
13. *Tenant*, p. 167.
14. Ibid., p. 165.
15. *Wuthering Heights* (Penguin edition, 1965, edited and with an introduction by David Daiches), p. 118.
16. Ibid., p. 122.
17. *Tenant*, p. 165.
18. Ibid., p. 215.
19. Ibid., p. 217.
20. Ibid., pp. 318, 330.
21. Ibid., p. 268.
22. Ibid., p. 252.
23. Ibid., p. 356.

24. Marion Shaw, *Anne Brontë: A Quiet Feminist*, Brontë Society Transactions, 21, Pt 4, 1994.
25. *Tenant*, pp. 437–8.
26. Ibid., p. 439.
27. Ibid., p. 446.
28. Ibid.
29. Michael Wheeler, *Death & The Future Life In Victorian Literature & Theology* (Cambridge: Cambridge University Press, 1990), p. 32.
30. *Tenant*, p. 486.
31. For a full discussion of *Ruth* in this context, see Siv Jansson, 'Elizabeth Gaskell: Writing Against The Angel In The House', *The Gaskell Society Journal*, 10 (1996).

3

Double Blessedness: Anna Kingsford and *Beatrice*

Peter Merchant

Although recognition in the standard literary and intellectual histories of the nineteenth century still eludes her, Anna Kingsford
(1846–88) could certainly claim to be a pivotal figure in the Victorian
representation of women of faith. She might even count as two
pivotal figures, since in 1863 – some years before she took the name
by which she is generally not recognized – it is possible to meet her,
already writing fiction, as plain Annie Bonus. The title-page of
Beatrice: A Tale of the Early Christians[1] further diminishes the Annie,
in fact, to an initial; and the (at most) 25,000 words of text make
Beatrice a slim volume indeed. But released in this apparently
modest début were an integrity and a fervour rivalling those of the
designated heroine. The idea of the female martyr had so seized
Annie Bonus's imagination that, for *Beatrice*, she devoted all of her
resources to restating and refurbishing it in an impressively
compact fictional narrative – and then extended this, I shall argue,
into a determined effort to realize it afresh in her own subsequent
career.

Beatrice is only able to surprise us with its sweeping sense of a
tradition new-minted because Bonus has deliberately chosen one of
the obscurer martyrs of the primitive Christian Church. The very
bald account that appeared in the standard work of reference,
Alban Butler's *Lives of the Fathers* ..., plainly left scope for all manner
of impromptu additions:

SS. SIMPLICIUS AND FAUSTINUS, BROTHERS, AND BEATRICE
THEIR SISTER, MM.

The two brothers were cruelly tormented, and at length be-
headed at Rome in the persecution of Dioclesian, in the year 303.

Their sister Beatrice took up their bodies out of the Tiber, and gave them burial. She lay herself concealed seven months in the house of a virtuous widow called Lucina, with whom she spent her time, night and day, in fervent prayer, and in the exercise of other good works. She was discovered and impeached by a pagan kinsman, who designed to possess himself of her estate, which was contiguous to his own: she resolutely protested to the judge that she would never adore gods of wood and stone, and was strangled by his order in prison the night following. Lucina buried her body near her brothers on the side of the highway to Porto, in the cemetery called Ad Ursum Pileatum. Pope Leo translated their relics into a church which he built to their honour in the city: they now lie in that of St. Mary Major.[2]

So much was authorized; yet it is the largely unauthorized moments in Bonus's story which generate her best effects. She adds extra detail to Beatrice's appearance before the Roman prefect – having her receive her sentence with 'an expression of rapturous joy'[3] – and she supplies a sequence showing the avaricious kinsman, called Lysias, who denounces Beatrice subjected to 'all the terrors attendant on an evil conscience'. In his curtain he sees 'the figure of Beatrice in her white garments, standing immoveably before him, and gazing full in his face with bright piercing eyes'; in the mournful sounds of the rushing wind he hears 'the voice of the martyred virgin calling on him by name'.[4] Although Bonus protests her strict adherence to truth in, at least, 'the greater part'[5] of what she has written, historical accuracy inevitably concerns her less than the clarity of her narrative line and the power of each separate episode; 'not only in the *general* history of the early Church, but often in that of her individual members', she says, 'there are scenes pictured, and characters displayed which cannot fail to awaken at once our admiration and our sympathy'.[6]

Beatrice was most warmly welcomed by its own publishers, with an unsigned laudatory review in their journal *The Churchman's Companion*:

We must specially commend to our readers' notice a work entitled *Beatrice, a Tale of the Early Christians*, (Masters,) which has just been published, by a young and very promising author. It displays great research and a depth of fervent religious feeling, which is the more pleasing because wholly free from exaggeration. Although in these days it is rare that any are permitted to win the 'bright peculiar crown' of martyrdom through the baptism of blood; yet in the most quiet uneventful life there will ever be found occasions for stern self-sacrifice, and this well-told story of one who yielded up her life with joy for her Master's sake, cannot fail to brace the souls of others for their own conflict on the pathway of life.[7]

Bonus was owed no less, perhaps, since she had already contributed poetry to *The Churchman's Companion*, and *Beatrice* itself was at one time earmarked for inclusion in it too.[8] Apart from the brief interest shown in *Beatrice* at the time of its publication, however, the book has excited next to no critical comment;[9] and this is unfortunate as there are a number of levels on which it warrants examination. It could engage attention simply through the youth of its author, who was just 17 – one year younger than her heroine – when *Beatrice* appeared. With its fourth-century Roman setting (conceived at a time when, for many artists and writers, Imperial Rome uncannily prefigured Victorian Britain)[10] it might, more profitably, engage us as a representative and revealing example of the Victorian historical imagination at work. And the presence in the subplot of a converted Roman nobleman, Secundus, means, moreover, that it offers an intriguing approach to the patterns of the late nineteenth-century 'toga plays' recently reassessed by David Mayer.[11] But for present purposes the most interesting aspect of *Beatrice* is Bonus's procedure in constructing, for its centrepiece, a commanding image of the virgin martyr as Christian heroine.

An inexperienced writer might well feel that she needed help with this task. Bonus makes a virtue of necessity, since she exercises great tact and discrimination both in identifying possible models for her portrayal of Beatrice and then in applying them. These were years in which such models were accumulating thickly. Probably the richest source of all was Catholic educational literature: lives of the early martyrs or tales of the early Church, in volumes priced typically at three shillings. The middle 1850s had yielded two particular pillars of the genre, whose usefulness to herself Bonus could plainly perceive. The first, dealing authoritatively with Diocletian's Rome, was Cardinal-Archbishop Wiseman's novel *Fabiola* (1854). That Bonus profited by Wiseman's researches into 'the usages, habits, condition, ideas, feeling, and spirit of the early ages of Christianity'[12] is evident from her own recourse to the same general setting. He opens in September 302, with the pious widow Lucina;

she opens in July 303, and of course goes on to introduce 'the same Lucina'[13] in an important supporting role. In respect of the heroines themselves, the major difference is that Wiseman develops the character of a Christian convert – rejecting Rome's 'refined ... epicureanism'[14] and progressing to baptism and confirmation – where Bonus would explore the character of a Christian martyr. (It is not Beatrice herself who experiences conversion, but Secundus and Sergius and Alban; and it is not for Fabiola that the crown of martyrdom is reserved, but for others of whom Wiseman also writes.) There are passages of physical description, however, employing just the same markers of inner purity and radiance. Wiseman makes the martyred Agnes 'an angel of light' whose hair, when let loose, 'flowed down, in golden waves, upon her snow-white dress'.[15] Bonus's Beatrice also wears white and likewise has cascading golden hair: 'her hair ... suddenly uncoiled itself and fell in glossy waves over her shoulders, covering her like a mantle of golden coloured silk'.[16]

Fabiola was followed in 1856 by Newman's *Callista*, published, like Wiseman's novel, as part of the Popular Catholic Library. *Callista* has a different setting (Proconsular Africa, in the third century AD) but shares *Fabiola*'s concern with conversion. Furthermore, the two books are usually linked – as by Charlotte Crawford – on the grounds that both were designed 'to correct from a Catholic point of view the picture of Church history presented in Kingsley's *Hypatia*'.[17] Clearly Newman disagrees profoundly with Kingsley's analysis of early Christianity, and has a case to argue about that. But it is not from any general exposition of Church history that *Callista* fetches its special intensity; the novel's resonance derives instead from the use Newman makes in it of direct personal experience. For the excited entry of its convert heroine into 'a new world of thought',[18] while representing the dominant movement of mind – from paganism to Christianity – in the specified historical period, also reflects the very recent upheaval (1845) of Newman's own conversion to Roman Catholicism. And for many readers this distinct undertow of autobiographical reference is enough to make *Callista*, now as then, the most compelling of all Early Christian novels. Its impact on other Catholic converts was enormous – such, perhaps, that part of Hopkins's reason for feeling so moved by the tall German nun's call (as reported in *The Times*) 'O Christ, come quickly!'[19] was that it seemed to echo the dying cry of Newman's Callista, when stretched upon the rack: 'Accept me, O my Love, upon this bed of pain! And come to me, O my Love, make haste and come!²⁰ Annie Bonus was not as yet a convert to Catholicism – although, true to the example of Hopkins (whose family had lived just down the road from hers in Stratford, London), she took that step in her early twenties. Even so, when she wrote *Beatrice* she was able to appreciate all of the power with which Newman's novel had communicated religious experience, and to harness some of that power for her own account of a heroine persecuted and martyred. Bonus's Beatrice has the same innocent youthfulness as Newman's Callista ('a girl ... who had not yet seen eighteen summers'),²¹ the same saintliness and the same hunger for Christ; 'O my sweet LORD JESUS', she implores,²² 'take quickly unto Thyself, the soul that longeth to be with Thee, its loving Spouse and Redeemer!'

The final relevant instance of the persecuted heroine, in the fiction of the 1850s, is Elizabeth Gaskell's magazine story *Lois the Witch*, which appeared in three issues of *All the Year Round* in October 1859, during the run of *A Tale of Two Cities*. What hints for *Beatrice* were furnished by *Lois the Witch* can only be conjectured. Certainly Bonus faced artistic difficulties for which Gaskell, four years earlier, had found fit solutions. One such difficulty (writ slightly smaller for Bonus, in a story just two-thirds the length of Gaskell's) was that of deciding in how much detail a complex historical background should be indicated and how it might be balanced against the individual drama of the eponymous heroine. Here, moreover, each writer is centrally concerned with a young woman of 18, who – in the fevered atmosphere of mass trials and summary justice which the story succeeds in evoking – is denounced and killed because she chooses, in Lois's words, 'death with a quiet conscience rather than life to be gained by a lie'.²³ And Bonus, like Gaskell, makes the heroine's situation more poignant still by highlighting her vulnerability and isolation. Lois was 'very friendless', with 'no father nor mother left upon earth';²⁴ Beatrice is 'left almost alone, an orphan and a Christian, in the midst of a pagan people'.²⁵

Rather than shaping the sentiments expressed in *Beatrice*, however, or suggesting the setting and situation, the most crucial service that Bonus's various models could perform for her was to fix the pictorial style in which she writes. Bonus develops a habit of freezing her narrative from time to time, in order to hold and study its heroine in a suitably striking pose. At one point, the 'motionless figure' of Beatrice is tinted by the moonlight with a hue that made it appear rather like a piece of exquisite statuary than a living form. How beautiful she looked standing there in the pale light, her countenance soft and fair with the impress of innocence, and her hands crossed peacefully on her bosom, as one of the immortals stands, in the brighter light of heaven![26]

The proleptic detail of the crossed hands, plainly presaging Beatrice's death, completes the picture; and the reaction of an observing Roman noble – 'Secundus gazed at her with a feeling of admiring awe, almost amounting to adoration'[27] – then frames it for the reader. The method is the one to which Bonus accustoms us as soon as she first introduces the heroine, at the trial of her brothers, and in so doing invites us to 'read' a carefully constructed visual image. What we are shown as Beatrice enters is

a young girl of about eighteen ... whose appearance though her dress was of the plainest kind, denoted high birth. Her beautiful face was calm, but colourless as the white marble pillars around her, and in her eyes, like wells in their depth and darkness, lay almost hidden a sad sweet look, which told at once of keen mental suffering and of holy trust.[28]

That account of Beatrice attending the trial of Simplicius and Faustinus may seem subtly reminiscent of Mary Barton, in Gaskell's novel, attending the trial of Jem Wilson: 'her face was deadly white, and almost set in its expression, while a mournful bewildered soul looked out of the depths of those soft, deep, gray eyes'.[29] If so, the likely reason is that behind the two passages lies a common source.

For Gaskell, in her next paragraph, continues her description of Mary Barton's courtroom ordeal as follows: 'I was not there myself; but one who was, told me that her look, and indeed her whole face, was more like the well-known engraving from Guido's picture of "Beatrice Cenci" than any thing else he could give me an idea of.' This picture (in which today we no longer see Guido's hand, but Guercino's) was greatly admired by many Victorians. It had been described by Dickens, two years previously, as

a picture almost impossible to be forgotten. Through the transcendent sweetness and beauty of the face, there is a something shining out, that haunts me. I see it now, as I see this paper, or my pen. The head is loosely draped in white; the light hair falling down below the linen folds. She has turned suddenly towards you; and there is an expression in the eyes – although they are very tender and gentle – as if the wildness of a momentary terror, or distraction, had been struggled with and overcome, that instant; and nothing but a celestial hope, and a beautiful sorrow, and a desolate earthly helplessness remained.[30]

In the following year, 1847, Bentley's *Miscellany* had printed the 'well-known engraving' to which Gaskell refers; and James Whittle, in an accompanying article,[31] had discussed the picture along exactly the same lines as Dickens. It is, says Whittle, 'one of the most perfect productions of Guido's pencil', capturing 'such a look of wild sorrow in the eyes, such feminine sweetness in the mouth, and such an expression of hopeless misery and despair, that the spectator's gaze is riveted, and the remembrance of that lovely face lingers in the mind, awakening a powerful and harrowing interest'.[32] The article proceeds to relate 'the history of the beautiful and ill-fated Beatrice'; and although on the surface this is nothing at all like a tale of the early Christians Whittle explicitly encourages just such a connection:

> she allowed no tear to escape from her eyes, no sigh from her breast, but, *like the martyrs of other days*, she continued to pour forth prayers to her Saviour; her beautiful countenance lightened with an expression of noble courage and resignation, shewing to all that she was resolved to die as became a Roman [emphasis mine].[33]

Finally, for the benefit of any artist or writer now tempted to transfer to 'the martyrs of other days' the 'powerful and harrowing interest' awoken by the sixteenth-century Beatrice, Whittle even prescribes a particular physiognomy and physique:

> Beatrice was only twenty years of age, rather below than above the middle stature; her limbs round, and well-formed; her eyes small, but full of expression, and her cheeks dimpled; and even after death she wore the same sweet smile as in life; her mouth was small, and her fair hair, which curled naturally, falling in luxuriant ringlets over her shoulders, added greatly to her beauty.[34]

This list of features quite accurately describes the Beatrice – name-sake of the beautiful and ill-fated parricide – about whom Annie Bonus writes. Throughout the tale, Beatrice's expressive eyes – which are 'radiant'[35] and in marked contrast to the 'small serpent eyes' of Lysias[36] – receive special attention; and so does her golden hair, which is as lustrous as Mary Barton's and which tumbles onto her shoulders because (as Bonus reminds us in a footnote)[37] 'flowing hair was a sign of the maiden state'. Beatrice's 'fair, golden hair, and deep earnest eyes' accordingly make 'a beautiful picture' in the second chapter;[38] and in the final chapter (where Lysias, rather than Secundus, is the observing Roman noble whose reaction is noted) they plead like angels against the iniquity of her death sentence:

Lysias … saw her pass majestically by him, her bright golden hair falling in rich waves over her white dress, and her full sublime eyes gazing fixedly upwards, as though in the contemplation of some heavenly vision … the miser recoiled and shrunk into himself, as her garments rustled by him, and he felt as though he would fain have hidden from her view, so glorious and holy she appeared.[39]

Superimposed upon the necessarily oblique allusions to Guido or Guercino, there is also a more straightforwardly contemporary di-mension to Bonus's use of the visual arts. Much is borrowed, in *Beatrice*, from the prevailing Pre-Raphaelite images of women: the rapt intensity of a heroine who typically is seen 'absorbed in her own thoughts',[40] or 'in ecstatic contemplation',[41] as well as the freely flowing hair. One obvious possible point of reference, Rossetti's *Beata Beatrix*, had yet to be painted; so there could be no conscious and visible twinning of Beatrice with any second namesake. But Millais's famous painting *Ophelia* (1852)[42] was of course available to Bonus, and contributes very powerfully at the tale's climax, when the Tiber yields up

the corpse of a young girl, her pale hands crossed upon her motionless breast, and her loose white robes floating heavily round her upon the dark, black river. Her head was thrown back upon the water, and the fair golden tresses of her hair streamed around her neck, and fell here and there in damp clusters upon it, while her countenance wore a sweet expression of perfect and unbroken peace, and her eyes seemed closed rather in slumber than in death. So quietly and calmly she lay pillowed on her watery couch, that had it not been for the marble paleness of her face, and the dark lines round her eyelids, one might have fancied her asleep, so little was there in the expression of her features to denote the presence of the King of Terrors.[43]

Bonus seems indebted to Millais both for the density of detail in this scene (the clothes, for instance, swelling in the water) and for the frankly lyrical quality with which the whole is suffused.

The fact that one specific 'young girl', of just the same age as Beatrice, had modelled for Millais's *Ophelia* further strengthens the already strong relationship between the story and the painting. That part of Beatrice which is Lizzie Siddal may still, however, not amount to as much as that part of her which is, quite simply, Annie Bonus. Bonus's heroine is a composite figure, after all, into the form of whose character it might be positively expected that – alongside the memories of Ophelia or Callista or Lois (or George Eliot's Romola, even more recently, with her lily-white brightness and hair of rippling gold) – a young, first-time novelist should incorporate some fragments of herself. Sure enough, we find in Beatrice as complete and precise a portrait of the writer, both temperamentally and physically, as the idealizing conventions of heroine description will allow. Beatrice's beautiful fair hair and beautiful deep eyes, together with her proneness to reverie,[44] all at least recur in accounts of Bonus herself, who reportedly went through her own teenage years – and into womanhood – with the same 'profusion' of 'golden' hair and the same 'deep-set' and 'dreamy' eyes.[45] Although there is an ultimate contradiction in form between martyrological narrative and autobiographical narrative, in that the one makes the death of the protagonist inevitable within the story and the other makes it inconceivable, that seems to have been no bar at all to this author's eager imaginative identification with her heroine.

It also seems that the heroine in question was rather more to the author than merely a reflection of her existing attributes; she represented, in addition, a reservoir of possibility for the future. By including elements of herself in her characterization of the martyred Beatrice, Bonus prospectively wrote herself, as a 17-year-old, into a role whose limits she then indeed proceeded to test, refining and reaffirming, throughout the 25 years of life remaining to her. It was a very varied and eventful life, too, that turned Annie Bonus

the budding author into Anna Kingsford the public figure. It saw
her marry her cousin, four years after *Beatrice*, and move away from
London when her husband left the Civil Service to retrain for the
Anglican ministry and take charge of a rural parish in Shropshire.
She herself became a Catholic convert in 1870, and a doctor of medi-
cine ten years later. Many more stories appeared in the meantime,
interchanged with bursts of activity in the fields of journalism and
political campaigning. She became increasingly committed to causes
and movements – among them vegetarianism and psychical science
– less dangerous than Christianity in Diocletian's Rome yet almost
as likely to isolate their adherents. After 1874, however, Kingsford
had a devoted friend and collaborator in Edward Maitland.
Together they wrote a book called *The Perfect Way*, in which
'Christian and Buddhist, Parsee and Hebrew, Greek and Egyptian,
are brought into harmony, and shown to be only so many different
dialects of one Catholic language'.[46] Although Kingsford was still a
self-styled 'Catholic Christian',[47] she used both words not 'in the
accepted sense of these terms', but 'in their original and true
sense'.[48] So it was that, by her final year, she 'was little more than
nominally a member of the Roman Church';[49] and reports in the
Catholic press that she had returned to it upon her deathbed were
strenuously denied by her associates.[50] They remembered the other
descriptions she had offered of herself: 'a spiritualist', 'a mystic and
an occultist', 'a Hermetist'.[51] Her aim as President (from 1884) of the
Hermetic Society was nothing less than 'to reform the Christian
system and start a new Esoteric Church'.[52]

There neither is nor can be, perhaps, any definitive conspectus of
a career taking in such various sorts of writing and research, and
combining (or seeking to combine) so many opposed religious traditions. Today, we risk either overlooking altogether an achievement
so difficult to categorize or stressing Kingsford's interest in the
occult in such a way as to make her appear both more marginal
than she may deserve and more ridiculous.[53] The only detailed
treatment is Edward Maitland's monumental hundred-year-old
biography, or biography-cum-history of Anna Kingsford's religious
opinions, which justifies itself as much by the warmth of the
writer's regard for his former colleague as by the accuracy of his
recall. Just as Dickens, when pondering the unforgettable portrait of
Beatrice Cenci, could sense 'a something shining out' of it, so
Maitland, as soon as he has met Anna Kingsford, notes a mysterious
'Something radiating from within'.[54] The book that he eventually

writes about her looks nearly as much like a saint's life as *Beatrice* had done. Maitland's elevated view of his subject, from the moment of their first meeting onward, is conveyed with a rhapsodic insistency which quite overrides fascinating developments – and fascinating tensions – in Kingsford's view of herself.

Maitland credits her, for instance, with 'a face, brow, and wealth of flowing golden hair, which a goddess might have envied', going on to speak of her as 'a goddess, too, not merely in outward seeming, but also in faculty and power'.[55] And this is sheer obfuscation. The fact that her biographer can cast her so freely in roles so glorious may prevent us from noticing where a role has been deliberately and independently assumed by Kingsford herself. Her own claims sometimes seem not quite to be pitched where Maitland pitches his. But certainly she regarded herself as blessed with an exceptionally privileged access to truth. In her dreams, she said, she had regularly received 'priceless insights and illuminations';[56] and on that basis she pronounced herself a 'prophetess'.[57] Kingsford was not one to demur, evidently, when – contrary to the general custom among men (of unjustly excluding women from 'the prophetic office', she considered, and arrogating 'all the credit to themselves') – Maitland began to marvel at her 'faculty of seership'.[58]

Kingsford's sense of being specially singled out apparently extended to a conviction that she was 'an appointed instrument' of higher powers.[59] Her campaigns turned into crusades, like the 'anti-vivisection crusade' in which Maitland enthusiastically participated,[60] and she hoped to become the pioneer of some great new awakening. For the lofty endeavour to which she was called resembled nothing so much as the 'mission ... of rescue and deliverance' entrusted to one of her former selves, she believed, in fifteenth-century France.[61] To Kingsford, in fact, Joan of Arc became a 'patron saint' or 'guardian angel';[62] an 'extraordinary correspondence in character, faculty, and experiences' united them.[63] In thus recognizing Joan of Arc as a kindred spirit, Kingsford effectively recognized the ardent desire for martyrdom that she herself was nursing. It is no accident that the other historical figure for whom she professed this passionate admiration and affinity was Anne Boleyn; 'how like me! how like me!' she exclaimed, except that Anne Boleyn's crown of martyrdom had been won sooner and more easily than hers would be.[64] Maitland celebrates Kingsford's life, therefore, as – from the very first – one of peculiar 'suffering and toil', undergone for the sake of 'some great and necessary work ... to be accomplished

by her'; she was plagued, in such a way 'as to make her life a martyrdom', with 'unclean insects and impure diseases', which added
extra and exceptional hardships to the 'personal persecution' she
already endured from her human enemies.[65] Kingsford's other
friends and relatives tended to endorse this talk of martyrdom. The
fact that she herself ascribed her final decline to 'an expedition in
rain and wind – disastrous indeed – to find Pasteur's Laboratory'
gave her brother good cause to state that 'she died a martyr to the
scrupulous conscientiousness with which she followed M. Pasteur's
experiments and processes, the fallacies of which, as she considered
them to be, she was desirous to make patent to all'.[66] Twenty-five
years after projecting Beatrice as a woman of faith and principle
whose status as martyr was validated by an enraptured and adoring
male onlooker – Secundus first of all, when he saw 'the light of faith
and holy love' in 'her radiant eyes'[67] – Kingsford, through the awed
admiration of her brother and her biographer, had become exactly
that herself.

With the heroine of her first book, consequently, Kingsford maintained that same deep connection – that same close 'correspondence
in character, faculty, and experiences' – which she enjoyed with Joan
of Arc. Not only had she written about the early martyrs' world of
patient service, sore trial and heroic sacrifice, but she and others
were in the end wholly persuaded that she as good as inhabited that
world. The remote Roman past could come alive again, it seemed, in
a contemporary context. Another type of writer, perceiving this,
might have wanted to use Rome as an example, to send a warning to
Victorian Britain. In 1863, indeed, Kingsford had duly offered the
ominous observation that 'Rome in all her grandeur and opulence
fell, for her power was not of GOD';[68] but thereafter she dwelt rather
upon the positive individual example – of Beatrice as a young
woman holding strongly, 'in the midst of a pagan people',[69] to the
faith which makes her an outcast – and used it for personal purposes, to reinforce her own resolve and to focus her own aspirations
to martyrdom. As if applying to herself the advice she had given her
first readers, that they should 'imitate' as well as 'esteem' the beauty
and constancy of 'the early Christian character',[70] she re-enacted
parts of Beatrice's inspiring history. Very seldom, or seldom until
Edward Maitland produced a book of his own about her which was
'by its very nature at once a biography and an autobiography',[71] can
the respective lives of a heroine and author have grown so hard to
disentangle. Never, despite its declared determination (as in *Fabiola*)

to show the nineteenth century as vitally continuous – and even in
some senses 'identical' – with 'the three first centuries',[72] had the
martyrological novel been so much a blueprint for the way the
novelist might think and act in the world of today. *Beatrice* in that
respect sees a future 'prophetess' going into print with her very first
prophetic statement, perhaps, at the age of only 17. For many of the
positions later adopted by Anna Kingsford are predicted and prepared in the published work of the young Annie Bonus.

NOTES

1. A. Bonus, *Beatrice: A Tale of the Early Christians* (London: Joseph
    Masters, 1863). All subsequent references are to this, the only edition
    of *Beatrice* which ever appeared.
2. Alban Butler, *The Lives of the Fathers, Martyrs, and Other Principal
    Saints*, 12 vols (London: John Murphy, 1812–15), vii, p. 377.
3. *Beatrice*, p. 108.
4. Ibid., p. 110.
5. Ibid., p. 4.
6. Ibid., p. 1.
7. *The Churchman's Companion*, 34 (November 1863), 400.
8. Edward Maitland, *Anna Kingsford: Her Life, Letters, Diary and Work*,
    third edition, edited by S.H. Hart, 2 vols (London: John M. Watkins,
    1913; original 1896), i, p. 4.
9. This paper draws upon my own recent essay 'Magnifying
    Martyrdom: Annie Bonus's *Beatrice* and the Victorian Vision of the
    Early Church', *Recusant History*, 22 (1994), 222–30; but I know of no
    other discussion than mine. Bonus and *Beatrice* are absent even from
    Royal W. Rhodes's definitive account of nineteenth-century fictional
    representations of the primitive Christian Church, *The Lion and the
    Cross: Early Christianity in Victorian Novels* (Columbus: Ohio State
    University Press, 1995), which appeared after the present paper had
    been written and delivered.
10. See George P. Landow, 'Victorianized Romans: Images of Rome in
    Victorian Painting', *Browning Institute Studies*, 12 (1984), 29–51.
11. See David Mayer, ed., *Playing Out the Empire: 'Ben Hur' and Other Toga
    Plays and Films, 1883–1908. A Critical Anthology* (Oxford: Clarendon
    Press, 1994), passim.
12. Nicholas Wiseman, *Fabiola; or, The Church of the Catacombs* (London:
    Burns and Lambert, 1855 [i.e. 1854]), p. viii.
13. *Beatrice*, p. 86.
14. Wiseman, *Fabiola*, pp. 17–18.
15. Ibid., pp. 314, 317.
16. *Beatrice*, pp. 29–30.
17. See Charlotte E. Crawford, 'Newman's *Callista* and the Catholic
    Popular Library', *The Modern Language Review*, 45 (1950), 219–21.

18. John Henry Newman, *Callista: A Sketch of the Third Century* (London: Burns, Oates, & Co., 1881), p. 326.
19. See Sean Street, *'The Wreck of the Deutschland': An Historical Note*, with an introduction by Charles Tomlinson (Budleigh Salterton: Interim Press, 1987), p. 15.
20. Newman, *Callista*, p. 369.
21. Ibid., p. 323.
22. *Beatrice*, p. 93.
23. *All the Year Round*, 1 (1859), 621 (issue no. 26, 22 October).
24. *All the Year Round*, 1 (1859), 564 (issue no. 24, 8 October).
25. *Beatrice*, p. 103.
26. Ibid., p. 30.
27. Ibid.
28. Ibid., p. 13.
29. Elizabeth Gaskell, *Mary Barton: A Tale of Manchester Life*, 2 vols (London: Chapman and Hall, 1848), ii, p. 198.
30. Charles Dickens, *Pictures from Italy* (London: Bradbury and Evans, 1846), pp. 211–12.
31. James Whittle, Esq., 'Beatrice Cenci, The Parricide', *Bentley's Miscellany*, 22 (1847), 105–18.
32. Ibid., p. 105.
33. Ibid., p. 116.
34. Ibid., p. 118.
35. *Beatrice*, p. 30.
36. Ibid., p. 35.
37. Ibid., p. 63, n.1. Cf. Wiseman, *Fabiola*, p. 317.
38. *Beatrice*, p. 18.
39. Ibid., p. 108.
40. Ibid., p. 30.
41. Ibid., p. 89.
42. An excellent colour reproduction appears in Jan Marsh, *Pre-Raphaelite Women: Images of Femininity in Pre-Raphaelite Art* (London: Weidenfeld and Nicolson, 1987), pp. 136–7.
43. *Beatrice*, p. 111.
44. Ibid., p. 89.
45. See Maitland, *Anna Kingsford*, i, p. 2; i, p. 31; and ii, p. 371 (quoting from an issue of *Light* dated 10 March 1888).
46. Ibid., ii, p. 56.
47. Ibid., ii, p. 124.
48. Anna Bonus Kingsford and Edward Maitland, *The Perfect Way; or, The Finding of Christ*, revised and enlarged edition (London: Field and Tuer, 1887), pp. 25–6.
49. Maitland, *Anna Kingsford*, ii, p. 308.
50. Ibid., ii, pp. 376 and 379–99.
51. Ibid., ii, pp. 60, 312, 328.
52. Ibid., ii, p. 187.
53. See, for instance, Derek Jarrett, *The Sleep of Reason: Fantasy and Reality from the Victorian Age to the First World War* (London: Weidenfeld and Nicolson, 1988), pp. 114ff.; Ronald Pearsall, *The Worm in the Bud: The*

World of Victorian Sexuality (Harmondsworth: Penguin Books, 1971), pp. 601–2.

54. Maitland, *Anna Kingsford*, i, p. 44.
55. Ibid., i, pp. 44, 250.
56. Anna Bonus Kingsford, *Dreams and Dream-Stories*, ed. Edward Maitland (London: George Redway, 1888), p. 8.
57. Maitland, *Anna Kingsford*, ii, p. 167.
58. Ibid., i, p. 183; i, p. 3. See Diana Basham's discussion of Anna Kingsford as prophetess, in her book *The Trial of Woman: Feminism and the Occult Sciences in Victorian Literature and Society* (Basingstoke and London: Macmillan, 1992), pp. 67–72.
59. Maitland, *Anna Kingsford*, ii, p. 370.
60. Ibid., i, p. 427; ii, p. 8.
61. Ibid., ii, p. 245.
62. Ibid., i, pp. 15, 229; ii, p. 133.
63. Ibid., i, p. 437.
64. Ibid., ii, pp. 59, 244.
65. Ibid., i, pp. 2, 419, 424, 426.
66. Diary entry for 17 November 1887, quoted by Maitland in *Anna Kingsford*, ii, p. 342; letter from John Bonus, quoted by Charles W. Forward in his book *Fifty Years of Food Reform: A History of the Vegetarian Movement in England* (London: The Ideal Publishing Union, and Manchester: The Vegetarian Society, 1898), p. 123.
67. *Beatrice*, p. 30.
68. Ibid., p. 4.
69. Ibid., p. 103.
70. Ibid., p. 5.
71. Maitland, *Anna Kingsford*, i, p. 34.
72. Wiseman, *Fabiola*, pp. 217–18, 362.

4

Sisterhood is Powerful: Christina Rosetti's *Maude*

Frederick S. Roden

In the past 20 years of Christina Rossetti criticism, the Victorian poet has been reclaimed from an image of a gentle, renunciatory spinster fearful of the world and unsuccessful in love.[1] Concurrent with the developments in feminist literary theory and criticism has been work in feminist theology seeking to reclaim a feminine voice in relationship to the Divine. In the nineteenth century, in the writings of Christina Rossetti and other religious women, this voice was present in a tradition similar to one that can be traced back to female mystical experience in medieval Christianity. While still in her teens, Christina Rossetti wrote a short work of prose and verse called *Maude*, perhaps the most neglected work in her canon. Rossetti also composed a huge amount of devotional prose and poetry which has only recently received greater scholarly attention as the ways in which her religiosity infuses her more 'secular' poetry have begun to be appreciated. I suggest we likewise consider *Maude* with Rossetti's unique brand of Christianity in mind. Written in the form of a spiritual journey, this nineteenth-century *Pilgrim's Progress* for a young, intellectual, High Church woman anticipates the essential link between spirituality and sexuality that the poet fleshes out in both incarnation and transubstantiation throughout her later great sensual poetry.

Maude is concerned with the spiritual life of High Church women. The work raises the question of the new option made available to them by the re-institution of religious sisterhoods in the Church of England during the mid-nineteenth century. The sisterhoods' significance cannot be underestimated in terms of gender politics, issues of women and community, and the re-vision of the concept of the family which they helped to engender in nineteenth-century English culture. They truly paved the way for the *fin-de-siècle* 'liberated' New Woman. In all of Rossetti's writings, both poetry and prose, the single woman's spirituality is contrasted with a married or marrying 'sister's'. Much of the negative response that the religious sisterhoods elicited involved the threats such phenomena posed to the Victorian patriarchal family, undercutting the authority of a father, brother or husband in favour of the authority of a feminine equal, a 'sister'. The 'law of the father' became second to the authority of the Father in heaven, before whom all mortals stand equal regardless of gender. The acceptance of the spiritual bridegroom in place of the relationship with and authority of a man on this earth likewise undermined the family and rejected the supreme sanctity of married life as it had been constructed in England during the more than 300 years since the Protestant Reformation.

The notion that the single devotional life could be holier than the married state incited 'nervous reactions', to utilize Michael Taussig's terminology, concerning gender in this culture. This point is evidenced by the numerous and diverse critical responses to the sisterhoods' destabilization of normative structures. Even contemporary writers such as Dinah Mulock Craik, who were sympathetic to the religious sisterhoods, strongly maintained that woman's primary duties were to her biological family. Sisterhood, for Craik, was a potential answer to the 'surplus woman' question. In considering notions of the family in relation to Christina Rossetti, many of the early biographical studies of the poet and readings of her work have been more detrimental than helpful. It is nevertheless significant to locate her relationship as 'High Priestess' of the Pre-Raphaelite Brotherhood with respect to domestic ideology. Excluded as she was from such a community of artists because of her gender, the potential *communitas* offered by sisterhood can be seen to have been a fruitful alternative.

In the nineteenth century, the presence of individuals actively rejecting heterosexual marriage in favour of life in a same-sex religious community brought accusations of the 'perversions' associated with Rome, as High Anglican men were branded 'effeminate' and communities of women 'unhealthy'.[2] As in the medieval period, 'unnaturalness' in theology was connected with 'unnaturalness' in sexuality by the Victorians. Each is equally subversive to the 'naturalness' of the contemporary socio-political matrix. Communities of men were founded earlier than sisterhoods in the High Church movement. Homosociality, devoted same-sex friendship and similar rejection of heterosexual marriage were hallmarks of Anglo-Catholicism, and as potentially subversive for men as they were for women. However, the brotherhoods never equalled the many sisterhoods in membership. By the end of the nineteenth century a huge number of orders and religious houses for women existed. Nevertheless, male religious communities set the stage for the introduction of those for women, recalling the convents of pre-Reformation England and looking to Catholic models of monastic rule. The religious model even inflected the utopian visions of the *fin-de-siècle*. Oscar Wilde, in his 1890 essay, 'The Soul of Man Under Socialism', envisaged an ideal society similar to monastic *communitas*, a community in which all ties of family, bonds of patriarchal/hierarchical familial systems and heterosexual marriage mean nothing in comparison to a true family of spiritual 'free-love'.

The nineteenth-century sisterhoods, unlike many communities of men, reversed traditional emphases of monasticism. The goal was not *contemplatio*, but action, activity and involvement in and with the world. Sisterhoods in the Church of England gave women an opportunity to connect with and more freely take action for those concerns to which they were otherwise forbidden direct access. They worked to recover 'fallen' sisters, a job thought to be too 'pathogenic' for most lay women. Sisters also took on those concerns to which secular women were themselves devoted, such as the care of orphans and nursing the sick.[3]

Despite the prominence of the active charity work of the Anglican sisterhoods, the majority of the literature of the period concerning the nun focuses on her life as a contemplative rejecting the world. Such male poets as Matthew Arnold, Coventry Patmore, Gerard Manley Hopkins and Ernest Dowson wrote works about the nun's renunciatory calling. Similarly, in the art of the period, in which the 'pretty young nun' painting was but a variation upon the 'pretty young woman' theme, the emphasis is upon leaving the world behind. Rather than being actively involved in the world's affairs through the practice of one of the few middle-class 'careers' open to her outside of marriage, such as governess or 'lady novelist', the nun is represented as shut behind cloister walls. Perhaps such an enclosure was meant to reflect her marital and indeed genital sexual inaccessibility to men. Such literary imprisonment in the creative imaginations of male artists would also seem to be one such way to contain and hence ultimately control what was seen as the threatening activity and self-empowerment of religious women.

The role of the sister, defined in the arts of the period as simultaneously erotic and 'safe', asexual, necessarily located her in a liminal
space.

Empowering herself through a religious vocation though never
taking the veil, Christina Rossetti was probably a secular 'outer
sister' of at least one Anglican order.[4] She was involved in charity
work with Magdalene homes, run by Anglican sisters for the
purpose of 'recovery' of fallen women. Indeed, Rossetti's *Goblin
Market* has been suggested to have been written for reading to
'refugees' in such a community.[5] Rossetti's sister Maria herself professed in the Anglican Society of All Saints in 1875. In Christina
Rossetti's poetry we find a subtle reconfiguring of familial relationships. Her work consistently portrays women's preference for
spiritual bridegrooms over love of husbands on earth. Rossetti's
nun poetry, despite her Anglicanism and antipathy to the Church
of Rome, most often sketches women who have renounced
the world rather than choosing to improve it, setting their sights
upon the ultimate spiritual authority and bliss with a Spiritual
Bridegroom – often conjoined with an earthly man – in eternity.[6]
Although divorced from active physical sexuality, Rossetti's religious women are very spiritually erotic in their relationship to the
Divine. Whoever Rossetti may have been, her nuns are not 'asexual'
Anglican nursing or philanthropic women.

From a theological perspective, Rossetti's stance is truly radical,
seizing an authoritative spiritual voice from which to speak. She
envisages an egalitarian life beyond the grave despite accepted
inequalities between the sexes in this world. Rossetti's trust in her
own religious voice, leading her to write some 2000 pages of
immensely popular devotional literature for a primarily female
audience, is worthy of comparison to Hildegard of Bingen or Julian
of Norwich. In her devotional writings, the poet articulates her
belief in the superiority of the spiritual life of the single woman
to that of her married 'sister'. In her reflection on the Ten
Commandments, *Letter and Spirit*, Rossetti writes that women who
marry do 'well'; those who choose to be brides of Christ do 'better'.[7]
Her prose demonstrates both an erudite, theologian's knowledge of
the Bible and a complex and ordered theology, a willingness to
engage the discipline on its own terms. Both subverting the model
of the patriarchal family in this world and basing her spirituality on
such a paradigm, Rossetti perhaps can be claimed as a foremother
of contemporary feminist theology. The single woman's spiritual

life is everywhere elevated in Rossetti's prose, offering an alternative vocation to marriage and motherhood.

Here on earth, Rossetti's theology is perhaps not as egalitarian as the modern feminist theologian might hope for in an ancestor. Rossetti's theological paradigm maintains the superiority of men over women in this world.[8] Nevertheless, she writes in *Seek and Find,*

> but if our proud waves will after all not be stayed, or at any rate not allayed (for stayed they must be) by the limit of God's ordinance concerning our sex, one final consolation yet remains to careful and troubled hearts: in Christ there is neither male nor female, for we are all one (Gal. iii.28).[9]

This thesis is central to Rossetti's idea of relationships between the sexes and before God. Rossetti compares Christ, in his humility and humanity, with woman herself, as in the works of the 'body theology' mystics of the late medieval period. 'Women must obey; and Christ "learned obedience"'; 'She must be fruitful, but in sorrow, and He, symbolised by a corn of wheat, had not brought forth much fruit except He had died'; woman must be 'subordinate: and He came not to be ministered unto but to minister; He was among His own "as He serveth"'; like Christ, she is to be a helpmeet, 'And well may she glory, inasmuch as one of the tenderest of divine promises takes (so to say) the feminine form: "As one whom his mother comforteth, so will I comfort you" (Is. lxvi.13)'.[10] As Caroline Walker Bynum has demonstrated in her work on medieval women's devotion, it is through the body that Rossetti similarly reaches to Christ and God as Father.[11]

The articulation of a religious voice and articulation of an authorial one are one and the same for Christina Rossetti. *Maude* emerges out of a youth of great poetic promise, a tradition of women writing in the genre of the novel, and a religiosity offering the suggestion of some kind of vocation. The novella offers a foretaste of Rossetti as a religious writer who unifies the sensual and spiritual. Written before she was out of her teens, *Maude* was not published until after the poet's death.[12]

The work exemplifies the power to be found in relationship with the Divine that is central to Rossetti's richest and most sensual later poetry that rejects the loves of this world. Maude's almost pathological religious behaviour of '*Domine, non sum digna* (Lord, I am not worthy)' is evidence of her fervour: more specifically, her passion. This sensation of spiritual passion burns through *Maude* in the sexuality of the young woman, her relationship to God attained through love from her body, and, ultimately, the role of her poesis in connecting the spiritual and sensual realms. In Rossetti, the poetic voice, reaching for the Unknowable, exists in an ecstatic scriptural relationship to the Divine.

Maude opens as a tale of adolescent restlessness and ennui. The title character is about 15 at the start, located in the liminal state between Victorian girlhood and mature womanhood, with all its expectations and duties. She is a writer of poetry. Rather than contemplating marriage as her foils in the work are doing, Maude instead looks to her art. Her writing book, kept locked, 'was neither Common-Place Book, Album, Scrap-Book, nor Diary; it was a compound of all of these'.[13] Maude's life, future and present, is kept secure within the locked book. She seeks control and self-determination, which she finds in enclosure. The young woman locks herself away just as she secures her words.

Maude is characterized as a silent, unseen woman. Unlike her cousin Mary, she is not for public consumption. She does not craft her appearance to be beautiful:

> The two made a strong contrast: one was occupied by a thousand shifting thoughts of herself, her friends, her plans, what she must do, and what she would do; the other, whatever might employ her tongue, and to a certain extent her mind, had always an undercurrent of thought intent upon herself.[14]

Maude is, most significantly, a contemplative, perhaps more intelligent than her cousin. She is not meant for marriage, family or the nurturing of others. Her advances to a baby frighten it. The poet's contemplative spirit is in some ways flawed. Her concentration is forever on herself, not on God or occupied with the welfare of others.

At a birthday party for Mary, three significant foils to Maude are presented. Mary, the first, like Christ's mother, is destined to marry and have a family. Agnes, her sister, like the *Agnus Dei*, is indeed Agnes of God. Mild and gentle as a lamb, she ultimately takes on a Christ-like salvific role. Magdalen Ellis is a young woman who, like Maude, shows no interest in marriage and family life. She later devotes herself to Christ's love alone, becoming a religious sister.

We are left to imagine whether Magdalen has a past as salacious as her famous namesake's. The name 'Maude' is an interesting variation of Magdalen: while derived from the French 'Madeleine', hence also suggestive of both past transgression and ultimate devotion to God, the name also hints at 'maudlin'. Somehow, Maude's personality is overly emotional, too self-absorbed to achieve the utter devotion of a Magdalen. The charity houses for recovering fallen women in Victorian England were called Magdalen homes. The biblical story of the Magdalen was well known in the nineteenth century.

At the party, only Agnes, Magdalen and Maude engage in *bouts rimés*, a poetry-making game. They are also the three main characters in the story who do not marry. Poetry-writing is suggested as antithetical to marriage for women. By 'Part 2nd' of the novella, the women have grown up. 'Agnes had a more womanly air than at their last meeting ... Mary had outgrown her sister and ... both were remarkably good-looking.'[15] Mary exclaims to Maude, '"Why, Maude, you are grown quite a woman; but you look more delicate than ever, and very thin: do you still write verses?"'[16] Mary's first and second observations are clearly connected in her ultimate question. As a woman who expects to marry and have children, Mary associates Maude's writing with youth and suggests that her prolonged literary activity, like a protracted adolescence, may contribute to her physical frailness. Her writing may be unhealthy or perhaps make her unattractive. Mary shares news of '"poor Magdalen ... done with Albums and such like ... she has entered her noviciate in the Sisterhood of Mercy"'.[17] Magdalen has gone from writing to praying. Maude assumes that Magdalen is very happy. Mary paints a bleak picture of life in a religious sisterhood. Although she does not specifically mention it, we can assume that Mary also objects to the absence of men, marriage and family ties. '"Surely you would not like such a life ... Is that to your taste?"' Maude declares, '"You cannot imagine me either fit or inclined for such a life; still I can perceive that those are very happy who are".'[18]

Maude responds to the sisters' news of Magdalen's vocation by giving them a poem for her. Her work praises '"old, brown, common earth"',[19] '"Lie on earth and take your ease: / Death is better far than birth, / You shall turn again to earth"'.[20] The poem celebrates, ultimately, the benefits of enclosure. While Magdalen found her freedom through death to the world in the enclosure of the convent and Maude strives for hers through her locked book, both landscapes are compared to final bodily entombment in the ground. All things pass away, so '"[l]et us wait the end in peace"'.[21] In a burst of religious fervour, the speaker looks positively to '"the last trumpet call",' when '"the quick and dead shall all / Rise"'.[22] Her attachment to the metaphor of death is paradoxically empowering, as it gives hope for some kind of freedom from a patriarchal familial hegemony.[23]

On Christmas Eve, Maude retires to her room complaining of a headache. Agnes finds her 'before the locking manuscript-book', looking 'pale, languid, almost in pain'.[24] She asks to read the poem Maude had entered into the book, which her cousin permits. The work opens, 'Vanity of vanities, the Preacher saith, / All things are vanity.'[25] 'The eye and ear / Cannot be filled with what they see and hear.'[26] It bemoans the drudgery and meaninglessness of life, how all things pass away. The biblical quote cited has been taken out of context to permit a slide into despair.

The second sonnet Agnes reads is spoken in the first person. The speaker describes a visit to a church in which the sensual experience of the service does not bring the pilgrim-heart to Christ. She observes, 'I ask my heart with a sad questioning: / "What lov'st thou here?" and my heart answers me: / "Within the shadows of this sanctuary / To watch and pray is a most blessed thing." / To watch and pray, false heart? it is not so.'[27] The narrator second-guesses her own intentions. The watching and praying mode of the prior work is not enough. The speaker doubts. Maude as poet does not doubt her faith, but rather the justifiability of poetry-writing as a career. She cannot be a Magdalen, renouncing the world and accepting Love Divine, which, to her, is the correct answer to 'What lov'st thou here?' Taken without works, love of God does not satisfy her. Love for earthly man is not preferred. Thus Maude condemns and chastises herself for her desire to write poetry: 'Vanity enters with thee, and thy love / Soars not to Heaven, but grovelleth below.'[28] Devotion and love to man or even to God alone can be justified for a woman. Devotion to herself, a poetic career, cannot be. 'Vanity keepeth guard, lest good should reach / Thy hardness; not the echoes from above / Can rule thy stubborn feelings or can teach.'[29] The poet sees her devotion to her art as somewhat blasphemous or sacrilegious. It is crucial to remember that these events take place on the eve of the feast celebrating the incarnation of God into human form. That which is adored in the sanctuary of the poem, what Maude finds herself shrinking from, is the reality of the presence of God. He is the beloved here.

Maude's primary concern is that her cousin should stay through Communion on Christmas Day. Maude reveals that she herself will not be receiving Holy Eucharist at church. If she is blocked from the Body of Christ, she wishes to assure that Agnes, a 'sister', truly a second self, will be able to receive Him in her place. Communion is read as an erotic act for the virginal women. Agnes states, '"Mary and I have been thinking how nice it will be for us all to receive together".'[30] In her spiritual crisis, Maude judges her body impure: by forgoing the sacrament, '"at least I will not profane Holy Things".'[31] She proves her belief in the Real Presence at the Eucharist through her concern about coming into communion with Christ at a time when she believes herself to be stained with sin. Agnes counters '"if the struggle is so hard now, [think] what it will be when you reject all help".'[32] The 'help' that Maude is rejecting is a powerful God-force: a specifically masculine Divine, in Agnes's eyes, who is capable of sustaining her like a husband would, emotionally as well as physically. Poesis itself, according to her theology, cannot sufficiently feed a young woman.

As a saving sister, Agnes willingly volunteers to serve as Maude's double in her relationship with Christ. On praying, Agnes tells Maude, '"if there is anything you miss and will tell me of, I will say it in your stead".'[33] Thus although Maude finds herself incapable of religious sisterhood in community, the saving power of a 'sister' is nevertheless available to her. The narrator comments, 'Deep-rooted indeed was that vanity which made Maude take pleasure, on such an occasion, in proving the force of arguments against herself. Still Agnes would not yield; but resolutely did battle for the truth.'[34] The determination of Agnes to save an endangered 'sister' prefigures the devotion which Lizzie offers Laura through her salvific act in Rossetti's later *Goblin Market*. Both 'sisters' fight to save souls that have fallen victim to different kinds of temptations. In her supposed vanity, Maude maintains that '"[n]o one will say that I cannot avoid putting myself forward and displaying my verses".'[35] Her verses are comparable to sexual wares, like Laura's transaction of her body with the goblin men. Maude's religious scrutiny about her poesis goes beyond concern for the sin of 'pride'. She is anxious about the propriety of putting herself, her work, forward.

Agnes posits that '"we must all die – what if you receive the Blessed Sacrament no more?"'[36] Refusing Communion is to refuse sustenance of God the lover in both worlds. She fears for her cousin's soul. Maude, however, sees her period of suffering, 'abstinence', as celibacy to make herself conducive to correction. She awaits the time when she will be '"purified indeed and weaned from the world"', so that she '"may be fit again to approach the Holy Altar"' without '"dishonouring"' it.[37] 'Weaning' suggests motherhood: here the poet anticipates a separation from her mother – in this case, the world, her poetry – in order to accept the love of a husband, Christ. The crisis is marital and her fears conjugal. Maude is not prepared to renounce her writing as a form of self-expression, which could be seen as self-indulgence or gratification according to some schools of spirituality as well as nineteenth-century expectations for an adult woman. The chapter and 'Part 2nd' conclude as Christmas morn is rung in with a carol celebrating the Incarnation.

Soon after, the poet prepares for a journey to attend her cousin Mary's wedding. She leaves her home absolutely enclosed and physically contained. 'Enveloped in two shawls, though it was the height of Summer, [she] stepped into a cab; promising strict conformity to her mother's injunction that both windows should be kept closed.'[38] The major event of this narrative takes place outside the space of the text. The reader is told very simply that '[h]alf an hour had not elapsed when another cab drove up to the door; and out of it Maude was lifted perfectly insensible. She had been overturned; and, though no limb was broken, she had neither stirred nor spoken since the accident.'[39] This 'accident' is Maude's 'climax', with all the erotic resonance the term implies. Instead of receiving the Blessed Sacrament or marrying a man, she is 'overturned'. The moment is a culmination of numerous forces acting upon and within her. Although presumably independent of her own volition, the accident is spoken of as if she, and not the cab, had been physically assaulted. We know, given from the statements she makes during her spiritual crisis, that Maude believes sickness and suffering to be modes of correction. The accident hence serves as her true 'conversion' experience.

Before being packed off to be mortally wounded, Maude had asked her mother about becoming a nun. The mother tells her that it would bring her great grief. Maude had already rejected marriage, as her poetic leanings were too strong for such a vocation. Hence the only way that she is able truly to receive God is through mortification of her flesh in death. She must return to the earth, as in the poem given to Magdalen. Maude cannot bear children as a holy mother Mary or renounce and take the veil as Magdalen. The poetess writes to Agnes some weeks later, '"You have heard of my mishap?"'[40] She then continues at great length about how grave the injuries were that she has suffered. '"My side is dreadfully hurt; I looked at it this morning for the first time, but hope never again to see so shocking a sight. The pain now and then is extreme, though not always so".'[41] She exclaims, '"Ugh, my side!"'[42] The wound to the side is blatantly evocative of the wounds of Christ. To receive God, she has become like Christ, physically wounded. Many descriptions of Christ's side in medieval women's mystical writings, such as the works of Mechthild of Magdeburg, liken it to a vagina or nursing breast. Maude's 'side' has been penetrated, achieving Communion with the Divine. In the course of her letter Maude reveals a continued preoccupation with religious sisters. Oddly, she has written three poems on nuns to serve as an epithalamium for Mary's marriage. The moral implied is that each woman has her own vocation. Maude's is poesis. Her writing, which she earlier thought to be an obstacle in her spiritual life, has become a means of union/communion with the Divine. Maude's 'effort' in writing results in a subsequent 'enclosure'.[43] It is through illness that Maude writes her best poetry. The pain of birthing poetry through her 'wounds' becomes her own Christ-like self-sacrifice. Her 'confinement', to use the Victorian euphemism, enables Maude to nurse others with her poetry.

Maude's 'overturn[ing]' is equated with her religious faith. 'Converted', the weaker she becomes physically, the more powerful she is spiritually. The same young woman who frightened an infant at the beginning of the story exclaims about her married cousin, '"how I should love a baby of hers, and what a pretty little creature it ought to be"'.[44] If 'Mary' is substituted for the pronoun Maude uses in the above quote, the object of her devotion is clearly defined as Christ. Any carnal affections she may now have are directed at Him. The mystical theology of this relationship recalls the fifteenth-century visionary Margery Kempe, who wrote of her ecstatic pleasure in caring for the infant Christ. Deprived of physical health and hence full biological 'womanhood', procreative sexuality, through her wounds Maude crossed the threshold to female adulthood. However, she looks to the family beyond the grave rather than one on earth for her gratification. At last, Maude's death to the world has come to justify her writing.

By the third chapter of 'Part 3rd' of Maude, the young woman has fully accepted the Holy Trinity. In particular, she has embraced the third [male] 'member', the Holy Spirit, as her poetic and spiritual guide, a type of divine muse.[45] Her heavenward reach has been satisfied, and Maude is able to embody the transient essence of the

Body of Christ in her religious poetry. Of the three options open to young women in this story, if Mary embodies God in humanity, Christ the Son, and Sister Magdalen relates to God the Father through her faithful profession to Him, Maude's process of conversion involves the Holy Spirit. The Paraclete has worked through her body, enabling her to use her poetic talents in a way that she might be united with God. She embodies Spirit in poetry and at last may write with a clear conscience, knowing that her work is infused by Whom she has embraced.

In the concluding chapter of the novella, Maude recounts the terms of her conversion. Her heart was changed even before her accident. By her confession to Mr Paulson of her parish church, Maude was able to receive Holy Communion, to take God into her body orally, on Easter Sunday. '"That was indeed a Feast",'[46] she writes. Through the mediation of an earthly man, Maude is able to return to the Body of Christ. However, and significantly, the feast of Easter determines her relationship to the Divine. While she abstains from Him when His humanity is celebrated at Christmas, she is finally able to receive Him again on the holy day when His divinity, that which sets Him apart from us, is acknowledged: a time when He too transcends this world for heaven. She receives Communion when Christ's triumph over both death and sin are celebrated, again reinforcing the theme of pilgrim's progress. Maude has chosen to renounce completely all earthly love relationships, including the paradox of God-in-man. Her renunciation, embodying the Divine as Spirit through her poetic corpus, enables her to triumph over pride and death. If there is no hope for her in a solely poetic vocation as a woman poet deprived of both Divine and human companionship, Maude is prepared to accept death and the powers it may bring through her relationship with the Holy Spirit. She was 'Barren through life, but in death bearing fruit'.[47] The enigmatic longing of this poem's speaker has been fulfilled; she has crossed the bar and achieved the Divine through writing.

In my consideration of Christina Rossetti's *Maude*, I have emphasized the title character's realization of her poetic vocation, resulting in death to the world both literally and symbolically. I have not delved into the connection between Maude and the psyche of the young artist who created her, as many other critics have.[48] Certainly, there are ways in which the young Rossetti resembled this creation of her imagination. Both were devout Anglican women of tremendous poetic gifts but likewise profoundly uncomfortable with the propriety of publicly realizing their voices. The acceptance of a religious voice and the power to be found in the authority attained by transcending to the Divine through spiritual writing came to define Rossetti's aesthetic. The journey of Maude would seem to recount this discovery. This early work clearly contains seeds of the later devotional writer and religious poet, well-aware of the empowering possibilities of the religious sisterhoods for women. Given the time of composition, the novella might even have functioned in the poet's growth and self-acceptance as a woman writer able to utilize her religiosity as a vehicle for self-empowerment and speech. As Diane D'Amico has pointed out, if Rossetti created and hence in part was Maude, she also found within herself the voice of Agnes, one practical, positive, and sure in her faith.[49] Perhaps Maude can be read as a kind of spiritual journey for Rossetti the young poet. It is a passage through the mystic's dark night of the soul, during which the heart is watchful, to the attainment of a spiritual aesthetic and poetic vocation that gave her the power to write in her incomparable later art.

NOTES

1. See L.M. Packer, *Christina Rossetti* (Berkeley: University of California Press, 1963) for the 'classic' tale of Rossetti's lost love. Early feminist critics did not necessarily look upon Rossetti favourably, such as S. Gilbert and S. Gubar, *The Madwoman in the Attic* (New Haven: Yale University Press, 1979). They read her poetry as that of self-abnegation.

2. See David Hilliard, 'Unenglish and Unmanly: Anglo-Catholicism and Homosexuality', *Victorian Studies*, XXV (1982), 181–210, for an excellent discussion of this subject. For further discussion of the sisterhoods as 'unnatural' and the depiction of nuns in Victorian art, see S. Casteras, 'Virgin Vows: The Early Victorian Artists' Portrayal of Nuns and Novices', *Victorian Studies*, XXIII (1981), 157–83.

3 For further on the religious sisterhoods and their effects on women's lives in Victorian England, see B. Heeney, *The Women's Movement in the Church of England* (Oxford: Clarendon, 1988); M. Hill, *The Religious Order* (London: Heinemann, 1973); J.S. Reed, '"A Female Movement": The Feminization of Nineteenth Century Anglo-Catholicism', *Anglican and Episcopal History*, LVII (1988), 199–238; M. Vicinus, *Independent Women: Work and Community for Single Women 1850–1920* (Chicago: University of Chicago Press, 1985).

4. Diane D'Amico, '"Choose the stairs that mount above": Christina Rossetti and the Anglican Sisterhoods', *Essays in Literature*, XVII (1990), 204.

5.   See D.M.R. Bentley, 'The Meretricious and Meritorious in *Goblin Market*: a Conjecture and an Analysis', in David A. Kent, ed., *The Achievement of Christina Rossetti* (Ithaca: Cornell University Press, 1987).

6.   'The Convent Threshold' is perhaps the best example of this, although many of Rossetti's works, including *Monna Innominata*, present a woman's transcendence to love of God via the earthly man whom she renounces.

7.   Christina Rossetti, *Letter and Spirit: Notes on the Commandments* (London: SPCK, 1883), p. 90.

8.   Rossetti's earthly gender politics are not, however, without a subversive twist. In a famous letter to suffragist Augusta Webster, Rossetti declares: 'The fact of the Priesthood being exclusively man's leaves me in no doubt that the highest functions are not *in this world* [my emphasis] open to both sexes ... On the other hand if female rights are sure to be overborne for lack of voting influence, then I confess I feel disposed to shoot ahead of my instructresses, and to assert that female MPs are only right and reasonable' (M. Bell, *Christina Rossetti: A Biographical and Critical Study* (New York: Haskell House, 4th edn, 1971) pp. 111–12).

9.   Christina Rossetti, *Seek and Find: A Double Series of Short Studies of the Benedicite* (London: SPCK, 1879), pp. 31–2.

10. Ibid., pp. 30–31. Compare this passage to an excerpt from Hildegard of Bingen's *Symphony of the Harmony of Celestial Revelations*: 'O feminea forma, soror Sapientie, quam gloriosa es (O form of woman, sister of Wisdom, great is your glory)!' B. Newman (trans.), *Symphonia: A Critical Edition of the Symphonia Armonie Celestium Revelationum* (Ithaca: Cornell University Press, 1988), pp. 264–5.

11. See Caroline Walker Bynum, *Holy Feast, Holy Fast: The Religious Significance of Food to Medieval Women* (Berkeley: University of California Press, 1988).

12. Recent availability of *Maude* has been equally scarce. The work was reissued in 1976 in an edition edited by R.W. Crump. Elaine Showalter in 1993 included the work in a volume containing works of Dinah Mulock Craik. *Maude* has received little critical attention despite the great interest in Rossetti and nineteenth-century women writers during the last 20 years.

13. Christina Rossetti, *Maude*, in *Maude, On Sisterhoods, A Woman's Thoughts About Women*, edited by Elaine Showalter, (New York: New York University Press, 1993), p. 4.

14. Ibid., p. 6.

15. Ibid., p. 15.

16. Ibid., p. 16.

17. Ibid.

18. Ibid.

19. Ibid., p. 17, line 12.

20. Ibid., p. 18, lines 22–4.

21. Ibid., line 36.

22. Ibid., lines 47–8.

23. For an excellent study of the cultural milieu surrounding the treatment of death in Victorian literature, see M. Wheeler, *Death and the Future Life in Victorian Literature and Theology* (Cambridge: Cambridge University Press, 1990).
24. *Maude*, p. 23.
25. Ibid., lines 1–2.
26. Ibid., lines 2–3.
27. Ibid., p. 24, lines 5–9.
28. Ibid., lines 10–11.
29. Ibid., lines 12–14.
30. Ibid., p. 24.
31. Ibid.
32. Ibid., p. 25.
33. Ibid., pp. 24–5.
34. Ibid., p. 25.
35. Ibid.
36. Ibid.
37. Ibid.
38. Ibid., p. 30.
39. Ibid.
40. Ibid., p. 31.
41. Ibid.
42. Ibid., p. 32.
43. Ibid., p. 31.
44. Ibid., p. 31.
45. Rossetti's *Monna Innominata*, subtitled 'A Sonnet of Sonnets', perhaps a deliberate play on the title of the Song of Songs, offers further consideration of the earthly/heavenly muse of the Renaissance sonnet tradition.
46. *Maude*, p. 41.
47. Ibid., p. 43, line 30.
48. See, for example, Angela Leighton, '"When I Am Dead, My Dearest": The Secret of Christina Rossetti', *Modern Philology*, LXXXVII (1990), 373–88. Book-length studies that take *Maude* into account are few and far between, and very few articles have been written on the work.
49. Diane D'Amico, 'Christina Rossetti's Maude: A Reconsideration', *University of Dayton Review*, XV (1981), 136.

5

Fedalma – 'The Angel of a Homeless Tribe': Issues of Religion, Race and Gender in George Eliot's Poetic Drama, *The Spanish Gypsy*

Joss West-Burnham

In 1868 George Eliot published *The Spanish Gypsy*, a 'tragic play in blank verse, laid in 1487'.[1] The poem in the original Blackwood edition has 28 lines to a page and runs into some 358 pages. It is divided into five separate books. Although the poem is in the main in blank verse it still retains the semblance of a dramatic production, mirroring its original draft inception, begun in 1864–5, laid aside by Eliot and rewritten and amplified in 1867 after a visit to Spain. There are explicit 'scene-setting' locations and character changes with 'stage' descriptions and 'sets' written into the text. The blank verse is largely as dialogue between characters, internal monologues of the principal protagonists with further insertion of longer narratives of geographical topography. Within the verse form of the poem are assimilated various lyrics and songs which are performed by the poet, Juan, and a lame boy, Pablo. These lyrics serve particular dramatic ends in linking the past, present and future events with an especial emotional resonance similar to the function of the chorus within classical literature. Other features of the composition include the rupture of the blank verse with a transition to prose narrative and the occasional use of the epistolary form to act as a device to bring together the various sub-plots within the piece. For continuity *The Spanish Gypsy* will hitherto be described throughout this chapter as a poetic drama in order to retain and signify these attributes.

The Spanish Gypsy had a mixed critical reception, but five editions were published during the nineteenth century. There was no twentieth-century edition until 1989 with Lucien Jenkins' publication through Skoob Books of *George Eliot, Collected Poems*. There are still very few substantial works on George Eliot's poetry and no fully annotated critical commentary on *The Spanish Gypsy* in particular. This is surprising considering the vast George Eliot industry with respect to critical works on her fictional writings.[2] In some respects this was actually anticipated by the author herself, who remarks in a letter to Mrs Charles Bray that people have become accustomed to her as a novelist and one which they 'hitherto have found readable and debatable but will now find her becoming unreadable'.[3] She also mused later in a letter to John Blackwood, the publisher, that a phrase of Balzac's was particularly apposite to her venture into poetry which was, 'When I want the world to praise my novels, I write a drama: when I want them to praise my drama, I write a novel.'[4] These concerns with regard to authorial intention and influences upon the use of form are largely issues outside this particular work and discussions of these can be found elsewhere.[5]

The execution of *The Spanish Gypsy* was, as has been suggested previously, undertaken by George Eliot over a period of approximately three years and was a very considered intellectual enterprise at a moment in her career when 'money making' was no longer a prime consideration. In another letter to her friend Mrs Charles Bray she writes, 'how people who consider writing simply as a money getting profession will despise me for choosing a work which I could only hope to get hundreds for when for my novels I get thousands'.[6] She also maintains that she has been lucky in having a 'husband' like George Henry Lewes and 'his urging me to produce a poem rather than anything in a worldly sense more profitable'.[7] Other correspondence of George Eliot's is enlightening with respect to the influence of classical literature upon her and this particular poems construction. This is illustrated when she provides an explanation for her choice of title, 'The Spanish Gypsy' to her publisher. She says in a letter to John Blackwood, 'I chose the title, "The Spanish Gypsy", a long time ago, because it is a little in the fashion of the elder dramatist with whom I have perhaps more cousinship than with recent poets.'[8] The density of classical literature and composition appealed to George Eliot's aesthetic sensibilities and thus becomes a model adopted here in *The Spanish Gypsy*. Central here were ideas and views on tragedy. Eliot records how:

A good tragic subject must represent a possible, sufficiently probable, not a common action; and to be really tragic, it must represent irreparable collision between the individual and the general ... The collision of Greek tragedy is often between hereditary entailed Nemesis and the peculiar individual lot, awakening our sympathy of the particular man or woman whom Nemesis is shown to grasp with terrific force.[9]

These thoughts on tragedy and the impact on Eliot of Titian's paintings, *The Annunciation*, during one of her trips to Venice in 1864 can be seen as important corequisites towards the composition of *The Spanish Gypsy*. In Titian's painting George Eliot saw the representation of:

a young maiden believing herself to be on the eve of the chief event of her life – marriage – about to share the ordinary lot of womanhood, full of young hope, has suddenly announced to her that she is chosen to fulfil a great destiny, entailing a terribly different experience from that of ordinary womanhood.[10]

This intention forms the basis of the plot of the poetic drama. The story of Fedalma who, having been brought up in a Spanish Christian household of some privilege, on the eve of her marriage to a Spanish Duke, Don Silva, renounces her 'ordinary lot' and carries out the wishes of her (newly known) gypsy father, Zarca, to become 'the angel of the homeless gypsy tribe'.[11] By this invocation of the analogy of 'angel' George Eliot can be seen to extend the now familiar nineteenth-century territory and representations of the idealized space *of* and *for* the middle-class woman, as angel of the hearth to that of woman as a leader and guardian angel of a race.

The particular historical period of the poetic drama's setting is the fifteenth century. This is also highly significant and, as mentioned previously, specified by the author, as 1487. The moment which Eliot herself states:

in Spanish history when the struggle with the Moors was attaining its climax and when the gypsy race present under such conditions as would enable me to get my heroine and the hereditary claim among the gypsies. I require the opposition of race to give the need for renouncing the expectation of marriage.[12]

So, Fedalma, the heroine, the Spanish gypsy, renounces her personal and private life for the sake of others; in order to do her duty. And, perhaps, this is what one has come to expect from George Eliot's heroines, or, at least, those more familiar to us from her novels. The self-renunciating heroines like Dorothea, in *Middlemarch*, who embarking into womanhood and marriage full of hope to change the world ends up actually foundress of nothing, subsumed back into the dominant ideal of womanhood – as loving wife and doting mother. Dorothea thus becomes the embodiment and conformation of the dominant stereotype as angel of her domestic hearth. One critic has suggested with respect to Fedalma and *The Spanish Gypsy* that 'renunciation is the keynote of the poem'.[13] However, this can be seen as a partial view, for, with the depiction of Fedalma, one can begin to suggest and reveal the possibilities of other readings and interpretations. One can see, for example, the construction of a different kind of role for woman as 'angel' who, though still idealized, leaves the safety and the known security of the home and the domestic hearth to embark on a mission to lead her peoples into the unknown 'home' of Africa. Fedalma's role as leader is further extended within the poetic drama from angel to madonna with Fedalma referred to as mother to her tribe. So, while one can agree that renunciation is featured within this work the emphasis and the effect of it works differently from that on offer in the fictional works of George Eliot. The renunciation of the individual lot as angel of the hearth has been undertaken as a duty for the greater good of others. Thus, Fedalma forgoes her personal life in order to become the saviour of the gypsies. In *The Spanish Gypsy* the use and evocation of religious symbolism and significance is highly important for it reflects one can suggest George Eliot's own shift in belief from Evangelical Christian believer to agnostic. For in her own renunciation of faith she, like her heroine Fedalma, nevertheless retains and shares the ideas about duty and responsibility to others encoded within the evangelical tradition.[14]

Fedalma is presented as a heroine who rejects submission to patriarchy, who rejects being part of the Christian Spanish hierarchy and who, ultimately, rejects power which can only be obtained through marriage to someone else who wields it. She chooses instead to become a leader of people (a nation in fact) in her own right. This 'right' is problematized for us because it is passed on to her as a birthright – an inheritance – from father to daughter, rather than in accordance with the nineteenth-century practice of primogeniture. This is to feature again in Eliot's work with the subsequent composition and publication of the novel *Felix Holt*. Within the narrative plot of this novel it is the character of Esther who 'can choose her inheritance and her class'.[15] Fedalma's inheritance however is markedly different from Esther's for it is not an economic inheritance but a racial one, as a gypsy. In line with the argument of the poetic drama, it becomes her inheritance to lead the gypsy tribe to their homeland in Africa. This juxtaposition of race and gender thus becomes crucial to any interpretation of *The Spanish Gypsy*.

So what Eliot appears to be offering here is a reversal of what can be viewed as familiar gender roles and attributes usually offered during the Victorian period. Of course, many of Eliot's novels are concerned with issues of inheritance and, in many ways, one could claim that *The Spanish Gypsy* is a first draft of her later novel, *Daniel Deronda*, where issues of race, inheritance and duty are further explored with specific reference to Judaism; except here, the female heroine carries the role of 'saviour' for a race which has been largely marginalized within Western culture and history. In addition, unlike other fictional George Eliot heroines, Fedalma does not renounce or give away her inheritance but follows what is expected of her to the end.[16]

Fedalma, then, inherits her role from her father through her blood ties, but, in the end, is offered as not just a leader, but as angel and mother to her gypsy tribe. The use of these secular and religious signifiers with respect to angel and mother make explicit the importance of the religious dimension within *The Spanish Gypsy*. For the struggling factions within the dramatic action of the poetic drama represent not only different races and different nationalities but also different religious affiliations and beliefs. The period Eliot is writing about here was one, 'when a common bond of persecution united the Moors, Jews and Gypsies is late fifteenth-century Spain during the reign of Ferdinand and Isabella'.[17] This period was marked by the beginnings of a consolidated campaign for the expulsion of these races from Spanish territory through the declaration of Royal Edicts. This common struggle thus forms the historical backdrop for *The Spanish Gypsy*, but Eliot is also to take these issues further and explore, through character illustrations, the ultimate differences between these groupings in their resistance to oppression. It is within this context that Fedalma and her actions are to be placed.

The reader is alerted to the possible 'difference' of Fedalma from the very first introduction of her in *The Spanish Gypsy*. She is described appearing in the Place Santiago where there is music playing and people gathering as:

> Sudden, with gliding motion like a flame
> That through dim vapour makes a path of glory
> A figure lithe, all white and saffron-robed
> Flashed right across the circle, and now stood,
> With ripened arms uplift and regal head,
> Like some tall flower whose dark and intense heart
> Lies half within a tulip tinted cup ...[18]

Fedalma has been drawn to the square from her domestic space and appears to be under the spell of the music being played. We are told:

> But she, sole swayed by impulse passionate,
> Feeling all life was music and all eyes
> The warming quickening light that music makes,
> Moved as, in dance religious, Miriam,
> When on the Red Sea shore she raised her voice
> And led the chorus of the people's joy;
> Or as the Trojan maids that reverent sang
> Watching the sorrow-crowned Hecuba:
> Moved in slow curves voluminous, gradual,
> Feeling and action flowing into one,
> In Eden's natural taintless marriage-bond;
> Ardently modest, sensuously pure,
> With young delight that wonders at itself
> And throbs as innocent as opening flowers
> Knowing not comment – soilless, beautiful ...[19]

The passage continues describing Fedalma's dance. A dance of joy. A dance of pure sensation. A sensual dance. The dance of the innocent. Just as here Fedalma has been related to biblical and mythical icons, so it continues with her being described variously as, at one point, having 'virgin majesty' and another as, 'a goddess quitting earth again'.[20] To begin with, the reactions of the accumulated crowd to 'Lady' Fedalma's dancing are subdued. They are not sure what to think or how to react, whereas we, as modern readers, 'know' that dancing with abandon in the streets is something beyond propriety for a lady. However, the scene continues, and everyone becomes seduced by the passionate delight of music and dancing.

As has been suggested, then, this early act signals Fedalma's 'difference' from the normative expectations of a Spanish Lady, and when her dance is interrupted by the procession through the square of the gypsy prisoners, lead by their chief, Zarca, her fate is sealed. The act of intrusion is offered as a violation – innocence arrested by experience and the past and has startling dramatic resonance:

> But sudden, at one point, the exultant throng
> Is pushed and hustled, and then thrust apart:
> Something approaches – something cuts the ring
> Of jubilant idlers – startling as a streak
> From alien wounds across the blooming flesh
> Of careless sporting childhood. 'Tis the band
> Of Gypsy prisoners.[21]

Fedalma's eyes, we are told, meet those of the gypsy Chief, whose eyes

> Seem to her the sadness of the world
> Rebuking her, the great bell's hidden thought
> Now first unveiled – the sorrow's unredeemed
> Of races outcast, scorned and wandering.
> Why does he look at her? Why she at him?
> As if the meeting light between their eyes
> Made permanent union?[22]

– which of course it does because here Zarca realizes is the body of his daughter, lost long ago, stolen from the gypsy encampment (in the depiction Eliot appears to be inverting a commonly held nineteenth-century myth of gypsies stealing babies). All of this is later revealed to Fedalma and, initially, she is unconcerned, believing that she can continue with her marriage to Don Silva and then use her position as his wife to get her father released. It is Zarca who points out the hypocrisy and error of such thoughts:

> A woman's dream – who thinks by smiling well
> To ripen figs in frost. What! Marry first

And then proclaim your birth? Enslave
Yourself
To use your freedom? Share another's name,
Then treat it as you will? How will that tune
Ring in your bridegroom's ears – that sudden song
Of triumph in your Gypsy father? [23]

Hence, ultimately, Fedalma renounces her marriage plans to Don
Silva and works to get her father released another way. But here
events do not really go as expected because Don Silva, unlike
Fedalma, is prepared to try and sacrifice everything for the sake of
Love; for her he is prepared to sacrifice his religion, his race, his
status and his power. He is prepared to follow her, in fact, to Africa,
and become one of her tribe of followers. Don Silva tells Fedalma
that his love for her is that which reverences and protects, "'Tis
what I love determines how I love./ The goddess with pure rites
reveals herself / And makes pure worship.'[24] So in worshipping her
he cannot stand by and let her lead the life of a wandering gypsy
alone. Don Silva therefore, for Fedalma, renounces his Spanish
origins to take an oath of brotherhood and allegiance: 'she was my
good – what other men call heaven.'[25]

Fedalma is concerned at his renunciation; it is she who makes the
point that it is difficult, and might in fact be impossible, to change
from being a patriarch, a ruler, to having to submit to another man's
law. However, Don Silva is not to be deterred and it is only through
time and experience of solitude and isolation within the gypsy community that he begins to realize that it is not actually that easy to
throw off the past. The culmination of this awareness takes place
when the gypsies have sacked Bedmar and have killed many of his
friends and family. The moment of crisis comes when he is witness
to the killing of his uncle, and with the words, 'I am a Catholic
Knight – A Spaniard who will die a Spanish death',[26] kills his lover's
father. The killing of Zarca thus denies forever Don Silva's claims
that 'Love comes to cancel all ancestral hate / Subdues all heritage,
proves that in mankind / Union is deeper than division.'[27] He has
not been able to evade the past nor renounce wholly his duties and
his responsibilities; similarly with Fedalma.

For each of them, Don Silva and Fedalma, personal renunciation
brings sorrow and emptiness. Whilst Fedalma leads her doomed
race to Africa, Don Silva is to go to Rome to seek absolution for his
misdemeanours and to be allowed to take up the sword again as a

Spanish knight. Neither the acts of hero nor heroine have then achieved anything permanent in the way of bringing about change or reconciliation between the different factions. Fedalma sums up their fate:

> Vengeance! She does but sweep us with her skirts –
> She takes large space, and lies a baleful light
> Revolving with long years – sees children's children,
> Blights them in their prime ... Oh, if two lovers leaned
> To breathe one air and spread a pestilence,
> They would but lie to vivid victims dead
> Amid the city of the dying. We
> With our petty lives have strangled one
> That ages watched for vainly.[28]

Theirs has been a missed opportunity, and not just in personal terms of reconciliation but between races and different religious groups. Don Silva thus returns to his old life and Fedalma to her task of leadership; both swear faithfulness to each other and to the memory of their youthful, innocent love. This faithfulness is an important signifier with respect to gypsy lore and custom, for Zarca has pointed out to his daughter that whilst the gypsies are believed to have no faith, their belief is actually in fidelity to one another:

> Our people's faith
> Is faithfulness; not the rote-learned belief
> That we are heaven's highest favourites,
> But the resolve that being most forsaken
> Among the sons of men,
> We will be true
> Each to the other, and our common lot.[29]

In this same passage, Zarca also points out the similarities and differences between the gypsies and Jews. Whilst both races are presented as persecuted and in search of their common homelands, there is a different cultural positioning of the gypsies, for, 'If the Jews were a wandering people because of the Crucifixion of Christ, the Gypsies were a wandering people because according to legend, they refused shelter to Mary and Joseph on the flight to Egypt'.[30] Another essential difference between them is that the latter held no religious belief in common, save in metempsychosis – the trans-

migration of souls after death into a new body of the same or different species.[31] Zarca, however, encapsulates faithfulness to each
other as an important bonding element, and this is significant if one
returns to an earlier point with regard to George Eliot and her writings on religion. The religion of humanity offered by Feuerbach,
and of profound influence on Eliot, is being very closely described
here within the gypsy race, and so Fedalma renounces all to carry
out her racial and 'religious' obligations:

> ... Fedalma walked
> Tearless, erect, following the dead – her cries
> Deep smothering in her breast, as one who guides
> Her children through the wilds, and sees and knows
> Of danger more than they, and feels more pangs
> Yet shrinks not, groans not, bearing in her heart
> Their ignorant misery and their trust in her.[32]

The ambiguity of the poetic drama with respect to issues of race,
gender and religion – which we can only begin to explore here – is
pertinent in relation to dominant stereotypes (of gender in particular) during the nineteenth century; and in beginning to draw
towards a conclusion it is useful here to revisit some work published
in 1977 by Carol Christ (in Martha Vicinus's important collection of
essays on changing roles of Victorian women, *The Widening Sphere*).
Christ was concerned in her essay, 'Victorian Masculinity and the
Angel in the House', to reassess the then current scholarship on
Patmore's poem; she deconstructs one section, and notes how
culturally significant it becomes 'for the clarity with which it represents the male concerns that motivate fascination with that ideal',
and also notes how 'Patmore associates woman with a complex of
traditionally feminine values – love, intuition, beauty, virtue. Each of
these values, however, results from a woman's lack of desire to act.'[33]
Conversely, though, 'Man ... is defined precisely by the desire to
achieve, but that desire brings him only anxiety and pain.'[34]
Ultimately for Christ then, Patmore's poem is about the 'ambivalence' of these gender positions – a questioning of the achievements
of men and the supposed freedom from action given to the 'ideal' of
womanhood. She also works with the issues of sexuality in the
poem, with man offered as the hunter and woman idealized and
respected by him, 'as long as she resists. Once she accepts his offers,
she loses the moral stature that is her power.'[35] Hence, 'woman's

frigidity assures man's continual striving for a higher morality as well as a conviction of his lack of it'.[36] So the male is motivated by his pursuit of the Angel, and this can provide him with the means of transcending the tension over male achievement and male sexuality.[37] Patmore's poem then, for Christ, is not wholly about the Angel in the House but the use made (by men) of this idealized creature.

It is interesting to analyse Christ's work here and to look across to George Eliot's *The Spanish Gypsy*. So far research has not divulged for certain whether Eliot was familiar with *The Angel in the House* itself, but one can assume a shared cultural context (while, of course, allowing for a different gender perspective). Eliot has a position to negotiate in society as woman as well as writer, and earlier comments which place *The Spanish Gypsy* at a stage in her career where she has already achieved success and acceptance become particularly important to consider. This provides a crucial element in any twentieth-century reading of this poetic drama, for Eliot herself had already transgressed the social mores of the Victorian age by running away and living openly with a married man; this lived act of defiance, when contrasted with her fictional self-renouncing heroines whom she often denies active, passionate self-hood, poses a conundrum. With Fedalma, these issues are still not straightforwardly resolved. Fedalma is presented as sexually alive and passionate; she is also active outside the domestic realm. However this personal life is still only a 'half life', for Fedalma cannot have both love and fulfil her duties and responsibilities to her people who depend on her.

The ending of *The Spanish Gypsy* and Fedalma's plight remains enigmatic. She is represented thus: 'For me – / I am but as the funeral urn that bears / The ashes of a leader'.[38] She is the barren daughter of her father, who can nurture her tribe as mother but not add to the race she leads. Her power is also offered as a limited one:

> They loved their Queen, trusted Zarca's child,
> Would bear her o'er the desert on their arms
> And think the weight a gladsome victory;
> But the great force which knit them into one,
> The invisible passion of her father's soul,
> That wrought them visibly into its will,
> And would have bound their lives with permanence
> Was gone.[39]

The law of the Father is hence articulated as something much more powerful than that of the dutiful daughter. Fedalma can be the angel who leaves the domestic sphere to act as a madonna to her tribe, but the cost of this in personal terms is represented as great. The suggestion appears to be, therefore, that if the angel does leave the house the power she wields may be but a temporary one. Just as the mother's role is to empower and nurture her children to stand alone, so with Fedalma: her role is to lead her people to a new beginning at the cost of her own future.

NOTES

1. G. Haight, ed., *Selections from George Eliot's Letters* (New Haven: Yale University Press, 1985), p. 313.
2. Some references to *The Spanish Gypsy* can be found in, for example, R. Ashton, *Selected Critical Writings of George Eliot* (Oxford: Oxford University Press, 1992); K. Brady, *George Eliot* (London: Macmillan Press, 1992); and G. Beer, *George Eliot* (Brighton: Harvester Press, 1986). More detailed references are available from G. Haight, *George Eliot: A Biography* (Harmondsworth: Penguin Books, 1985); G. Haight, *Selections from George Eliot: A Biography* (Harmondsworth: Penguin Books, 1985); Joss West-Burnham, 'George Eliot's *The Spanish Gypsy*, a Neglected Work', *George Eliot Fellowship Review*, 21 (1990); and Joss West-Burnham, *George Eliot's 'The Spanish Gypsy': an Introductory Reading* (Keele University, M.Litt Thesis, 1988) held in the George Eliot Special Collection, Nuneaton Library, Nuneaton. A recent publication, B. Semmel, *George Eliot and the Politics of National Inheritance*, (Oxford: Oxford University Press, 1994), focuses in particular on issues of race and inheritance in George Eliot's writings.
3. Haight, *Selections ...*, pp. 346–7.
4. Ibid., p. 350.
5. Note 2 refers to some of these but in particular see Joss West-Burnham, *George Eliot's 'The Spanish Gypsy': an Introductory Reading*.
6. Haight, *Selections ...* p. 354.
7. Ibid., p. 346.
8. Ibid., p. 343.
9. F.B. Pinion, ed., *A George Eliot Miscellany* (London: Macmillan, 1982), p. 127.
10. Haight, *George Eliot: A Biography*, p. 376.
11. George Eliot, *The Spanish Gypsy* (London: William Blackwood & Sons, Standard Edition, 1868), Book 1, p. 147.
12. Haight, *George Eliot: A Biography*, p. 376.
13. G. Potter, *Annals of a Publishing House*, Vol. 3 (London: William Blackwood & Sons, 1928), p. 376.

14. An important point of debate here is also the recognition of the influence of George Eliot's reading and translation of the work of Feuerbach, in particular his emphasis on the 'religion of humanity'.

15. Beer, p. 140. Beer also suggests that this 'inheritance' plot within *Felix Holt* works to challenge 'the patriarchal succession of genealogy'.

16. For a much fuller discussion of these issues see Semmel, in particular chapter 5.

17. J. Wiesenfarth, *George Eliot: A Writer's Notebook, 1854–1879* (Charlottesville: University Press of Virginia, 1981), p. xxix.

18. Eliot, *The Spanish Gypsy*, Book 1, pp. 63–4.

19. Ibid., p. 64.

20. Ibid., p. 65.

21. Ibid., p. 69.

22. Ibid., p. 71.

23. Ibid., p. 148.

24. Ibid., p. 112.

25. Eliot, *The Spanish Gypsy*, Book 4, p. 315.

26. Ibid., p. 345.

27. Eliot, *The Spanish Gypsy*, Book 3, p. 288.

28. Eliot, *The Spanish Gypsy*, Book 5, p. 368.

29. Eliot, *The Spanish Gypsy*, Book 3, p. 288.

30. Wiesenfarth, p. xxiv.

31. Ibid., p. xxix.

32. Eliot, *The Spanish Gypsy*, Book 4, p. 354.

33. Carol Christ, 'Victorian Masculinity & the Angel in the House', in M. Vincinus, ed., *A Widening Sphere* (London: Methuen, 1980), pp. 147 and 149.

34. Ibid., p. 149.

35. Ibid., p. 151.

36. Ibid., p. 152.

37. Ibid.

38. Eliot, *The Spanish Gypsy*, Book 5, p. 369.

39. Ibid., p. 360.

6

Angel or Eve?: Victorian Catholicism and the Angel in the House

Anne Hogan

The influence of the conflicting and contradictory Victorian imagery for women – Angel in the House or Eve, sexual temptress – is evident in George Moore's presentation of Evelyn Innes, an acclaimed opera singer, as illustrated in this scene where she is about to sing Cherubini's *Ave Maria*:

> There were on that afternoon assembled in the little white chapel of the Passionate Sisters about a dozen elderly ladies ... and perhaps three or four spare women who wore a little more colour in their hats; these might be spinsters, of ages varying between forty and fifty-five. Amid these Evelyn was surprised and glad to perceive three or four young men ... Even though she was converted, she did not wish to sing only to women, and it amused her to perceive that something of the original Eve still existed in her.[1]

In this description of a small Catholic congregation, another image for Victorian women is suggested, that of pious single celibate: the 'three or four spare women who wore a little more colour in their hats'. In her comments after singing for the sisters, Evelyn reveals her awareness that as an unmarried Catholic, she is expected to be ignorant of sexual desire: 'She had never known how much of her life of passion and desire had entered into her voice ... her voice must have shocked them a little ... For all her life was in her voice ... her voice would be always Evelyn Innes – Owen Asher's mistress.'[2]

Mrs Humphry Ward, although not widely read today, was a popular and influential writer in the Victorian period, and her

novel *Helbeck of Bannisdale* (1898), which was published in the same
year as *Evelyn Innes*, also takes the struggle with Roman Catholicism
as a major part of the characterization of its main heroine. She
wrote of *Helbeck*, in *A Writer's Recollections* (1918), 'I was never more
possessed by a subject, more shut in by it from the outer world'[3]
and, throughout the winter of 1896, she absorbed herself in Catholic
literature in preparation for writing the novel. As Mrs Ward's
daughter and first biographer, Mrs Trevelyan, points out, the many
Catholic books in which she browsed gave her the grip of detail in
matters of belief or Catholic ritual, 'without which she could not
have approached her subject ...'[4] Although a review appearing in
the *Athenaeum* of June 1898, complained of the 'Catholic' theme
being 'too overdone, too strong',[5] Trevelyan writes that this novel
was thought to be probably the one on which her mother's fame as
a novelist 'will stand or fall'.[6]

Laura Fountain, the heroine of the novel, is the daughter of a
Cambridge lecturer in an obscure scientific subject; she has been
brought up with no religious training and with a positive contempt
for ritual and superstition, and 'from her childhood it came natural
to her to hate bigoted people who believed in ridiculous things'.[7]
When her father dies, Laura reluctantly accompanies her ailing
stepmother back to her old family home of Bannisdale Hall, where
her stepmother's brother, Alan Helbeck, maintains a long tradition
of Catholicism. Despite her deep repugnance towards his Catholic
faith, Laura becomes attracted to Helbeck, who with his romantic,
dark appearance was compared by one reviewer to Brontë's
Rochester.[8] This scene shows the immediate attraction which they
feel for each other:

> 'I fear that Bannisdale is not a very gay place for a young lady
> visitor?' He smiled. And so did she; though his tone, with its
> shade of proud humility, embarrassed her.
> 'It is as beautiful as a dream!' she said, with sudden energy ...
> And he turned to look, as she was looking, at the river and the
> woods. 'You feel the beauty of it so much?' he asked her, wonder-
> ing. His own strong feeling for his native place was all a matter of
> old habit and association. The flash of wild pleasure in her face
> astounded him. There was in it that fiery, tameless something
> that was the girl's distinguishing mark, her very soul and self.
> Was it beginning to speak from her blood to his?
> She nodded, then laughed.

'But, of course, it isn't my business to live here. I have a great friend – a Cambridge girl – and we have arranged it all. We are to live together, and travel a great deal, and work at music.'

'That is what young ladies do nowadays, I understand.'

'And why not?'

He lifted his shoulders, as though to decline the answer, and was silent – so silent that she was forced at last to take the field.

'Don't you approve of "new women", Mr Helbeck? ...'

'I wasn't thinking of them,' he said simply. 'I was thinking of the life that women used to live here ... of my mother and my grandmother.'

She could not help a stir of interest. What might the Catholic women of Bannisdale have been like?[9]

This passage also draws a contrast between the late nineteenth-century New Woman, who campaigned for equal rights, and Catholic women, who could now be portrayed as more closely maintaining the Victorian ideal of female piety.

In the earlier years of the Victorian period the inherited suspicions and animosity towards Catholicism continued to create a general attitude of prejudiced hostility. These deep suspicions may have found their origins in the long association of Catholicism with England's traditional enemies Spain and France, and the accepted picture of Rome demanding an unwavering and unthinking obedience,which seemed incompatible with central nineteenth-century English principles, such as political and religious freedom, and an allegiance to Crown and country.[10] The novels of this earlier period, where Catholicism provided an unfailing source of material for popular novelists, such as Mrs Frances Trollope's *Father Eustace, A Tale of the Jesuits* (1847), contrast with the portrayal of Catholics in novels of the 1880s and 1890s when a greater period of tolerance prevailed. The melodramatic appeal of anything Roman had faded and the subject of Catholicism is handled by writers like Mrs Ward and George Moore in the more thoughtful way anticipated by John Henry Newman, where the greater emphasis is placed on the spiritual and psychological significance of holding a belief.

One might wish to ask: what had changed by the 1890s that allowed a more sympathetic view of Catholics to emerge? By the last decade of the nineteenth century the impact of Darwinism, with what was perceived as its challenge to many of the basic principles of Christianity, tended to unite those with religious convictions against what appeared to be a common enemy. It is significant that in *Helbeck of Bannisdale* the conflict is between an orthodox Catholic, Helbeck, and Laura, who is representative of a new generation of women brought up in a spirit of free inquiry. By 1898, it had become apparent that there was not going to be a Catholic revival in England on a wide scale, and in consequence Catholics were no longer seen as a direct challenge to the authority of the established Church; rather, a spirit of uneasy tolerance towards Catholics prevailed. It is within this particular historical context that Mrs Ward gives a sympathetic portrayal of a devout Catholic.

Helbeck is close to 40 and has lived an almost monastic life: 'it was fifteen years since a woman's voice, a woman's presence, had mattered anything at all to him.'[11] During a moment of crisis in their relationship, Helbeck confesses to Laura that several years earlier he had been on the verge of an illicit love affair, but the woman in question saved him by entering a convent; and, were it not for his responsibilities as a landowner, he would have become a Jesuit. Although Helbeck is portrayed sympathetically, his is a stern, austere character and the reader is able to appreciate Laura's conflict in reconciling herself to his beliefs. Helbeck is portrayed as a more rigid Catholic than his local bishop, and he holds fiercely to his motto, 'No salvation outside the Church.'[12]

In her delineation of Helbeck's character, Mrs Ward drew upon her knowledge of her own father's religious history. Thomas Arnold (the second son of Dr Arnold, headmaster of Rugby School) vacillated painfully between reliance on authority and independence; embraced Roman Catholicism as a convert; then abandoned it to return to the Church of England; then reconverted and remained in the Catholic Church until his death. The whole family suffered considerable social and financial discomfort by his conversion, but Mrs Ward remained very close to her father. Some years after *Helbeck's* first publication she wrote that her greatest satisfaction had been her father's praise of the novel: 'I had said nothing to hurt that Catholic sensibility, at least, which I most dreaded to hurt, nothing consciously unjust to his side of that great controversy.'[13]

Helbeck is therefore a rare and quite convincing portrayal of a profoundly devout Victorian Catholic; that such a man should suddenly announce his engagement to a proclaimed sceptic appears incredible to Helbeck's Catholic friends and, no doubt, to Ward's readers. How then does Mrs Ward account for Helbeck falling in

love with Laura? Laura is portrayed as both beautiful and charming, and it is her feminine qualities that are shown to attract even a
man like Helbeck to her regardless of her advanced views: this
attraction is convincingly portrayed in the novel: 'Helbeck saw her
come in with a start of pleasure. Augustina [her stepmother]
fidgeted uncomfortably. She thought that Laura might have
dressed in something more quiet and retiring to meet a guest who
was a religious, almost a priest.'[14] If Laura is finally more convincing
as a conventional romantic Victorian heroine than as a sceptic, it is
perhaps partly accounted for by Mrs Ward's views that women are
not primarily intellectual beings: this is shown in this passage from
the novel:

> [Laura] represented forces of intelligence, of analysis, of criticism
> … But when in this new conflict – a conflict of instincts, of the
> deepest tendencies of two natures – she tried to lay hold upon
> the rational life … it failed her everywhere. She had no tools, no
> weapons. The Catholic argument scandalised, exasperated her;
> but she could not meet it.[15]

The plot concludes tragically with the traditional nineteenth-
century nemesis for transgressive females, when Laura, unable
finally to unite her agnosticism and feminist views with her love for
Helbeck, commits suicide: 'the tyrant river that she loved, had received her, had taken her life.'[16] In Laura's fictional suicide Mrs
Ward might be seen to comment on the limitations, as she saw
them, of the new views being expressed on the woman's role; the
'Woman Question', as it became popularly known, was an increasing preoccupation of late Victorian society. Mrs Ward saw these
views as responsible for encouraging women to reject their 'natural'
role as supportive wife and mother, and she felt moral chaos would
be the outcome of any merging of the gender roles. She was ap-
palled, as Elaine Showalter puts it, by the 'selfish individualism'[17] of
the campaign for women's suffrage and she opposed it,where possible, in her fiction.

Helbeck is described as an example of Catholicism at its best 'a
type sprung from the best English blood.'[18] However, unlike Laura,
he is shown to have the security of his faith, but when he loses her,
he learns that, as a Catholic, compromise is impossible and that he
has no real place in the modern world. There would seem to be no
better fictional solution for him, after Laura's death, than that

described by the Cambridge professor, Dr Friedland, a minor character who probably best expresses Ward's own views: 'Always I have felt myself in the presence of a good and noble man. In a few months or even weeks, they say he will have [joined] the Jesuits ... It gives me a deep relief to think of it.'[19] It is Dr Friedland who also places the conflict in the perspective of the revolution of modern morality, felt by some to be taking place in the later decades of the Victorian period: 'At present what one sees going on in the modern world is a vast transformation of moral ideas ... And the net result in the best moderns is at once a great elaborating of conscience – and an almost intoxicating sense of freedom.'[20] In 1898, when *Helbeck* was published, Catholicism was, as we have seen, no longer considered a subversive force in society, and Mrs Ward portrays it as an archaic faith, but a faith which might be cautiously admired for still holding to traditional values, particularly in relation to the role of women. In a changing late nineteenth-century world of 'intoxicating freedom', a much greater threat for the middle-class heroine than conversion to Rome by a handsome Jesuit, for a conservative Anglican like Mrs Ward, was presented by feminism and agnosticism.

George Moore's novel *Evelyn Innes* is singled out by Margaret Maison as 'a valuable study of a Catholic girl's conquest of passion by faith, wherein a genuine and sympathetic interest in Catholic ideals ... replaces the ... melodrama of earlier novels on this theme.'[21] In *Helbeck of Bannisdale*, Ward writes about Catholicism in the informative, discursive way expected of the 'problem novel'. George Moore's interest is not in writing fiction to educate his readers but rather in experimenting with the novel form itself. On his eightieth birthday a letter of congratulation appeared in *The Times* signed by most of the principal writers and artists of the day who greeted him as 'a master of English Letters' and as one who 'has not ceased to labour ... on the perfecting of his craft.'[22] Moore's process of experimentation with new styles is reflected in both *Evelyn Innes* and its sequel *Sister Teresa* (1901). A review of *Sister Teresa* which appeared in *The Academy* of July 1901, comments on how, in the novel, the reader is 'given not just an artistic array of picturesque facts, but also a sense of the innermost vitality of the characters'.[23]

In *Evelyn Innes* the conflict explored in *Helbeck* is reversed: here the eponymous heroine an opera singer, is torn between her sensual love for Sir Owen Asher, an atheist and an aristocratic sophisticate,

and her Catholic conscience and duty to her father. The novel could
be seen to reflect the quest for a centre, or code of values, for the late
nineteenth century which would reconcile the age old conflict – the
desires of the flesh and the spirit. Moore imaginatively evokes in
Evelyn Innes the web of emotionally charged duties that complicate
personal and ethical decisions. Asher makes it a condition of paying
for Evelyn's tuition as an opera singer that she leave her widowed
father and become his mistress in Paris. Evelyn has to choose
between her father and ambition; between love for Asher and duty
to a parent who depends solely on her as his contact with and
shelter from the everyday world. Evelyn has thus far spent her life
in the conventional manner of a typical nineteenth-century heroine
in putting her father's needs above her own, and she prevents, for
example, any intrusion into Mr Innes' privacy, which he devotes
exclusively to the study of medieval liturgical music.

After considerable soul-searching, Evelyn chooses Owen Asher
who, having been brought up a Catholic, has successfully argued
God out of existence; life for his social set in Paris is devoted to the
satisfaction of all sensual desire. Asher dictates that the full force of
her creative instincts be channelled into interpretative art, rather
than the traditional roles for women of marriage and motherhood.
He encourages her to identify totally with the character she is
portraying by imposing aspects of herself on the role. '[H]er Isolde
would have an intense and personal life that no Isolde had had
before.'[24] Art therefore becomes Evelyn's means of expressing the
potent sexuality that through Asher she has discovered in herself;
her acting becomes a studied demonstration of the power of
instinct. This is the personal mark of her interpretation of Wagner's
heroines, especially Isolde, and gains her great critical and popular
acclaim.

However, Evelyn is shown as unable to overcome her moral scruples completely, and eventually she goes back to Dulwich to plead
for her father's forgiveness. As she asks her father's pardon, she is
still mentally acting out a scene from Wagner's opera, and she
pleads in the words of Brunnhilde to Wotan. As the familiar music
plays in her ears, she loses all powers of discrimination between
reality and the play-acting of penitence: 'She knelt at her father's or
at Wotan's feet – she could not distinguish.'[25] Thus it is shown how
music has become for Evelyn a way to escape her conscience, and
she is suddenly fearful that her artistic life has corrupted her soul.
To achieve lasting success on the stage, Evelyn will have to distance

herself more firmly from her religious beliefs, but as Moore illustrates, for a Catholic that is to sacrifice eternity for the satisfaction of
the moment.

After this scene with her father, where they are reconciled,
Evelyn begins a long review of her past life. Her increasing dissatisfaction with Asher as a lover makes her critical of his principles, and
of their influence on the course her life has taken. 'Her mistake from
the beginning', she decides 'was in trying to acquire a code of
morals which did not coincide with her feelings.'[26] At one point she
tells Monsignor Mostyn – a religious and friend of her father's, who
becomes her spiritual mentor as she begins to review her personal,
professional and spiritual lives – that 'what we feel matters much
more than what we know'.[27] She renounces as arid the aesthetic
intellectualism which occupied so much of her time with Asher.
What she feels now is that she can free herself from Owen's
influence, not by using her conscience as a means to control her
passion, but only by total renunciation of the world; and, finally,
she decides that it is, 'by denial of the sexual instinct that we
become religious'.[28] The novel concludes with her decision to enter
the convent of the Passionate Sisters.

In *Evelyn Innes*, Moore examines various aspects of contemporary
culture; for example, Evelyn assimilates aspects of Walter Pater's
aestheticism and the fashionable cult of religiosity that followed in
the wake of the growing enthusiasm for Wagner's operas. Another
aspect of contemporary culture which Moore explores is the position of women. Patricia Stubbs argues that Moore's work, like
Thomas Hardy's, 'shows a deliberate attempt to break away from
the sexual stereotypes of mid-Victorian culture',[29] and Robert Lee
Wolff describes Evelyn Innes as the 'last of the Victorian and the
first of the wholly modern Catholics'.[30] Certainly, she is not portrayed as the traditional desexualized nineteenth-century heroine
and is drawn with a passionate nature and a 'sexual instinct'; and
yet nor is she characterized in an entirely new mould. If she is considered as a portrait of a religious heroine, there are aspects of her
characterization which reveal the continuing influence of traditional Victorian values, and the Angel in the House; an image
which, it would seem, kept a strong hold on the creative imagination even of a writer of realistic, experimental fiction such as Moore.

Lloyd Fernando summarizes here the central conflict of the
novel: 'Moore has brought this heroine ... to confront the moral
problem which Victorians could only see as a pair of mutually

opposed alternatives, chastity or immorality. Neither Evelyn Innes or her creator found a resolution to this dilemma.'[31] Lloyd Fernando also argues that while never happier than in the company of women, Moore 'never held a brief for women's liberation, entertaining the traditional fear that they would be "unsexed" by it.'[32] Although, publicly, Moore did not share Mrs Ward's conservative views and had distanced himself from the Catholic faith in which he was brought up, his personal opinions on the subject of the Woman Question prove, then, to be surprisingly similar to her own; according to Fernando, Moore expressed 'his denial of equal status to women in much the same terms as might be used in some quarters even today'.[33] When Evelyn is portrayed as entering a convent, in an effort to renounce her lover and a successful career, it seems a personal defeat for her; a denial of self. In this ending, we are also shown how a pious Victorian woman is unable, finally, to reconcile both her religious and sexual selves; the dichotomy between sexual temptress and idealized wife and mother continues, therefore, even at the end of the nineteenth century.

As she wrote *Helbeck* in 1898, it has been demonstrated here that Mrs Ward was clearly more anxious about the outcome, as she saw it, of the declining influence of the Angel in the House rather than any influence which Catholicism might have gained. As another century draws to an end, however, it is clear today that rather than waning away, the persuasive and enduring influence of the imagery of Angel or Temptress – with the Augustinian view of women which it embodies – is still evident in the continuing debate about the role which 'the Second Sex' should play in the church generally, and, in particular, within the discourse of orthodox Catholicism. In an essay entitled 'The Death of the Moth' Virginia Woolf suggested we should attempt to kill the self-effacing image of the Victorian Angel in the House,[34] if women are ever to play a truly equal part in society; it would seem, however, that she has still to be expelled from many parishes.

NOTES

1. George Moore, *Evelyn Innes* (London: Fisher Unwin, 1898), p. 453.
2. Ibid., p. 453.
3. Quoted in Mrs G.M. Trevelyan, *The Life of Mrs Humphry Ward* (London: 1923), p. 3.
4. Ibid., p. 146.

5.　'Review of *Helbeck of Bannisdale*', *Athenaeum* (11 June 1898), 3685, 751.
6.　Trevelyan, p. 143.
7.　Mrs Humphry Ward, *Helbeck of Bannisdale* (London: Smith, Elder, & Co., 1898), p. 33.
8.　Quoted in Mrs Trevelyan, p. 143.
9.　Mrs Ward, pp. 146–7.
10.　See E.R. Norman, *Anti-Catholicism In Victorian England* (London: Allen & Unwin, 1968).
11.　Mrs Ward, p. 139.
12.　Ibid., p. 114.
13.　Originally in the Introduction to the Westmoreland edition of *Helbeck*, quoted in V. Colby, *The Singular Anomaly: Women Novelists of the Nineteenth Century* (New York: New York University Press, 1970).
14.　Ward, p. 298.
15.　Ibid., pp. 317–18.
16.　Ibid., p. 459.
17.　Elaine Showalter, *A Literature of Their Own: British Women Novelists From Brontë to Lessing* (London: Virago, 1982), p. 227.
18.　Ward, p. 367.
19.　Ibid., p. 464.
20.　Ibid., p. 389.
21.　Margaret Maison, *Search Your Soul, Eustace: A Survey of the Religious Novel in the Victorian Age* (New York: Sheed & Ward, 1961), p. 161.
22.　The letter 'To George Moore on his Eightieth Birthday' was printed in *The Times* on 22 February 1932. It is cited in full, but without the list of signatures, in J.M. Hone, *The Life of George Moore* (London: Victor Gollancz, 1936), p. 437.
23.　'The Review of *Sister Teresa*', *The Academy* (20 July 1901), 1524, 53.
24.　*Evelyn Innes*, p. 153.
25.　Ibid., p. 212.
26.　Ibid., p. 337.
27.　Ibid., p. 335.
28.　Ibid., p. 469.
29.　Patricia Stubbs, *Women & Fiction: Feminism and the Novel 1880–1920* (Brighton: Harvester Press, 1979), p. 88.
30.　Robert Lee Wolff, *Gains and Losses: Novels of Faith and Doubt in Victorian England* (London: John Murray, 1977), p. 106.
31.　Lloyd Fernando, *'The New Woman' in the Late Victorian Novel* (University Park & London: Pennsylvania State University Press, 1977), p. 104.
32.　Ibid., p. 85.
33.　Ibid.
34.　Virginia Woolf, 'The Death of the Moth', quoted in *Killing the Angel in the House: Seven Essays* (London: Penguin Books, 1995).

7

From Hearth to Heath: Angelic Transformations in May Sinclair's Major Novels

Terry Phillips

This chapter focuses on May Sinclair's three best-known novels: *The Three Sisters, Mary Olivier: A Life* and *Life and Death of Harriett Frean*. Technically, Sinclair's work falls outside the parameters of this volume, since she began writing in 1897, and wrote her more significant contributions to the English novel between 1914 and 1922. However the central characters of the three novels I wish to discuss are fictional representations of products of a Victorian upbringing, an upbringing shared by Sinclair herself. I intend to argue that two of these characters challenge and rewrite the Victorian ideal of womanhood, as exemplified by the Angel in the House.

All three novels deal to varying degrees with the angel. *Life and Death of Harriett Frean*, published in 1922, is the account of the life of the only daughter of upper middle-class parents whose life is roughly contemporaneous with that of Sinclair herself, and who is very clearly educated for the role of Angel in the House. A religious authority underpins the role, to be confused in the infant Harriett's mind with the parental role. As a very small child, Harriett is being comforted and cosseted by her mother for a particularly angelic piece of conduct: 'Suddenly a thought came rushing at her. There was God and there was Jesus. But even God and Jesus were not more beautiful than Mamma. They couldn't be.'[1]

From her mother Harriett learns to regard God as a surrogate parent figure, offering and withholding approval. Harriett's mother's religious beliefs provide the framework within which she can train her daughter to be as she is, as the nineteenth-century patriarchal family needed her to be, a model of a particular kind of femininity. For if Harriett is to behave like an angel, not the heroic, 'angel of the Lord', but his/her unrecognizable nineteenth-century descendant, she must learn to be unselfish, for example allowing her 'little guest'[2] to play with her favourite doll, her fantasy child, an act which causes her such pain that she 'buries' the doll in a cardboard box, a burial which symbolizes the burial of the self which the call to angelic self-sacrifice demands.

After a childish act of disobedience, Harriett's father tells her that her parents want her 'To behave beautifully'.[3] The emphasis on surface appearance, rather than innate moral qualities, strikes a sympathetic chord within Harriett, who has already learnt that 'being good was being beautiful like Mamma'.[4] The phrase carries its own irony, created by the incongruity of the terms, and is the false premise on which Harriett conducts her entire life, confusing appearance with morality. The equating of beautiful behaviour with morality underlines the superficial attractiveness of the etherealized sexuality of the Victorian angel.

The one point of choice in Harriett's life, she decides negatively, in accordance with the doctrine of self-sacrifice and surrender with which she has been imbued. When her best friend's fiancé proposes marriage to her, Harriett can only refuse. Years later, when Harriett reflects on this, 'She felt a thrill of pleasure in her beautiful behaviour, and a thrill of pride in remembering that he had loved her more than Priscilla.'[5] For Harriett angelic behaviour is not the heroic sanctity of biblical angels but rather behaving beautifully. The end of the novel points this up with grim comedy. Harriett undergoes an operation, walking to the theatre with tightly compressed lips, lest she say anything improper under the anaesthetic. The penultimate section of the novel is a single line which reads, 'She had behaved beautifully',[6] a superbly ironic phrase, utterly inappropriate in Harriett's life and death situation, achieving the dimension of a comment on Harriett's entire life.

Life and Death of Harriett Frean is in many ways a depressing novel, the story of a woman who emphatically does not challenge or rewrite the idea of the angel, enlivened only by the narrative's undercutting of the central character. Within the context of Sinclair's work, it may therefore be seen as an ironic challenge to the formation of the Victorian angel, and as part of a revisionary project directed at the religious and social education of women.

A revisionary project implies some degree of rewriting, of recovery. Is it possible to rewrite the model of the angel so that it produces an altogether different kind of religious woman? Two of Sinclair's earlier novels suggest this possibility. *The Three Sisters*, published in 1914, owes some of its inspiration to Sinclair's series of introductions to the Dent editions of the Brontë novels published between 1907 and 1914 and to her full-length study of the Brontës, *The Three Brontës*, published in 1912. The similarity in title, as well as the setting of the Yorkshire moors, suggests the partial model of the Brontë sisters' circumstances. The novel is primarily about women's sexuality, which is represented as repressed by the strongly patriarchal figure of the sisters' father, Mr Carteret, the Vicar of Morfe. The central character and middle sister, Gwenda, in her strength of character and her love for her natural surroundings, can reasonably be regarded as modelled in part on Emily Brontë. She becomes the object of the only eligible male in the parish, the local doctor, but moves away in the hopes that he will marry her love-obsessed younger sister, Alice; in fact, her elder sister Mary ensnares him into marriage, while Alice finds escape in a scandalous marriage to a local farmer. Such a plot summary is distorting in its simplicity. Gwenda's motives are mixed. They may be attributed to sublimation (the primary interest of the novel is psychoanalytical) or to the inadequacies of the doctor, or perhaps any man, as a suitable husband for an independent young woman. I shall focus here on particular aspects of the portrayal of Gwenda and her elder sister, Mary.

Mary is the archetypal Angel in the House, what Harriett Frean might have become with a husband and a little more cunning, while Gwenda, I shall suggest, is a different and very unorthodox sort of religious woman. Mary Carteret, the Angel in the House, is ironically linked throughout the text with the words 'goodness' and 'sweetness', but the irony is not so much directed at Mary as at the terms themselves. On one occasion a direct criticism of Mary is made by Rowcliffe, the doctor she eventually succeeds in marrying:

Why, on earth, he wondered, had she [Gwenda] gone away and left him with this sweet and good, this quite exasperatingly sweet and good woman who had told him nothing but lies? He was aware that Mary Carteret was sweet and good. But he had found that sweet and good women were not invariably intelligent. As for honesty, if they were always honest they would not always be sweet and good.[7]

The criticism of Mary and her 'goodness' and the suggestion of self-deception is made obvious by the doctor's reflections on intelligence and honesty. However the reflection does not apply to Mary alone but is given general application. It is not Mary alone who is at fault, but the virtues of 'goodness' and 'sweetness' as they are commonly perceived. The term 'sweetness', almost invariably associated in the novel with 'goodness', evokes qualities of pliability and prettiness. The combination of both words strongly suggests the long enduring legend of the Angel in the House. It is this very 'goodness' and 'sweetness' which later ensnares Rowcliffe, his earlier clarity on the subject forgotten.

In fact, even a passing acquaintance with the plot of the novel will have suggested to most readers that 'good' is not a term to be applied to Mary's conduct, although she is commonly regarded in the neighbourhood as the only one of the three sisters who is a good woman. *The Three Sisters*, unlike *Harriett Frean* is not a full-length portrait of an Angel but nevertheless, through the character of Mary, the construct of the conventional and virtuous woman within the patriarchal family, patient, compliant, gentle and dedicated to the domestic comfort of others is effectively satirized. Inevitably Mary is contrasted with her sister Gwenda who represents the very real possibilities of rewriting the religious woman.

There are two central points in my definition of the religious woman; evidence of actions informed by conscience, and a belief in some kind of transcendence. Gwenda Carteret certainly has no time for orthodox religion, having suffered at the hands of her repressed and repressive father, the Vicar of Garth. She does however have a strong moral sense, never explicitly drawn out in the novel but expressed in her actions. When the scandal of Alice's pregnancy is revealed, it is Gwenda who stands by her, offering an alternative morality to that of her sanctimonious family. Her central act of self-sacrifice, whatever the mix of motives which may inform it, is primarily undertaken out of pity for her sister Alice.

Not only is Gwenda portrayed as a highly moral person, but the novel hints at some kind of awareness of the transcendent. In this respect, the setting of the novel, the Yorkshire moors, is very important as Gwenda's awareness of the transcendent is based on her awareness of the landscape:

> She saw the long straight line of Greffington Edge, hiding the secret moon, and Karva with the ashen west behind it. There was

something in their form and in their gesture that called to her as if they knew her, as if they waited for her; they struck her with the shock of recognition, as if she had known them and had waited too.[8]

There is an echo here, of course, of Emily Brontë. On one level it is the familiar Romantic celebration of nature, but it also carries some suggestion of the pantheism which often informs such Romantic writing, for the personification is more than a figure of speech and 'the shock of recognition' suggests that the elusive spirit of the place calls to something already within Gwenda.

Gwenda continues to display an absorption in her natural surroundings, but towards the end of the novel, when she is left alone to look after her sick father, with only the occasional and carefully rationed companionship of Rowcliffe this grows into something different. One night she takes a walk with him and sees what she describes as a vision:

The moon was hidden in the haze where the gray day and the white night were mixed. Across the bottom on the dim, watery green of the eastern slope, the thorn trees were in flower. The hot air held them like still water. It quivered invisibly, loosening their scent and scattering it. And of a sudden she saw them as if thrown back to a distance where they stood enchanted in a great stillness and clearness and a piercing beauty.

There went through her a sudden deep excitement, a subtle and mysterious joy. This passion was as distant and as pure as ecstasy. It swept her, while the white glamour lasted, into the stillness where the flowering thorn trees stood.[9]

The vision may be placed in a female tradition by its link with nature,[10] although the link with nature also suggests a Wordsworthian Romanticism, as does the reference to light and water. Words such as 'ecstasy' and 'mysterious' point to the spiritual nature of the experience. Unusually, for such experiences, it is shared by her companion, thus serving to suggest that the experience is beyond themselves and links them with some transcendent power.

Moments of vision, always associated with the thorn trees occur only towards the end of the novel, after Gwenda's rejection of sexual passion. Feminine passion for nature is often linked with

what recent critics have attempted to define as a new feminine
spirituality, often sensual and focusing on joy and plenitude.
Gwenda's thorn tree visions suggest rather a much older mystic
tradition of ecstasy in its original meaning of 'out of the body',
stressing the opposition of flesh and spirit which has its roots as far
back at least as second-century gnosticism. In one general passage
this is made quite explicit:

> Cut off from all contacts of the flesh, it turned to the distant and
> the undreamed. Its very senses became infinitely subtle; they dis-
> cerned the hidden soul of the land that had entranced her.
>   There were no words for this experience. She had no sense of
> self in it and needed none. It seemed to her that she was what she
> contemplated, as if all her senses were fused together in the sense
> of seeing and what her eyes saw they heard and touched and
> felt.[11]

In fact, the two strains of mysticism – ecstasy and sensuality – are
paradoxically both present here. The escape from the flesh leading
to the 'hidden soul of the land' seems to eschew the materiality of
both woman and landscape only for the experience to be expressed
not through language but through the senses. Kristeva's distinction
of the semiotic and symbolic seems relevant here. The account
certainly points to an extra-linguistic dimension.

Seven years later, Gwenda, whose life of isolation is relieved only
by her reading and by solitary walks, experiences another vision
prompted by the thorn trees. This time the mysterious vision does
not go uninterpreted. Her sister Alice's husband, Jim Greatorex,
tells her:

> 'I knaw what yo mane about those thorn-trees. 'Tisn' no earthly
> beauty what yo see in 'em.'
>   ... 'I can tell yo this for yo coomfort. Ef yo soofer enoof mebbe it'll
> coom t' yo again. Ef yo're snoog and 'appy sure's death it'll goa.'
>   ... 'I'll tell yo anoother quare thing. 'T'assn't got mooch t'do wi'
> good and baad. T'drink 'll nat drive it from yo, an' sin'll nat drive
> it from yo. Saw I raakon 't is mooch t'saame thing as t'graace o'
> Gawd.'[12]

Jim's experience although described through language, is a long
way removed from philosophic abstractions, and might more

readily be ascribed to the realm of the semiotic, or at least tending towards such a realm, which serves as a reminder of the dangers of ascribing the semiotic purely to female experience. Having said this, it is also true that Greatorex uses culturally-specific language, speaking of the grace of God, words which Gwenda herself does not use, but serving to confirm the link between this sort of experience and the cultural constructions which contribute to orthodox religious belief. This is further underlined by the association of the experience with flowering thorn trees, clearly suggesting the idea espoused by Christian and other religions of growth through suffering and particularly suggesting the biblical crown of thorns.

Greatorex argues that what he calls the grace of God is not dependent on being good. A close analysis of his conduct in the novel, and of Gwenda's conduct, suggests rather that the experience has little to do with what *the world* calls being good. Many critics have argued that Gwenda's self-sacrifice is mistaken, while others, myself included, would suggest that it is a rejection of a flawed sexual partner who would challenge Gwenda's sense of her self. In any event the issue can be passed over here. What I wish to argue is that Gwenda rejects the domesticated angelic role of goodness and sweetness, exemplified by her sister Mary, as ultimately immoral, moving from the domestic hearth quite literally onto the heath where, remaining true to herself and her own moral instincts, she finds confirmation, not just in self-affirmation but in the presence of a transcendence which is beyond herself.

The rewriting of the angelic role which can be seen in the character of Gwenda is made much more explicit in *Mary Olivier: A Life*. The novel is generally regarded as autobiographical, and Sinclair herself acknowledged autobiographical elements.[13] It traces the life up to middle age of Mary, the only girl in a family of four, in that sense paralleling the structure of *Life and Death of Harriett Frean*. However, the novel, focalized by the consciousness of the central character, Mary, is written in a much fuller style than the highly economical *Harriett Frean*, providing detail on the process of socialisation by which Mrs Olivier seeks to turn Mary into a dutiful daughter.

The daughter's account of her infancy and childhood abounds with religious references, snatches of hymns sung by the servants, prayers learnt at her mother's knee, the keeping of Good Friday. However the message is substantially the message of Mrs Frean: self-sacrifice. Just as Harriett was reprimanded for refusing to share her doll, so Mary, even before her fifth birthday, is reprimanded by her mother for wanting a kitten which has been given to her brother, Mark: ' "God," she said, "hates selfishness and self-will. God is grieved every time Mary is self-willed and selfish. He wants her to give up her will." '[14]

The difference between Mary and Harriett is Mary's resistance which takes place in two ways. One is through a traditionally masculine route, independence of mind and the application of logic. Mary's childish mind is sharp enough to perceive that the God of whom she is taught is an unpleasant, authoritarian figure, a perception which is conveyed by her frequent association of her ill-tempered father with 'Jehovah'. This view is confirmed by her interpretation of the meaning of the Passion: 'The Passion meant that God had flown into another temper and that Jesus was crucified to make him good again'.[15] The object of the irony created by the child's comical and incongruous connection of the revered deity of Christian worship with undignified behaviour such as flying into a temper, is the crude notion of 'atonement', which remains Mary's chief stumbling block as far as orthodox Christianity is concerned.

Like many women of her generation, Mary has little formal education, being mainly educated at home by her mother. However, she is more intelligent and intellectually curious than her mother, as well as being spurred on by her dislike of the doctrine of the atonement. Like other independent-minded heroines such as Maggie Tulliver, she turns to the family library, beginning with Locke's *Essay Concerning Human Understanding*, and, as she grows older, working through Spinoza, Plato, Kant, Schopenhauer and Hegel, as well as studying Buddhism and The Upanishads. The intellectual turning point of her life occurs when she is 14, and discovers Pantheism and the ideas of Spinoza in the *Encyclopaedia Britannica*, proclaiming indignantly: 'You had been told one lie on the top of another.'[16] This moment is the crucial influence in her intellectual life, to which through all her philosophical readings she returns again and again: 'The God of Baruch Spinoza was the God you had wanted, the only sort of God you cared to think about. Thinking about him – after the Christian God – was like coming out of a small dark room into an immense open space filled with happy light.'[17]

There is a second way in which Mary challenges orthodox Christianity. If Mary's first route to her own God is through the symbolic, and little can be more symbolic than the abstractions of

Kant and Hegel, then it could be argued that her second is through the semiotic or, to put it another way, it is not through male authority but through lived female experience. The first moment of such experience comes when Mary is seven years old:

> A queer white light everywhere, like water thin and clear. Wide fields, flat and still, like water, flooded with the thin, clear light; grey earth, shot delicately with green blades, shimmering. Ley Street, a grey road, whitening suddenly where it crossed open country, a hard causeway thrown over the flood. The high trees, the small, scattered cottages, the two taverns, the one tall house had the look of standing up in water.
>
> She saw the queer white light for the first time and drew in her breath with a sharp check. She knew that the fields were beautiful …
>
> The drawing-room at the back was full of the queer white light. Things stood out in it, sharp and suddenly strange, like the trees and houses in the light outside: the wine-red satin stripes in the grey damask curtains at the three windows; the rings of wine-red roses on the grey carpet …[18]

It is recognizable as a visionary experience, certainly not unique in literature, and like the visions of Gwenda Carteret, it may be placed in both a female tradition and the tradition of Wordsworthian Romanticism by its link with nature, and the reference to light and water. The account makes clear that the vision comes from within. It is the gift of knowledge: 'she knew that the fields were beautiful'. It is also important to note that while the natural scene prompts the vision, it continues once Mary is indoors, and in this way differs from Wordsworthian visions, and from those experienced by Gwenda.

Similar visions occur throughout Mary's childhood and adolescence, always represented by white light, always when she is by herself and always in some way associated with nature. She calls it her 'sudden, secret happiness'.[19] As is often the case with visionary experiences they are beyond Mary's control: 'It had happened so often that she received it now with a shock of recognition; and when it was over she wanted it to happen again. She would go back and back to the places where it had come, looking for it, thinking that any minute it might happen again. But it never came twice to the same place in the same way.'[20]

Mary is tempted to write her visions as poetry:

Poems made of the white dust, of the wind in the green corn, of
the five trees – they would be the most beautiful poems in the
world. Sometimes the images of these things would begin to
move before her with persistence, as if they were going to make a
pattern; she could hear a thin cling-clang, a moving white pattern
of sound that, when she tried to catch it, broke up and flowed
away. The image pattern and the sound pattern belonged to each
other, but when she tried to bring them together they fell apart.[21]

She compares the patterns of sound to those in a Greek poem she
has discovered in an old poetry book: 'She wished she knew Greek;
the patterns the sounds made were so hard and still.' These comments, foregrounding pattern and musicality and a language loved
only for its pattern, not its symbolic function, clearly privilege the
semiotic, recalling Kristeva's interpretation of Mallarmé's view on
poetic language: 'Indifferent to language, enigmatic and feminine,
this space underlying the written is rhythmic, unfettered, irre-
ducible to its intelligible verbal translation; it is musical, anterior to
judgement, but restrained by a single guarantee: syntax.'[22] Here I
wish to confine myself to the linguistic rather than psychoanalytic
implications. Suffice it to say that Mary's experience, represented
for us in language, is beyond language.
    As Mary grows older, these visions cease, to be replaced by
visions of another kind. Living an intolerably lonely and tedious life
with her mother, she is about to accompany some wealthy neigh-
bours to the south of France when she hears that her brother has
been taken ill. She is caught in a terrible dilemma between her love
and pity for her brother and her intense desire to make the journey
to the south of France. Adopting the conventional position of
prayer, kneeling beside her bed, with her arms stretched out on the
counterpane she pleads: 'If Anything's there – if Anything's there –
make me give up going. Make me think about Roddy. Not about
myself. About Roddy. Roddy. Make me not want to go to Agaye.'[23]
It is, whether or not Mary recognizes it as such, the prayer of
Gethsemane, 'take this cup away from me. Nevertheless, let your
will be done, not mine.'[24]
    Mary expects no answer to her prayer:

She didn't really believe that anything would happen. Her
mind left off crying. Outside, the clock on the Congregational

Chapel was striking six. She was aware of a sudden checking and letting go, of a black stillness coming on and on, hushing sound and sight and the touch of her arms on the rough counterpane, and her breathing and the beating of her heart. There was a sort of rhythm in the blackness that caught you and took you into its peace. When the thing stopped you could almost hear the click.

She stood up. Her white room was grey. Across the window the shoulder of the hill had darkened. Out there the night crouched, breathing like an immense, quiet animal. She had a sense of exquisite security and clarity and joy. She was not going to Agaye. She didn't want to go.[25]

This experience like Mary's earlier ecstasies may be described as visionary and, with its emphasis on rhythm and the senses, ascribed to the semiotic. There are, though, important differences. The experience is willed by Mary, or at least initiated by her prayer; it is characterized by darkness, not light; it takes place in her room, not outside; and it may be regarded as having some kind of outcome. The first and the last link it to the social order and define its difference from the other visions as being one of a moral dimension, of the self in relation to another. This social dimension relates the incident to darkness, and to the cultural space of the indoors. Mary's spiritual experience here is not one of plenitude but is in some ways the opposite, suggesting emptiness and enclosure.

Mary's narrative does not immediately associate her two apparently opposite kinds of vision. The darker vision is forgotten for 22 years, until another crisis in Mary's life when she recalls and repeats her previous act of willing. This time, the experience itself is apparently much more painful: 'It wasn't like this before. This is an awful feeling. Dying must be like this. One thing going after another. Something holding down your heart, stopping its beat; something holding down your chest, crushing the breath out of it ...' The comment can clearly be related to the notion common in Christian and other religious traditions of the death of the self. This is confirmed as the passage continues:

Let everything go except yourself. Hold on to yourself ... But you felt yourself going. Going and coming back; gathered together; incredibly free; disentangled from the net of nerves and veins. It didn't move any more with the movement of the net. It was clear and still in the blackness; intensely real.[26]

This places the experience, more emphatically than the previous dark vision, in a tradition completely opposed to those in which I have located Mary's other visions, either the High Romantic tradition, or the more recent traditions of female spirituality. It places it even more strongly than the manner in which Gwenda Carteret's experiences are described, within a much older mystic tradition of ecstasy as escape from the flesh. It may also however be linked to what I would describe as a tradition of radical spiritual resistance to the Victorian idea of the angel, manifested very clearly in the writings of Emily Brontë, recalling as it does 'The Prisoner':

> My outward sense is gone, my inward essence feels –
> Its wings are almost free, its home, its harbour found;
> Measuring the gulf it stoops and dares the final bound!
>
> Oh, dreadful is the check – intense the agony
> When the ear begins to hear and the eye begins to see;[27]

Mary does not express the regret at the return to the senses that the Brontë passage expresses but in other ways there are clear similarities. What Mary does move to is what I earlier described as an outcome. She moves to a point where she can will her mother's survival: 'Then it willed. Yourself willed. It was free to will.' The implication is clear. Mary's ecstatic experience has freed her from her more selfish desires; by dying to her self she has achieved a greater freedom.

I have, in the course of this chapter, identified two distinct and in some ways opposite trends in visionary experience, which are mirrored by opposite trends in Christian tradition: the one which begins with the experience of natural beauty and is characterized by joy and exaltation and a sense of fulfilment, associated with images of light, and the other which begins often in an enclosed space, characterized by pain and loss and associated with images of darkness. To return once more to Brontë, it is a duality expressed in the well-known stanza:

> Few hearts to mortals given
> On earth so wildly pine
> Yet none would ask a Heaven
> More, like this Earth than thine.[28]

Both variants on the visionary experience may be associated with Kristeva's notion of the semiotic in the linguistic sense that they are associated with the senses and with unformulated repetitions and patterns. This is more obviously true of what we may term the 'light' experiences, partly because the 'dark' experiences come when Mary is older and she analyses them. Nevertheless, in seeking to explain them both to her lover and herself she privileges the semiotic over the symbolic, being able to explain it to her lover only in terms of its 'queerness'. 'It isn't the thing people call willing at all. It's much queerer. Awfully queer.'[29] and later to herself: 'she had never been aware of it before; she had only thought about and about it, about Substance, the Thing-in-itself, Reality, God. Thinking was not being aware.'[30]

I am aware of a tendency in what I have said so far to use the word 'semiotic' to mean 'extra-linguistic' whereas in the psychoanalytical sense in which the term is developed by Kristeva it should be confined to the 'pre-linguistic'. All the visionary experiences I have discussed may, of course, be explained in these terms as echoes of both a lost plenitude, and of the death-drive. However to confine them to such explanations is to cut off other possibilities of the extra-linguistic, other ways to escape the tyranny of the rational-symbolic. Sinclair was well versed in both philosophy and contemporary psychoanalysis, being the author of two books on philosophy and articles on psychoanalysis,[31] but the terms in which Mary explains her visions owe more to her creator and original's adherence to Philosophic Idealism than to Freudianism. As the novel draws to a conclusion, the ecstatic visions return and Mary ascribes them explicitly to a transcendental presence: 'She had a sense of happiness and peace suddenly there with her in the room. Not so much her own as the happiness and peace of an immense, invisible, intangible being of whose life she was thus aware.'[32]

This, of course, is a much more distanced account than the earlier accounts of visionary experience. It is an explanation rather than an account; a return to the symbolic, which serves to remind us of my starting point, that Mary challenges and rewrites the idea of the angel through two routes: thought and experience.

One cannot deny the description 'religious woman' to Mary Olivier, although the religious beliefs she professes and practises are far removed from those of the Angel in the House, Harriett Frean. At the end of the novel, she comments on the orthodox

Christianity lived by women of her time which she sees as having become far too bound up with the patriarchal system which seeks to tie her to her mother's values, and to the prized feminine virtues of passivity, sweetness and gentleness. Thus she identifies with the Jesus she sees as brave, proud, impatient and ironic, the reverse of the virtues she has been taught. She rejects the notion of sin and atonement as both barbaric and having the undesirable effect of creating an oppressive burden of guilt.

She rejects this in favour of something less orthodox. Yet she retains a belief in a transcendent deity, not separate from herself, for she sees herself as part of God, but more than herself, which I take as the defining principle of transcendence. Although she argues for an absolutely un-moral beauty and rejects 'being good', one can only assume that this is a reference to the orthodox moral-ity of the time which she happily transgresses, for example in becoming Richard's mistress, since some of her moments of illumi-nation through darkness come at moments of placing the good of others, namely Roddy and her mother, before her own self-interest. These I would argue are the defining descriptions of a religious woman, a belief in transcendence and a moral code in relating to others.

In arguing that the characters of Gwenda Carteret and Mary Olivier represent revisions of the religious woman, transforming her from the angel of the hearth to a free and independent woman, who in the latter's case takes her place in the public arena, I am aware of certain problems. I have contrasted them with Harriett Frean, the exemplary daughter, but are they any different? All three women sacrifice an opportunity of marriage. I have based my definition of the religious woman in part on the presence of a moral sense, or conscience, which others may well argue takes us right back to the sacrificial role of the angel.[33] However, I wish to assert, that unless one is going to abandon the social altogether, the setting aside of one's own desires, self-sacrifice, self-denial, call it what you will, cannot be altogether avoided. What must be avoided are the Scylla and Charybdis of self-preoccupation and self-abnegation. The visionary experiences I have discussed, which I have attributed to awareness of transcendence can be separated into the sensual and the ecstatic, sometimes containing elements of both at once, indi-cating the necessity of both. Only by maintaining both can the twin perils of plenitude and denial be avoided. In discussing visionary experience I have drawn on the idea of the semiotic in the sense of the extra-linguistic. An important element in Kristeva's discussion of the semiotic is her notion of the thetic break, which is necessary to pass from the unformulated semiotic into the articulated symbolic.[34] Entrance into the symbolic is often viewed negatively, but the fact remains that the symbolic is necessary in order to relate. Therefore the thetic is necessary with its inevitable consequence of loss. At the point where Sinclair's spiritual heroines relate to others they experience the negative, the dark of the ecstatic visions, but this is only a part of their experience and a consequence of their very independence which marks them out from the traditional angel and rewrites them as strong defiant angels beyond the limiting constructs of femininity.

NOTES

1. May Sinclair, *Life and Death of Harriett Frean* (London: Virago, 1980; first published, London, 1922), pp. 15–16.
2. Ibid., p. 6.
3. Ibid., p. 23.
4. Ibid., p. 15.
5. Ibid., p. 67.
6. Ibid., p. 182.
7. May Sinclair, *The Three Sisters* (London: Virago, 1982; first published, London, 1914), p. 74.
8. Ibid., pp. 58–9.
9. Ibid., pp. 320–1.
10. See for example, Annis Pratt, 'Women and Nature in Modern Fiction', *Contemporary Literature*, 13 (1972), 476–491.
11. *The Three Sisters*, p. 340.
12. Ibid., p. 369.
13. May Sinclair, Letter to Marc Lodge, quoted and summarized by Theophilus Boll, *Miss May Sinclair: Novelist* (Rutherford: New Jersey, 1973), p. 226.
14. May Sinclair, *Mary Olivier: A Life* (London; Virago, 1980; first published, London, 1919), p. 14.
15. Ibid., p. 51.
16. Ibid., p. 100.
17. Ibid.
18. Ibid., pp. 48–9.
19. Ibid., pp. 75–6 and 93.
20. Ibid., p. 93.
21. Ibid., p. 125.
22. Julia Kristeva, 'Revolution in Poetic Language', in Toril Moi, ed., *The Kristeva Reader*, (Oxford: Blackwell, 1986), p. 97.
23. *Mary Olivier: A Life*, p. 260.

24.   Luke 22.42–3, Jerusalem Edition (London, Darton, Longman and Todd, 1966).
25.   *Mary Olivier: A Life*, pp. 260–1.
26.   Ibid., p. 351.
27.   C.W. Hatfield, ed., *The Complete Poems of Emily Jane Brontë* (London, Oxford University Press, 1941), p. 239.
28.   Ibid., p. 164.
29.   *Mary Olivier: A Life*, p. 366.
30.   Ibid., p. 378.
31.   May Sinclair, *A Defence of Idealism* (London, 1917) and *The New Idealism* (London, 1922).
32.   *Mary Olivier: A Life*, p. 375.
33.   See for example Jean Radford, Introduction, in *Mary Olivier: A Life*, and Sydney Kaplan, *Feminine Consciousness in the Modern British Novel* (Urbana, Illinois, 1975), p. 58.
34.   Kristeva, 'Revolution in Poetic Language', pp. 98ff.

8

The Angel in the House of Death: Gender and Identity in George MacDonald's *Lilith*

William Gray

This chapter seeks to address the theme of the 'Angel in the House' by exploring the representation of the female (and specifically the maternal) in *Lilith*, the fantasy novel by George MacDonald. The relevance of this approach to the theme is corroborated by Barbara Koltuv's *The Book of Lilith*, when in the chapter 'Lilith and the Daughters of Eve', she cites *in extenso* the passage in Virginia Woolf's essay 'Professions for Women' in which she talks about the need to kill the Angel in the House. Koltuv is a Jungian analyst who talks of 'the war between Eve and Lilith,'[1] or in less oppositional language 'the [endless] cycle of alterations between the Lilith and Eve aspects of woman's psyche'.[2] Another Jungian analyst, Siegmund Hurwitz, has taken Koltuv to task in his *Lilith – The First Eve*, ostensibly for scholarly inadequacies, but by implication as one of those who overlook the point that the Lilith material is 'above all about the anima problem of the Jewish male',[3] and 'only applies externally ... to the real woman in a secondary fashion'.[4] While I myself resist conversion to the Jungian *gnosis*, nevertheless I find it difficult to resist the analogy that George MacDonald's *Lilith* is about the problem (call it 'anima problem' if you will) of a Scottish male. However, there is something blatantly sexist in Hurwitz's assumption that male images of women only apply 'externally ... in a secondary fashion' to 'the real woman'. Surely the point of much feminist writing has been that male images generated by male problems have been foisted (no doubt 'in a secondary fashion') on women to such an extent that 'the real woman' is often

117

hard to find? There are of course different feminist responses to this situation. One such response which might be relevant to George MacDonald's work is that of Lynne Pearce in her book *Woman/Image/Text*, where she raises the question of whether reading Pre-Raphaelite art and literature 'against the grain' can in some cases only ever be a Pyrrhic victory.[5] The works in question leave so little space for a feminist reading that the game is simply not worth the candle. Whether MacDonald's work falls into this category remains to be seen. Another response which perhaps is only feminist under erasure is that of Julia Kristeva. Kristeva's writings are both provocative and suggestive from a psychoanalytical point of view, and what she does for example in 'Stabat Mater'[6] seems to offer a fruitful way of exploring patriarchal images and fantasies of 'women'. The approach she develops in her texts of the 1980s (*Powers of Horror*, *Tales of Love* and *Black Sun*)[7] seems to work particularly well with George MacDonald's fantasy writing.[8]

But to return for the moment to Virginia Woolf and the need to kill the Angel in the House, Koltuv sets up an opposition between the wild and murderous Lilith and the nurturing Mother Eve. She does not explicitly identify Eve with the Angel in the House, but there can be little doubt that they are closely associated if not identified. There is a strong suggestion that in a sense it *is* Mother Eve (the Eve of patriarchal construction) who needs to be killed for women to achieve freedom and dignity. In Kristeva's terms, the need for such matricide in the symbolic order is related in a complex way to the more primal need for the matricide which is, as she controversially puts it in *Black Sun*: 'our vital necessity, the sine-qua-non condition of our individuation …'.[9] For Kristeva, individuation as such demands the leaving, the losing, symbolically the killing, of the original all-embracing Mother or the *chora*. Failure to 'kill the mother' can result ultimately only in psychosis or suicide according to Kristeva. Matricide in this sense is a case literally, as Woolf puts it, of murder in self-defence.

George MacDonald's fantasy writing is transparently all about the Mother, as R.L. Wolff[10] and David Holbrook[11] in their different ways have shown. More specifically, as I have tried to show elsewhere,[12] MacDonald's fantasy writing is about the dilemma of losing or killing or taking leave of the Mother in order to be somebody *or* holding fast to the Mother, but at the price of not being somebody, that is, in psychosis or suicide. There is biographical evidence which suggests that the melancholy which per-

vades MacDonald's writing goes back to a traumatic primary experience with his mother;[13] but in any case the texts themselves
witness to an intense struggle with the figure of the Mother, a struggle literally to the death. This struggle is nowhere more evident
than in his last major work *Lilith*, published in 1895, when
MacDonald was 71. There are many similarities between *Lilith* and
Phantastes, MacDonald's other fantasy work, published nearly 40
years previously.

Both novels are dominated by a tension between various incarna-
tions, on the one hand, of the Angel in the House (in *Phantastes* this
is above all the wise old woman with young eyes in the magic
cottage), and on the other of a female demon (in *Phantastes* this is
the ogre in 'the Church of Darkness', but above all the Alder-
maiden, who, like Lilith, 'will smother you with her web of hair, if
you let her near you at night').[14] The 'Shadow' also figures in both
novels, though much more prominently in *Phantastes* – where the
plot mostly revolves around Anodos's attempts to become free of
his 'Shadow', the depression or melancholy which afflicts him. In
Lilith the 'Shadow' is in a sense much more 'objectively', if inter-
mittently, present as the consort of Lilith, and is even referred to as
Samoil, presumably a corruption of Samael, the Satan of the
Kabbalah. In contrast, in *Phantastes* the threat of the female demon
is certainly present, but it does not dominate the novel in the way
that it does in *Lilith*. *Phantastes* is clearly a *Bildungsroman*, concerned
with the formation of the young hero (and writer); but while the
narrator of *Lilith* is also a young man, the novel is not so much
about his formation as it is about the part he plays in a much larger
and age-old drama which culminates the overcoming and 'redemption' of Lilith. *Lilith* is certainly a psychological novel, but it is also a
mythological and perhaps a theological one.

Lilith is above all about two competing images or constructions
of 'woman': Lilith versus Eve. It is only gradually revealed to
the reader that Mr and Mrs Raven are Adam and Eve. But already
on his first meeting with Mrs Raven, the narrator, Vane, has a
numinous experience:

> The sexton [Mr Raven] said something to his wife that made her
> turn towards us. – What a change had passed upon her! It was as
> if the splendour of her eyes had grown too much for them to
> hold, and, sinking into her countenance, made it flash with a
> loveliness like that of Beatrice in the white rose of the redeemed.

Life itself, life eternal, immortal, streamed from it, an unbroken lightning. Even her hands shone with a white radiance, every 'pearl-shell helmet' gleaming like a moonstone. Her beauty was overpowering; I was glad when she turned it from me.[15]

The narrator's first encounter with Lilith (as yet unnamed) is also numinous:

Then I saw, slowly walking over the light soil, the form of a woman ... She was beautiful, but with such a pride at once and misery on her countenance that I could hardly believe what yet I saw. Up and down she walked, vainly endeavouring to lay hold of the mist and wrap it around her. The eyes in the beautiful face were dead, and on her left side was a dark spot, against which she would now and then press her hand, as if to stifle pain or sickness. Her hair hung nearly to her feet, and sometimes the wind would so mix it with the mist that I could not distinguish the one from the other, but when it fell gathering together again, it shone a pale gold in the moonlight.

Suddenly pressing both hands on her heart, she fell to the ground, and the mist rose from her and melted in the air. I ran to her. But she began to writhe in such torture that I stood aghast. A moment more and her legs, hurrying from her body, sped away serpents. From her shoulders fled her arms as in terror, serpents also. Then something flew up from her like a bat, and when I looked again, she was gone. The ground rose like the sea in a storm; terror laid hold upon me; I turned to the hills and ran.[16]

Eve and Lilith seem to represent binary opposites: immortal life versus sickness, pain and death; presence and plenitude versus disintegration and dispersal; the power of the gaze versus vulnerability to the gaze; and above all (echoing Woolf's 'Angel of the House' passage) purity versus impurity. And yet each of these is dangerous: the sacred and the taboo; the sublime and the abject; the perfectly self-same and the threateningly other; each seems to derive from a place which is uncanny and unfit for human life. Perhaps MacDonald's Eve and Lilith, split apart as they are, can only offer suicide or psychosis as the consequence of not successfully negotiating a break with the maternal body or chora in order to become somebody else.

Vane has a further glimpse of the as yet unnamed Lilith as a woman in 'the evil wood' urging on a 'strife-tormented multitude' in a furious battle.[17] A little later he hears Mara's version of the story of the evil princess (Mara is the daughter of, and very much identified with, Eve). Lilith herself first confronts him as what seems to be a corpse, a skeleton: 'a body it was however, and no skeleton, though as nearly one as body could well be'.[18] The naked, ghastly form seems very much to represent what Kristeva calls 'the abject', that is, the maternal body become a phobic 'object'.[19] Technically the 'abject' is not an 'object' at all, because it comes from the place that is prior to the split between 'subject' and 'object', between 'self' and 'other', which happens in the symbolic order. The 'abject' is the 'other' which is not yet properly distinguished from the 'self'; it is the 'outside' which is not yet properly distinguished from the 'inside', and is therefore threatening to the precarious emergent self. The 'abject' is the improper, the unclean: filth, waste (out of which Lilith, according to one Jewish tradition, was formed).[20] It is the corpse, and especially, as here, a corpse which is 'alive': the living dead. It is no surprise that Lilith turns out to be a vampire. And yet not only will Vane not abandon this repulsive female body; in a disturbingly necrophiliac gesture he goes to bed with this quasi-corpse:

> I crept into the heap of leaves, got as close to her as I could, and took her in my arms. I had not much heat left in me, but what I had I would share with her. Thus I spent what remained of the night ... Her cold seemed to radiate into me, but no heat to pass from me to her.[21]

In the three months Vane spends trying to resuscitate the corpse, he spends much time washing her (ritual purification of the taboo?) and trying to feed her. He dreams of her transformation into Eve:

> Every time I slept, I dreamed of finding a wounded angel, who, unable to fly, remained with me until at last she loved me and would not leave me; and every time I woke, it was to see, instead of an angel-visage with lustrous eyes, the white motionless, wasted face upon the couch.[22]

Yet ironically it is only when he is asleep that Lilith feeds off him, sucking his blood in the form of a great white leech. In psychoanalytical terms, this is surely a classic tale of the 'biter bit'. The anxiety and aggression involved in devouring the mother are projected on to the maternal figure in a situation where mother and infant are not yet clearly sorted out. And yet having preserved this repulsive yet fascinating female figure by unknowingly giving his blood, Vane is himself literally repulsed by her. She leaves him, yet:

> I followed her like a child whose mother pretends to abandon him. 'I will be your slave!' I said, and laid my head on her arm. She turned as if a serpent had bit her. I cowered before the blaze of her eyes, but could not avert my own.[23]

His dreams of finding an angel who will not leave him having been shattered, Vane nevertheless continues to pursue Lilith. At length, utterly exhausted, she does take him in her arms:

> Suddenly [her arms] closed about my neck, rigid as those of the torture-maiden. She drew down my face to hers, and her lips clung to my cheek. A sting of pain shot somewhere through me, and pulsed. I could not stir a hair's breadth. Gradually the pain ceased. A slumberous weariness, a dreamy pleasure stole over me, and then I knew nothing.[24]

The sexual aspect of his coming together with Lilith is even more explicit later in her palace when he regains consciousness out of a 'delicious languor', a floating in sheer pleasure, a dying. He finds Lilith, wearing 'a look of satisfied passion', on top of him,[25] a position which of course Adam would not stand for, though MacDonald does not make this point overtly. But at this stage in the narrative Lilith has had enough of Vane; she changes into a leopard, and speeds off to her palace.

It is there that Vane eventually catches up with Lilith, and before she comes to his bed, she gives her version of her story. Lilith's version is presented as mendacious; however one passage does ring true to the character of Lilith as revealed later. She says: 'I knew that, if you saw me as I am, you would love me – like the rest of them – to have and to hold. I would none of that either! I would be otherwise loved!'[26]

Despite the humiliation and castration that Lilith will have to undergo at the hands of Adam, Eve and the family, this cry rings strongly from the heart of the novel: 'I would be otherwise loved!'

The dramatic confrontation between Lilith and Raven, who finally reveals himself as Adam, occurs after Lilith follows Vane back into 'our' world in the form of a Persian cat. Raven reads aloud a poem recounting Lilith's story which provokes Lilith into revealing herself. Raven then appears as Adam and proceeds to give the 'definitive' patriarchal version of Lilith's story. Lilith was an 'angelic splendour' brought by God to Adam to be his wife. She however could only think of *power*, and counted it slavery to be one with Adam and bear children.[27] Lilith fled to the army of the aliens, ensnared the heart of the great Shadow so that he became her slave and made her queen of Hell. She is the vilest of God's creatures, living by the blood and lives and souls of men.[28] But then God gave Adam another wife – not an angel but a woman – who is to Lilith as light is to darkness. But there is hope for Lilith, for even she shall be saved by her childbearing.[29] This prophecy is fulfilled when Lilith's daughter, Lona, brings about her mother's fall from power,[30] a fall which in the patriarchal version naturally constitutes Lilith's 'redemption'. Adam then calls upon Lilith to repent. She defies him, saying: 'I will not repent. I will drink the blood of thy child.'[31] So Adam locks her in a cupboard. Lilith's magic enables her to escape, but she is pursued to her palace by an army of the so-called Little Ones led by Vane and her daughter Lona. Lona seeks to embrace her mother, but is dashed to the floor and killed. The 'murdering princess' is however captured, having reverted to the withered, wasted, corpse-like condition in which Vane first found her.[32] She is carried off in triumph to Adam, but *en route* the army stops at Mara's house, 'the House of Bitterness', where Lilith's re-education begins. Asked three times by Mara to repent, Lilith, now a 'seeming corpse', answers: 'I will not. I will be myself and not another.'[33] The dialogue continues, with Lilith sounding ever more like an existentialist feminist hero:

'Alas, you are another now, not yourself! Will you not be your real self?'
   'I will be what I mean myself now.'
   'If you were restored, would you not make what amends you could for the misery you have caused?'
   'I would do after my nature.'
   'You do not know it: your nature is good, and you do evil!'
   'I will do as my Self pleases – as my Self desires' …
   'You are not the Self you imagine.'

'So long as I feel myself what it pleases me to think myself, I care not. I am content to be to myself what I would be. What I choose to seem to myself makes me what I am. My own thought makes me me; my own thought of myself is me. Another shall not make me!' ...

'Such a compulsion would be without value. But there is a light that goes deeper than the will, a light that lights up the darkness behind it: that light can change your will, can make it truly yours and not another's – not the Shadow's. Into the created can pour itself the creating will, and so redeem it!'

'That light shall not enter me: I hate it! – Begone, slave!'[34]

But the light does enter Lilith, in the form of a 'worm-thing ... white hot, vivid as incandescent silver, the live heart of essential fire',[35] which creeps out of the fire to penetrate Lilith: 'The Princess gave one writhing, contorted shudder, and ... the worm was in her secret chamber.'[36]

Despite going through 'horror', 'torture' and 'the hell of self-consciousness' as the central fire of the universe radiates into her, Lilith nevertheless proves very difficult to break. She persists in her defiance, even when visited by 'an invisible darkness ... a horrible Nothingness, a Negation positive ... Death Absolute ... not the absence of everything, but the presence of Nothing'.[37] In this quasi-existentialist encounter with Nothingness: 'The princess dashed herself ... to the floor with an exceeding great and bitter cry. It was the recoil of Being from Annihilation.'[38] Still Lilith will not submit until she undergoes 'the most fearful thing of all' which is beyond knowledge and even imagination. She goes alone into the outer darkness, into living death, into a dismay beyond misery, a dismay beyond expression. Her face

sent out a livid gloom, the light that was in her was darkness, and after its kind it shone. She was what God could not have created. She had usurped beyond her share in self-creation, and her part had undone her. She saw now what she had made, and behold, it was not good![39]

If this glimpse 'into the heart of horror essential' must in theological terms be a vision of Hell, in psychoanalytical terms it recalls Winnicott's 'unthinkable anxiety'[40] located in a place prior to selfhood, let alone knowledge. And 'The light that ... in her was darkness' recalls the 'black sun', the primal unnameable horror, evoked by Kristeva not only in *Black Sun* but also in *Powers of Horror*.[41] Confronted by this horror far beyond mere annihilation, Lilith finally yields and begs to die. She is now ready to be taken to Adam and Eve in the House of Death. Her subjugation is not yet complete, however; the final humiliation is to have to beg to be symbolically castrated by asking Adam to sever her hand which she cannot open (could the Goethe-loving MacDonald have been unaware that the fist that must be cut off is in German *Faust*?). Using the sword which once guarded the gate of Eden, Adam severs the hand of Lilith, who is now finally allowed to die. Broken by the threat of psychosis, the unnameable horror, Lilith has finally submitted to a fate in which suicide seems to coincide with assimilation into the patriarchal symbolic order, that is, the House of Death.

Eve has triumphed over Lilith, and the angel in the house has not been killed but is as alive and as well as a woman can be in the House of Death. In Kristeva's terms, we might say that matricide has been avoided. The Mother has been preserved, but at the cost of suicide, what Kristeva calls 'the depressive or melancholic putting to death of the self ... instead of matricide. In order to protect mother I kill myself ...'[42] The suicide in question here is, of course, not only that of Lilith, but also that of George MacDonald, who is clearly 'of Lilith's party', perhaps without knowing it. MacDonald's suicide is not literal, but is expressed in the depression which haunted his life from his youth, when he is remembered as repeating 'I wis we war a' deid',[43] to the final lapse into five years of silence at the end of his life. The triumph of the Angel in the House represents the defeat not only of a woman who would be 'otherwise loved' but also of a man who would love otherwise. In theological terms, *Lilith* also seems to represent the failure of a Christian who would have faith 'otherwise'. The text is shot through with allusions to gnostic motifs; but in the end it seems that it is the 'martinet God' (as MacDonald once called him) who seems to triumph through his representative Adam and his angels in the house. But the book does not end without hope, if 'unconcludedness' can be read as 'not without hope'; for the 'final' chapter of *Lilith* is entitled 'The Endless Ending'. At the very last moment Vane is denied access to the throne of the Ancient of Days, and returns to his library, though at times he is literally uncertain where he is, or whether he is awake or dreaming.[44] Wherever he is, Vane waits and ponders MacDonald's favourite quotation from that great modern gnostic, Novalis: 'Our life is no dream, but it should and will perhaps become one.'[45]

It is significant that MacDonald's first fantasy novel, *Phantastes*, begins with a lengthy extract from Novalis, and his final fantasy novel ends with a quotation from the same author. To read MacDonald 'against the grain' would be to follow his ambivalent but deep-rooted attachment to the radical vision of Novalis. There, beyond the deathly double-bind of Eve or Lilith, we might find Sophia.

NOTES

1. B.B. Koltuv, *The Book of Lilith* (York Beach, Maine: Nicholas-Hays, 1986), p. 83.
2. Ibid.
3. S. Hurwitz, *Lilith: The First Eve* (Einsiedeln: Daimon Verlag, 1992), p. 12.
4. Ibid.
5. L. Pearce, *Woman/Image/Text* (London: Harvester Wheatsheaf, 1991), p. 139.
6. In T. Moi, ed., *The Kristeva Reader* (Oxford: Blackwell, 1986), pp. 160–186; also reprinted in *Tales of Love* (New York: Columbia University Press, 1987).
7. J. Kristeva, *Powers of Horror: An Essay on Abjection* (New York: Columbia University Press, 1982); *Tales of Love; Black Sun: Depression and Melancholy* (New York: Columbia University Press, 1989).
8. See W.N. Gray, 'George MacDonald, Julia Kristeva and the *Black Sun*', *Studies in English Literature 1500–1900*, Autumn 1996.
9. Kristeva, *Black Sun*, pp. 27f.
10. R.L. Wolff, *The Golden Key: A Study of the Fiction of George MacDonald* (New Haven: Yale University Press, 1961).
11. G. MacDonald, *Phantastes*, with an Introduction by David Holbrook (London: Everyman Paperback, 1983).
12. See Gray, op. cit.
13. In a secret drawer in MacDonald's desk were found, after his death, a lock of his mother's hair and a letter by her containing the following reference to his premature weaning: 'I cannot help in my heart being very much grieved for him yet, for he has not forgot it ... he cryed desperate for a while in the first night, but he has cryed very little since and I hope the worst is over now'; see Greville MacDonald, *George MacDonald and His Wife* (London: George Allen and Unwin, 1924), p. 32.
14. G. MacDonald, *Phantastes* (London: Dent, 1915), p. 10.
15. G. MacDonald, *Lilith* (Grand Rapids: Eerdmans, 1981), p. 32.
16. Ibid., p. 50.

17.　Ibid., p. 54.
18.　Ibid., p. 96.
19.　Cf. K. Oliver, *Reading Kristeva: Unraveling the Double-bind* (Bloomington: Indiana University Press, 1993), p. 58.
20.　Cf. Koltuv, p. 19.
21.　*Lilith*, p. 97.
22.　Ibid., p. 102.
23.　Ibid., p. 110.
24.　Ibid.
25.　Ibid., pp. 132f.
26.　Ibid., p. 130.
27.　Ibid., p. 147.
28.　Ibid., p. 148.
29.　Ibid.
30.　Ibid., pp. 184f.
31.　Ibid., p. 149.
32.　Ibid., p. 185.
33.　Ibid., p. 199.
34.　Ibid., pp. 199f.
35.　Ibid., p. 201.
36.　Ibid.
37.　Ibid., p. 204.
38.　Ibid.
39.　Ibid., p. 206.
40.　See D.W. Winnicott, *The Maturational Process and the Facilitating Environment* (London: Hogarth, 1965), p. 57f; and *Home is Where We Start From* (Harmondsworth: Penguin, 1986), p. 32.
41.　See *Powers of Horror*, pp. 34ff.
42.　*Black Sun*, p. 28.
43.　Greville MacDonald, p. 84.
44.　*Lilith*, p. 251.
45.　Ibid., p. 252. Original in Novalis, *Schriften*, ed. Kluckhohn and Samuel, dritter Band (Stuttgart: Kohlhammer, 1960), p. 281.

9

Quiet Angels: Some Women Hymn Writers*

J.R. Watson

The nineteenth century saw a huge increase in the writing of hymns and the publication of hymn books, and a great many of both were written by women. They wrote hymns because it was a respectable and lady-like thing to do, along with teaching in Sunday school or Bible class (Mercy Chant, in Hardy's *Tess of the D'Urbervilles*, is an uninteresting example). Their great exemplar, from the previous century, was Anne Steele, who did not publish under her own name, but who called herself 'Theodosia' to indicate her sex, and whose two volumes were prefaced with engravings making it clear that a woman was writing (even if the poems themselves do not discuss the problems of woman's writing as, say, those of Anne Finch or Mary Leapor do). A nineteenth-century writer described her thus:

> Anne Steele, both on account of an accident in girlhood and heavy attacks of illness at not infrequent intervals, loved the retirement of her Hampshire home. A quiet life suited her best. The garish foppery of fashion and the loud-voiced frequenters of life's dusty arena were little suited to her taste.[1]

The writer of this account, Mrs E.R. Pitman, clearly had a conception of a woman's role as quiet (perhaps in more than one sense). Her book, *Lady Hymn Writers*, published in 1892, is full of appreciations of a particular kind, unspoken assumptions about the way in which women (or rather 'ladies') were supposed to write. One chapter in her book, entitled 'Hymn Writers for the Quiet Hour', begins with women hymn-writers who 'write for the most part for sick and suffering ones, for sad and weary workers, for heart-broken penitents, and for bereaved, trembling mourners':

In all their poetry may be found touches of pathos, evidently wrung from the heart's deepest experiences, scraps of spiritual autobiography, and many snatches of 'songs in the night'.[2]

This pathos, which women hymn-writers were thought to feel to a greater degree than men, was often associated with their own experience of suffering. Indeed, Gilbert and Gubar's observation that in the nineteenth century women were leading lives that caused them to be ill, and that 'nineteenth-century culture seems to have actually admonished women to *be* ill',[3] is strikingly borne out in Mrs Pitman's pages. Anne and Emily Brontë died young; Frances Ridley Havergal 'had many sharp attacks of illness, and consequent journeys in search of health':[4] Eliza Fanny Goffe 'spent her girlhood amid country surroundings, on account of her delicate health';[5] Margaret Miller Davidson showed early signs of genius which 'was allied to a fragility of constitution and delicacy of temperament which resulted in early death';[6] Caroline M. Noel 'suffered a long illness of twenty years before the end came', and thus she 'learned in suffering what she taught in song'.[7]

An example is that of Charlotte Elliott (1789–1871), who wrote 'Just as I am, without one plea', which was first published in *The Invalid's Hymn Book* (second edition, Dublin 1841). She also published *Hours of Sorrow Cheered and Comforted* (1836), described on the title-page as being 'By a Lady'. After a severe illness in 1821, she became an invalid for the next 50 years, devoting some of the time to editing *The Christian Remembrancer Pocket Book*, and living with her clergyman brother. Her poem 'The Minstrel' suggests that the idea of a certain kind of woman poet was acceptable: the minstrel is a woman (as opposed to those in James Beattie's *The Minstrel* and in Scott's *Lay of the Last Minstrel*) who is prone to considerable mood-swings:

ever and anon I heard her sigh,
And ever and anon tears filled her eye.

This is because she is aware of 'care, suffering, strife', and of death waiting at the close of life. The woman minstrel's voice is soft and low; it is deeply sensitive to sadness, but also deeply moved by the consolations of religion:

The sunshine is from earth removed, that heaven more bright may seem,

The heart denied what most it loved, till there He reign supreme.

Women writers were thought to be especially sensitive to pain, suffering, and the misery of bereavement. For example, we may take a letter written by a stranger to Anna Laetitia Waring in 1856:

> I have a great desire to let you know what a source of comfort your 'Hymns and Meditations' have been and still continue to be to me, during long dark nights of affliction, and praise God that He has so instructed you, and feel the deepest communion of spirit with you. In the short space of six and a half years I have buried four sons and my dear wife.[8]

Such sensitivity was thought to be more appropriate than hard thinking. The memoir of Anna Laetitia Waring from which this is taken emphasizes experience and intuition rather than intellectual enquiry: 'The language of philosophy was alien to her. Speculation on ultimate realities had no attraction for her.'[9] Because she lived to a great age, dying in 1910, Waring had to realize that there was such a thing as doubt: 'The questionings of modern doubt must have reached her outward ears. She never heard an echo of their whisper within ...'[10]

It is this pattern of tender feelings allied to untroubled minds that characterizes many women hymn writers of the nineteenth century. They worked within the expected limitations of the age: they wrote hymns for the sick, or for the sad and sorrowing. They also compiled selections of hymns for them, such as Frances Mary Yonge's *A Child's Christian Year* (1841), and wrote books such as *Hymns for Little Children* (1848) by Cecil Frances Humphreys (later 'Mrs Alexander'). These were only two of a great number of women hymn-writers for children, beginning with Anne and Jane Taylor's *Hymns for Infant Minds* (1810), and continuing with many others – Jemima Luke, Mary Duncan, Emily Elliott, Jane Leeson. 'Women', wrote Mrs Pitman,

> – and especially women who were mothers – have excelled in the art of writing hymns for children. Somehow it needs mother-love to interpret divine love to the little ones.[11]

The parameters of women's hymn-writing seem fairly generally established in these patterns of sensitivity to suffering and anxiety

for the well-being of little children; above all, in the acceptance of a
subordinate role, in which the woman waits' and is passive rather
than works (which is the preserve of the man). A poem by Anna
Montague, called 'Women', sets it out clearly. The woman stands
by the master's vineyard, longing to go in and work; as she turns to
enter, she meets the 'Master', who tells her

> 'Daughter,
> I know thy longing heart,
> In the toil of my laden vineyard,
> Is eager to bear a part.'

The master tells her that her duty is to do 'no active labour'. She is
to stay in her cottage and 'sit with folded hands', so that the hymn
ends by adapting Milton for the condition of women –

> They also serve who patiently
> But fold their hands, and *wait*.

In the face of such submission it is clear why active and intelligent
women like Susanna and Catherine Winkworth campaigned so
hard for the higher education of women. They were exceptional
among hymn-writers in doing so; the majority accepted their submissive and subordinate role, sublimating it into the loss of self that
was demanded by religion: they described Jesus, again and again,
as 'Master'. They became expert at describing pain and suffering,
the impotence of having to sit with folded hands; they poured out
their frustrations in passionate avowals of love to the Saviour (as in
Sarah Flower Adams' 'nearer, my God, to Thee'); and, more safely,
they wrote hymns for children, combining their own memories of
childhood, before the conditions of Victorian society and marriage
closed in upon them, with their ideas of how children should
behave.

It is in the context of this hymnody of affliction that Charlotte
Elliott's 'Just as I am, without one plea' was written, on the text
'Him that cometh to me I will in no wise cast out' (John vi.37). It
proved an immensely popular hymn: it was published separately,
with illustrations and an exposition, and included in innumerable
hymn books. Its power lies in the repetition of the initial phrase,
and the simplicity of those words, 'Just as I am', with their craving
for acceptance, followed by the fulfilment, 'O Lamb of God, I come!'

It is the ancestor of many Victorian hymns in which the sinner is accepted, and ends up safe in the arms of Jesus: it is unusual in its ability to capture the movement of such a process so vividly and rhythmically – from the initial nakedness of 'Just as I am' to the climax of 'O Lamb of God, I come!'

The hymn represents a longing that turns into an ecstasy; although I imagine that any conscious sexuality was far from Charlotte Elliott's mind, the unconscious drive towards the Saviour represents a sexual sublimation of the highest order. Between the first phrase and the last in each verse, a parenthesis is developed, exquisitely and pleasurably delaying the hoped-for moment, and allowing the mind to dwell on the power of Jesus to accept and save. These parentheses begin with the saving blood – 'But that thy blood was shed for me' – and continue with the problems of human life –

> With many a conflict, many a doubt,
> Fightings and fears, within, without –

and ends, appropriately, with a contemplation of divine love:

> – of that free love
> 'The breadth, length, depth, and height' to prove,
> Here for a season, then above –

The pauses in the rhythm, the structures of the lines, are beautifully calculated, the mind and spirit poised at the end of the third line before being released into the joy of 'O Lamb of God, I come!' The process of coming to Jesus, repeated in verse after verse, ends in the triumphant final coming, the release from loss and pain, and the mystic's joy and wonder, safe in the everlasting arms. It is as passionate a representation of divine love, and human response, as Bernini's Saint Teresa, caught in her moment of ecstasy.

Elliott's hymn is an extreme example of the writing which sought an outlet for longing and hope. In everyday religious life, such energies went into church attendance and activities, especially the teaching of children; and many hymns were written for them. The best-known children's hymn writer was 'Mrs Alexander' (1818–95, so called after her marriage to the Bishop of Derry and Raphoe), who published her *Hymns for Little Children* in 1848. The 'little' was important: as she wrote in a later hymn –

We are but little children weak' –

and the word occurs again and again in the 1848 book, either spoken by children themselves, or by an adult. It is a good example of the way in which women hymn writers were able to write if they adopted a particular role – in this case either that of the Sunday school teacher, or that of the infant, with its wide-eyed innocence. 'Tiny' goes along with 'little' as the adult points something out to the children:

> Each little flower that opens,
>   Each little bird that sings,
> He made their glowing colours,
>   He made their tiny wings ...

The word 'little' has a respectable provenance, from Matthew 18 ('And Jesus called a little child'); but the chapter was exploited for its behaviourial possibilities and for its sentimental associations. Words such as 'dear', 'warm', 'soft' and 'little' encourage a certain deliberate naivety, a refusal to enter the grown-up world, especially when the words are spoken by children. They may have a certain charm, but it is a charm that has its disadvantages:

> We are little Christian children,
>   Saved by Him Who loved us most,
> We believe in God Almighty,
>   Father, Son, and Holy Ghost.
>
> We were only little babies,
>   Knowing neither good nor harm,
> When the Priest of God Most Holy
>   Took us gently on his arm.

We know that we are saved because we have been baptised:

> And he sprinkled our young faces,
>   With the water clean and bright,
> And he signed our Saviour's token
>   On our little foreheads white.

Children are often white in these hymns, most notably in heaven –

When like stars His children crowned,
All in white shall wait around.

It is not clear if these are the spirits of children who have died in
infancy, or if this is an image for innocence generally: it is part of
a strange atmosphere of Mrs Alexander's hymns, involving little
children, white angels, flowers and birds, the baby Jesus:

Mary was that mother mild,
Jesus Christ her little child.

Only occasionally does the voice of the adult take over from this
childlike, or childish, innocence; but when it does so the tone is that
of the bossy Sunday-school teacher, frightening and severe:

Little children must be quiet,
   When to Holy Church they go,
They must sit with serious faces,
   Must not play or whisper low.

For the Church is God's own Temple
   Where men go for praise and prayer,
And the Great God will not love them
   Who forget His presence there.

The threat of the withdrawal of love is uncomfortable evidence of
the steely discipline that surrounds the little heads and the dear
mothers. Behind the pretty pictures of little flowers and birds with
tiny wings there is a patriarchal law that Mrs Alexander subscribes
to with enthusiasm:

Do no sinful action,
   Speak no angry word,
Ye belong to Jesus,
   Children of the Lord.

Christ is kind and gentle;
   Christ is pure and true,
And his little children
   Must be holy too.

The children 'belong' to Jesus; and in his possession, the operative word is 'must':

> Christian children all must be
> Mild, obedient, good as he.

The problem, for Alexander as well as for others, is not just one of a restricted and repressive code of conduct, preaching unnatural subservience and quietness in the name of Christianity (of the kind which Isaac Watts and Blake attacked); it is also one of finding a satisfactory language for the moral commerce with the very young. Simplicity has an easy charm, but it also has its disadvantages, nowhere more so than in Alexander's comments on political economy. Addressing a poor child in a hymn on 'Give us this day our daily bread', she instructs it to kneel down and pray for 'all things needful':

> God made thy cottage home so dear,
>   Gave store enough for frugal fare:
> If richer homes have better cheer,
>   'Twas God Who sent it there.

This seems to involve the Almighty in a certain amount of inequitable distribution of the good things of this world, and it is not much comfort to be told:

> To the Holy Church we go,
> The dear Church of high and low,
> Where the poor man meanly dressed
> Is as welcome as the rest.

Alexander's simplicities here communicate themselves in an embarrassing condescension, and it surely cannot be right for children of any age to be told –

> The rich man in his castle,
>   The poor man at his gate,
> God made them, high or lowly,
>   And ordered their estate.

Such a commentary on Victorian society places the Church of
England alongside those who had a vested interest in preserving
things as they were; it is perhaps unfair to point out that
Alexander's book was published only a year before the Irish potato
famine, but such juxtapositions help to point out her limitations.
The 'rich man' verse transforms the final verse into a political statement – God made all things well, including the social system.

Alexander's conservative political economy is one in which
Christianity is intended to stifle any thought of incipient revolution:

> You must be content and quiet,
>   Your appointed stations in;
> For to envy, or to covet
>   Other's goods, is mortal sin.
>   ('The tenth Commandment')

Above all, however, these poems reveal a concept of the child that is
based on an adult's conception of what a child should be. This is
seen most clearly in the poem on the seventh Commandment,
which uses the figure of a snowdrop (this seems to have been a
common emblem for a small child in its innocence; a snowdrop
appears on the front cover of *A Child's Christian Year*):

> I love the little snowdrop flower,
>   The first in all the year,
> Without a stain upon its leaf,
>   So snowy white and clear.
>
> I love a little modest child,
>   That speaketh quietly,
> That blushes up to its blue eyes,
>   And hardly answers me.
>
> I sometimes think the Church's Saints
>   Are flowers so fair and bright,
> And that her little children are
>   Her snowdrops sweet and white.

This is an extreme example of a kind of nineteenth-century hymn-
writing for children that was all too common, gratifying the wishes
of adulthood and sweeping aside the real needs of children and
adolescents.

The real needs of women are nowhere more vividly perceived than in the hymn-writing of Dora Greenwell (1821–82). Like some other women writers, she suffered from ill-health for long periods. She told her friend Constance Maynard that 'only those who had experienced the utter helplessness of life reduced to its lowest point, to an exhaustion that was all but extinction, could tell what it meant'.[12] She may have been referring to a depression brought on by family problems: she lived for some 18 years with her tyrannical mother in Durham, from the age of 33 to the age of 51 (1854–71). She had received an inadequate education, too, although she was a proficient linguist: her brother William, who was a Canon of Durham Cathedral and a notable antiquarian, called it 'a very flimsy education for a sharp mind like hers':

> Philosophy, biography, medieval legends, political economy – nothing came amiss, and she read widely. But when she tried to express herself, everything had the same defect; all was so undisciplined, so unfinished![13]

When confronted with this kind of masculine complacency, it is not surprising that Constance Maynard, Greenwell's biographer and a pioneer in women's education (she was the first Principal of Westfield College, London), should have written of the 'constant pressure and thwarting' of Dora Greenwell's nature, probably because her mother apparently 'exerted a sort of passive resistance to any new acquaintances made by her daughter':[14] according to one of her friends –

> Her mother never thoroughly approved of her life, her occupations, or of her friends, and seemed to think it her duty to be always checking her impulses and keeping her straight.[15]

Her occupations – despite her poor health (which may of course have been psychosomatic) – included prison visiting, workhouse visiting and helping the poor. Her sharp and pointed, yet also jolly Christmas carol, 'If ye would hear the Angels sing', indicates her concern for philanthropy:

> If ye would hear the Angels sing,
>   Rise and spread your Christmas fare;
>   'Tis merrier still the more that share,
> On Christmas Day in the morning.

> Rise, and bake your Christmas bread:
>   Christians, rise! the world is bare,
>   And bleak, and dark with want and care,
>   Yet Christmas comes in the morning.

In her social work (like her friend Josephine Butler) she seems to have found a purpose that was denied to her by her family; but Jean Ingelow, who visited her in Durham, described her as living 'in a shaded world'.[16] Her frustrations occasionally showed: a new arrival in Durham was shocked by the freedom of her conversation, and 'found people rather afraid of Miss Greenwell, because she said such unexpected things'.[17]

It is not surprising, perhaps, that this living representative of the tragedy that George Eliot presented in Maggie Tulliver and Dorothea Brooke should have felt frustrated, nor that one of her best-known hymns should have begun with an image of herself as deskilled:

> I am not skilled to understand
> What God has willed, what God has planned;
> I only know at his right hand
>   Stands one who is my Saviour.

The point of the hymn is that she takes God at his word, simply, without trying to speculate: she reads the Gospel, and finds the need in her heart:

> I take God at his word and deed:
>   Christ died to save me, this I read;
> And in my heart I find a need
>   Of him to be my Saviour.
>
> And was there then no other way
>   For God to take? I cannot say;
> I only bless him, day by day
>   Who saved me through my Saviour.

The 'I cannot say' suggests that the theology is better left to the Canons of the Cathedral, such as her pompous brother William, who was continually telling her that she was no good as a writer:

I remember I read one book (I forgot which) and said, 'Dora, I cannot see your aim. What is it you want to tell people? You seem to be in earnest, but what is the conclusion? You roll your subject over and over, and then you stop. I don't believe you know yourself what you want to teach!'[18]

Dora Greenwell's work demonstrated, in a particularly acute and poignant form, that appetite for life which was denied by circumstances. She had a great sense of fun: her poem on 'The Saturday Review' appeared in *Punch*, and is still worth reading,[19] and she once held an impromptu dance in the kitchen of the house in Durham, out of earshot of her mother. At the same time, her health suffered from the strain of restraint and concealment. Her *Essays*, published in 1866 were prefaced by a quotation from Chaucer, which suggests that she saw herself as a loser in life:

That which is sent thee take in soothfastnesse;
The wrestling of this life doth ask a fall.

The fall is a failure of hope, the disappointment of expectations. In one of the poems from *Carmina Crucis* (1869), entitled 'The Playfellows', she recalled that

Love, Hope, Joy, and I together
Play'd, ah! many and many a day;

The game was hide-and-seek; but one day Hope and Joy

Hid so long and hid so well,
We found them not, though keenly chiding;

and the result was that

We knew that we had seen the last
Of Hope and Joy, no more together
Play we there in summer weather.

What remained was endurance and fortitude. Greenwell's emblem on the title-page of *Essays* (1866) and of *Carmina Crucis* was that of a hand holding a cross, with the words 'Et Teneo et Teneor' ('I hold and am held'). The dedication quotes Luther, taking for the symbol of his theology a seal

> on which I had engraven a cross, with a heart in its centre.The cross is black, to indicate the sorrows, even unto death, through which the Christian must pass; *but the heart preserves its natural colour*, for the cross does not extinguish nature, it does not kill, but gives life.

Dora Greenwell's poetry is a perpetual dialogue between the heart and the cross – the cross which gives life, but which is an emblem of suffering. Her own suffering included her unmarried state, which she wrote about in a remarkable essay, 'Our Single Women', published in the *North British Review* in 1862, where she speaks of the problems of a single woman in the nineteenth century – 'It may now, perhaps, be harder for her than it has ever been to make her wishes and her fate agree'.[20]

The last poem in *Carmina Crucis*, from which her best-known hymn is taken, is entitled 'Veni, veni, Emmanuel'; it demonstrates these conflicts with a directness that is peculiarly poignant.

> And art Thou come with us to dwell,
> Our Prince, our Guide, our Love, our Lord?
> And is thy name Emmanuel,
> God present with his world restored?

The hymn celebrates the abundant life that Dora Greenwell never knew:

> Thou bringest all again; with Thee
> Is light, is space, is breadth and room
> For each thing fair, beloved, and free,
> To have its hour of life and bloom.

The images are startlingly appropriate to her own circumstances, but also wonderfully true to the sayings of Jesus ('I am come that they may have life, and have it more abundantly'), and to the metaphors of rebirth and spring ('whereby the dayspring from on high hath visited us'). The coming of the spring ('to give light to them that sit in darkness, and in the shadow of death' – we may recall Jean Ingelow's impression that Dora Greenwell lived 'in a shaded world') allows the imagination to return to the hopes of childhood, flourishing in the warmth of the sun:

> Thy reign eternal will not cease;
> Thy years are sure, and glad, and slow;
> Within Thy mighty world of peace
> The humblest flower hath leave to blow,
>
> And spread its leaves to meet the sun,
> And drink within its soul the dew;
> The child's sweet laugh like light may run
> Through life's long day, and still be true;

The presence of God upon earth, Emmanuel, 'God with us', means that hope and joy will be found again in the game of hide-and-seek, although Dora Greenwell's imagery for this (in the first line of the penultimate verse) is a wistful acknowledgment of a life that she never knew:

> The maid's fond sigh, the lover's kiss,
> The firm warm clasp of constant friend;
> And nought shall fail, and nought shall miss
> Its blissful aim, its blissful end.

The verse moves towards the final happiness of this imagined consummation through images of human love ('blissful ... blissful'). With selfless courage, Dora Greenwell links the promise of human happiness with the eventual triumph of divine love ('and all shall be well, and all manner of thing shall be well') in the manner of a medieval mystic.

The last writer I shall consider here, Frances Ridley Havergal, stands apart from the other women hymn-writers of the nineteenth century, if only because of her energy and good health. Mrs Pitman's assertion that 'she had many sharp attacks of illness, and consequent journeys in search of health', already quoted, is only partly true. Although she did have periods of illness, she was a good walker and a good swimmer, and the 'journeys' were often hikes in mountains – Snowdonia and the Lake District – and on a number of occasions to the Alps, where she did some high-altitude climbing. For a Victorian woman, she was athletic and adventurous (she also sang hymns and preached to the other holiday-makers when on holiday). She was also a fine musician, and a poet whose energy found an outlet in all kinds of zestful verse – in acrostics, riddles, charades and poems on the names of her sisters and friends. Some of her enthusiasm found its outlet in Sunday school teaching, and she was a vigorous early supporter of the Young Women's Christian Association. Her delightful and ingenuous keenness is seen everywhere in her hymns:

> Who is on the Lord's side?
>   Who will serve the King?
> Who will be his helpers
>   Other lives to bring?
> Who will leave the world's side?
>   Who will face the foe?
> Who is on the Lord's side?
>   Who for Him will go?

In the great game of life, Frances Ridley Havergal was picking her side: during the last week of her life, by the seaside near Swansea –

> The donkey boy, Fred Rosser, remembers that Miss Frances told him 'I had better leave the devil's side and get on the safe side: that Jesus Christ's was the winning side; that He loved us and was calling us, and wouldn't I choose Him for my Captain?'[21]

To that side she gave total obedience, all her enthusiastic self thrown into the fray:

> Take my life, and let it be
> Consecrated, Lord, to Thee.

What might be thought of as metaphorical is literally true: it was as a fine pianist and singer that she wrote

> Take my voice, and let me sing
> Always, only, for my King.

And the verse

> Take my silver and my gold;
> Not a mite would I withhold

should be set beside her conduct when *Good Words* paid her £10 17s 6d in 1863. She gave £10 to her father for the church, 10/- to the Scripture Readers' collection, and kept the 7s 6d 'for any similar emergency'.[22]

On Advent Sunday 1873 she wrote:

> I first saw clearly the blessedness of true consecration. I saw it as a flash of electric light, and what you *see* you can never *un*see. There must be a full surrender before there can be full happiness.[23]

It was soon after this that she wrote the 'Consecration Hymn', 'Take my life, and let it be'. The word that she then used, again and again, was 'Master', to which she gave a particular interpretation as a woman, taking a submissive place. She saw that subordination as inextricable from love (as in the word 'obey' in the marriage service):

> 'O Master!' It is perhaps my favourite title, because it implies rule and submission; and this is what love craves. Men may feel differently, but a true woman's submission is inseparable from deep love.[24]

'Whose I am' thus begins

> Jesus, Master, whose I am,

and 'Master' is the key word in one of her best-known hymns:

> Master, speak! Thy servant heareth,
>   Waiting for Thy gracious word,
> Longing for Thy voice that cheereth;
>   Master! let it now be heard.
> I am listening, Lord, for Thee;
> What hast Thou to say to me?

In Havergal's work, as in that of Elliott, can be seen a sublimation of the self; and in each of the hymn-writers treated in this chapter can be seen attitudes of submission, or confinement within specific roles appropriate to the female gender. If the Angel in the House took to hymn-writing, she did so within well defined and clearly accepted limits.

J.R. Watson

NOTES

* The substance of this chapter is an extract from 'Victorian Women Hymn Writers', in *The English Hymn* (Oxford University Press, 1997). It is reproduced here by kind permission of Oxford University Press.

1. Mrs E.R. Pitman, *Lady Hymn Writers* (London, 1892), p. 69. The title is reminiscent of George Eliot's 'Silly Novels by Lady Novelists', without Eliot's sense of an ironic usage. The word 'Mrs' appears on the title-page and the cover of Pitman's book.
2. Ibid., p. 162.
3. Sandra M. Gilbert and Susan M. Gubar, *The Madwoman in the Attic*, (New Haven and London, 1979), p. 64.
4. Pitman, *Lady Hymn Writers*, p. 74.
5. Ibid., p. 176.
6. Ibid., pp. 210–11.
7. Ibid., p. 253.
8. Mary S. Talbot, *In Remembrance of Anna Laetitia Waring* (London, 1911), p. 29.
9. Ibid., p. 11.
10. Ibid., p. 15.
11. Pitman, *Lady Hymn Writers*, pp. 281–2.
12. Constance L. Maynard, *Dora Greenwell* (London, 1926), p. 40.
13. Ibid., p. 39.
14. Ibid., p. 68.
15. Ibid., p. 98.
16. Ibid., p. 128.
17. Ibid., p. 130
18. Ibid., p. 122.
19. It is printed in *Everyman's Book of Victorian Verse*, ed. J.R. Watson (London, 1982), pp. 186–8.
20. 'Our Single Women', *North British Review*, 1862.
21. *Memorials of Frances Ridley Havergal*, by her sister M.V.G.H. (Maria Vernon Graham Havergal) (London, 1880), pp. 295–6.
22. Ibid., p. 92.
23. Ibid., p. 126.
24. Ibid., p. 138.

10

Nonconformist Obituaries: How Stereotyped Was Their View of Women?

Linda Wilson

Nonconformity was a general term which, by the mid-nineteenth century, was used collectively of the evangelical dissenting churches and of Methodism and its offshoots.[1] The 1851 census, despite the difficulties in interpreting its data, showed that, measured in terms of Sunday attendances, Nonconformity had grown dramatically in the first part of the nineteenth century, and was challenging the dominance of the Established Church.[2] Well over half of those attending Nonconformist chapels would have been women, and to study Nonconformist women is therefore crucial for that reason alone.[3]

Obituaries, found in the denominational magazines, are a useful source for such an investigation. Varying in length from a few lines to several pages, they provide information about the lives of people within a denomination, especially but not exclusively about their conversion and last illnesses. A large minority of these obituaries were of women, and provide a useful source for women's religious history, yet they have been largely neglected by historians: Obelkevich, for instance, refers to them only briefly in his study of south Lincoln, whilst discussing women within Primitive Methodism.[4] Exceptions are Julia Werner, who makes more extensive use of obituaries when referring to women in her investigation of early Primitive Methodism, and Dorothy Graham, who uses them in her thesis on female preachers within the same church.[5]

The small amount of attention they have received could be due in part to the methodological problems involved in using obituaries for women's history. Not only were they designed for a specific purpose, to demonstrate a 'good life' and death, but the majority of

Linda Wilson

them were written by men. There was thus a danger that the women in them would be portrayed in a stereotypical manner as dutiful daughters, wives and mothers, who provided the spiritual centre of a loving and efficient home, and who eventually died confident of their place in heaven. This study will demonstrate that this was not always the case, and that even where there is an element of stereotyping, much useful information can be drawn from these accounts. Although written by men, women probably supplied much of the material for writing. In addition, a large number of obituaries quoted reported speech, and several included extracts from women's letters and diaries, allowing access to their own thoughts and opinions. Obituaries also provide valuable evidence about the lives of women, mainly ordinary women, which is usually not available in any other form. It is a reasonable assumption, too, that the contents and attitudes of these magazines had an influence on the Nonconformist reading public, and that obituaries and the examples of good Christian lives which they portrayed, would in particular have had a shaping effect on women's perceptions of their own lives.[6] It is worth studying them, therefore, both for the information they contain and as an account of their influencing role on Nonconformist thinking.

Denominations usually had their own magazines, often easily identifiable by their names. Samples of obituaries from five magazines, linked to four denominations, have been analysed for this study. The magazines used are the *Methodist Magazine* (Wesleyan Methodism), the *Primitive Methodist Magazine*, the *Baptist Magazine* (Particular or Calvinistic Baptists), the *Christian Witness* (which in 1872 became *The Congregationalist*) and the *Evangelical Magazine* (which was also mainly Congregationalist). All these magazines carried obituaries or memoirs which ranged from short 12-line paragraphs to reports of several pages. Congregationalist magazines tended to have just an occasional long memoir, Baptist ones had rather more, and Methodist and Primitive Methodists had 100 or more of varying lengths in one year's issues. I have studied 60 obituaries from each denomination, and some extra material from elsewhere, all of which were published between 1825 and 1875. This study investigates the extent to which these obituaries portrayed a stereotyped view of women.

The majority of women in the sample were married, although 19 per cent were unmarried and 3 per cent were widows. Of the 78 per cent who were married, 27 per cent were married to ministers. However, whilst 40 per cent of the Congregationalist sample were pastors' wives, amongst the Baptists the figure was 28 per cent, and the figure was lower still for Methodist women; only 10 per cent of Wesleyan Methodists and 5 per cent of Primitives were married to ministers. Thus whilst there were a considerable proportion of ministers' wives within the sample, there were also many ordinary church members.

What view did Nonconformists have of women? Sean Gill points out, apropos of theology in the nineteenth century, that it 'was both moulded by, and helped to create, the norms of the society in which it is practised', and this was as true for Nonconformist thinking as it was for the Anglican Church which was his focus.[7] The Anglican Hannah More at the turn of the century, and later Sarah Ellis, a Congregationalist, were amongst those who helped to influence and shape the ideal of women as the spiritual guardians of the home, and ultimately of the nation. Nonconformist preachers often echoed this view. For instance, John Angel James, a Congregationalist preacher at Carr's Lane, Birmingham, published his sermons on 'Female Piety' in 1852 which reinforced an evangelical version of Patmore. He believed that

> It is in the female bosom, however we may account for the fact, that piety finds a home on earth. She gladdens by her presence the solitary hours of man's existence and to some extent purifies and sanctifies him by making him feel how awful goodness is ... [and] woman lives to repair the wrong she has inflicted on man and lavishes upon him consolations which may sweeten the recent bitterness of sin, and warnings which may preserve from the future bitterness of hell.[8]

In James' thinking there is complete assent to the prevailing ideology of women. Charles Haddon Spurgeon, the well-known Baptist preacher (1834–92), also believed that women's role was a home-based and supportive one, though he himself could be quite domesticated, furnishing a new house whilst his wife was an invalid.[9] Several articles in the magazines also stress that women's role should be home-based, indicating that this view was widespread.[10]

At first sight, these conventional beliefs seem to be echoed in the obituaries, many of which appear to reinforce a definite characterization of the religious woman as the Angel in the House. In the

Primitive Methodist Magazine for 1850, the following obituary can be found, full of conventional formulae:

> Alice Milnes, aged 52 years, died at Bottoms, in the Halifax circuit, on Dec 20th 1849. About 12 years ago she *believed in Christ to the saving of her soul*, and was shortly *united with the people of God*; and since then she has been an *orderly and creditable* member of our society. The *sincerity of her piety* was displayed in all her deportment – at home and abroad. Her *ardent desires for the salvation of her family* were seen in her unwearied efforts to turn them to repentance, and in her *fervent prayers* in their behalf. It was her constant wish that her eldest child should be saved first, that he might be a pattern to the rest. About a year ago he was saved ... since then another child, a daughter, has been *brought into the fold of Christ*.[11]

The obituary concludes by saying that in her illness she knew 'the comforts of a strong and lively confidence in God'. This account stresses all the conventional aspects of Nonconformist spirituality. Following her conversion, Alice joined a church, and remained a reliable member of it, demonstrating her religion through her life, both in behaviour and in prayer. This was an example intended to be approved of and imitated.

Several obituarists stressed that women's virtues were particularly seen in the home. The image of a shining light was used several times in this context. So the obituarist of Elizabeth Cooper in the *Christian Witness* commented that 'It was especially in the family her virtues shone',[12] and a Methodist writer recalled of Mary Ann Maidment that 'her light shone out bright in the family circle'.[13] The implication is that outside the home the light would not be seen so clearly. In 1859, the obituarist of Harriet Green, a Baptist, explained that her life 'was passed as the life of a Christian wife and mother must be, in the quiet discharge of her family duties'.[14] This writer not only stressed that there was a clear link between Harriet's function and her faith, but went further and asserted that focusing on the home was an essential part of Christian womanhood. Running an efficient household was thus regarded as part of spirituality, along with personal and family devotions and public attendance at chapel.

The majority of women whose lives were portrayed in the obituaries were wives and mothers, and they are shown investing time, effort and prayers in nurturing these primary relationships. In the obituary of Mary Horsfield, a Congregationalist, the link between being a good wife and mother and spirituality was made explicit. 'She adorned the doctrine of God our Saviour in all the relationships of life. As a wife, a daughter, a sister and a neighbour, she was blameless, "showing piety at home".'[15] Her piety was regarded as directly linked to her behaviour in various relationships which were assumed to be an important means of expressing spirituality in practice. Several women in the sample were influenced by their own mother's piety and training, and many women with children spent time in instructing them in the faith, and praying for them. One example is the Primitive Methodist, Alice Milnes, whose obituary was quoted above. She had 'ardent desires for the salvation of her family' and made 'unwearied efforts to turn them to repentance', also praying for them. About a year before her death her eldest child was converted, which was what she had hoped for: 'that he might be a pattern to the rest'.[16] Thus, both in the practical running of the home, and the servicing of relationships in the family, women are often portrayed in conventional roles within the obituaries.

Death-bed scenes, too, were usually couched in standardized terms. The obituarists were often disappointed if the nature of the illness prevented a deathbed testimony, and many spent a considerable time recounting these pious women's experiences during their illness, and recording some of their last words. In one Wesleyan Methodist obituary of 22 lines, 17 were taken up with the account of an illness,[17] whilst in longer obituaries a page or more might be spent on a woman's last days. Their compliance with God's will, and lack of complaint when in pain, were frequently stressed. The obituary of Mrs Dickson, in the *Christian Witness* in 1849, is one of several which highlights the womanly and Christian characteristics considered appropriate during a long illness:

As Mrs D. [sic] lived when in health, she suffered and died. The temper and bearing of the Christian were ever evinced by her. During the whole of her lengthened illness she never once complained or murmured: the most subdued and cheerful resignation characterised her. She acknowledged the hand of God in the affliction she suffered, and felt assured that the dispensation which had been allotted to her, however painful to flesh and blood, was one of wisdom and love, and she submitted to it with meekness and submissiveness.[18]

The belief expressed in this obituary, that God had brought about the illness and was using it for his good purpose, often to purify the sufferer, was commonly expressed in obituaries, as was the approved response of resignation and compliance with God's will. These scenes clearly show women in a passive role.

There is more than this, however, to the portrayal of women in the obituaries. It is interesting that they are not only referred to in terms of their relationship to men, despite the absence of a Christian name in a small percentage of cases. Many accounts do start by citing the woman's relationship to others, for instance 'Jane, the beloved wife of John Fox, esq',[19] but not all do. Men, too, are often defined in terms of their parentage, with reference being made to a man's father, although rarely to his mother or wife. An occasional male obituary even refers to a female connection: the obituary of Edward Franceys of Liverpool mentions that he was the son-in-law 'of the late Mrs Byrom, a lady highly and deservedly esteemed in the circles of Wesleyan Methodism'.[20] The Congregationalist obituaries being largely middle-class, it might have been expected that Congregationalist women would be more frequently referred to in terms of their relations to others. However, although her father's job and often her husband's job were cited, in some obituaries husbands were barely mentioned, whilst in some Primitive Methodist ones, it is not even clear if the woman had a husband. The obituaries centred on the woman herself, and whilst women's role was perceived as specific in much Nonconformist culture, they were regarded as equal before God, and in their response to the gospel.

There was also an attempt within some of the obituaries to portray the spirituality and the thoughts of the woman, rather than just a stylized outline of her spiritual career. Several longer ones quote from letters or diaries or recount conversations. Sophia Jefferson, a Wesleyan Methodist, was one woman who kept a diary which was quoted from in her obituary.[21] In Elizabeth Cooper's obituary, in the *Christian Witness* of 1850, letters to a friend are referred to for evidence of her faith and religious experience.[22] The obituarist of Susanna Pickles, a Primitive Methodist who died in 1847, quoted a letter to him in which Susanna wrote that she thinks of Jesus coming to her house and 'taking a friendly cup of tea with us'.[23] These glimpses into women's thoughts demonstrate that obituaries were not all as standardized as at first appears.

Occasionally, these portraits of women who might appear too good to be true are qualified by an oblique reference to their faults, although they are rarely spelt out. Mrs Colcroft's obituary, in the 1852 *Baptist Magazine*, ended by explaining that she was not perfect: 'She had her faults. She knew them more fully than others did, and confessed them with great pain of mind.'[24] Other obituaries referred to spiritual depression and doubt, but only if there was resolution of any problems prior to death.

In the obituaries there is evidence of a Nonconformist ideal distinct from the concept of the Angel in the House, although there is some overlap. This ethos embraced the idea that women were more spiritual than men, their role being largely that of spiritual guardian to both family and society. It also involved the need for activity, a necessary part of life after salvation, contrasted with the passive nature of Angel ideology.[25] The overlap of these two stereotypes led to confusion in some conversion accounts. Belief in original sin was a basic tenet of evangelical faith, yet sometimes in these histories it is not very evident. Certainly none of these women had committed much in the way of obvious sin. Most of their repentance was connected with an awareness of their essential sinfulness as human beings, rather than with specific sins they had committed, and sometimes they were described as being unusually good in their childhood. Ann Selina Campbell strikingly illustrates this point. Her father, in an account of her life, wrote that 'she seemed to be sanctified from her birth',[26] almost contradicting the idea of depravity. Such women came very close to Patmore's ideal of woman as a superior spiritual being to man, and the accounts were in danger of undermining the traditional view of original sin.

At times acceptable Nonconformist women took the initiative regarding family worship, and a few examples of this are found in obituaries. For instance, Mrs Dickson, a Congregationalist, started family prayers when she was nineteen and 'for several years conducted it with the greatest propriety'.[27] Susannah Nichole, born 1810 in Hereford, who became a Primitive Methodist local preacher, started family worship in her house as soon as she was converted, and before long her mother, sister and father were all converted through her.[28] Women sometimes took the place of their husband in family prayers when they were away, and Mary Lang, a Baptist, took over the leading of family worship after her husband's death.[29] It is possible, however, to see this as an extension of the Angel ideal,

rather than as an alternative to it, being related to taking responsibility for spiritual development in the home.

Another aspect of obituaries which conforms to a Nonconformist
perspective, rather than the Angel one, is the intellectual side.
Nonconformist women were encouraged to study and develop
their thinking. This was especially the case with Bible study. One
example of this was Mary Parker, a Wesleyan Methodist whose
obituarist notes with approval that she 'had taken great pains to
cultivate her mind, by diligent attention to reading'. She read the
Bible, commentators and Methodist works:[30] and this was at a time
when Sarah Ellis was complaining of the frivolity of girl's education
in England![31] Similarly, the anonymous obituarist of Mrs Mary
Emma Turquand approved of her learning Greek so she could be
better equipped to teach her Sunday school class.[32] Women's contribution within Nonconformity was regarded as distinctive, but by
no means frivolous.

Some obituaries reveal more than just an alternative view of
women, and several recorded instances where, consciously or
unconsciously, they acted in a way that challenged the ideal of the
Angel in the House. A few women defied parents or husbands in
pursuit of their faith. Kezia Geden was brought up by her aunt and
uncle, and loved cards and dancing until she came into contact with
Methodists. Her obituarist records that her uncle was opposed to
her new interest, disinherited her and temporarily turned her out of
the house for standing by her beliefs.[33] For Kezia, her faith was
more important to her than obedience to her guardians, and this is
shown clearly, and approved of, in her obituary. This was true also
for some women with regard to submission to their husband's
wishes. A Wesleyan Methodist, Jane Miles, had opposition from her
husband: she prayed with her servants twice a day, but because her
husband disapproved 'for many years she was accustomed to take
the servants up to the garret for prayer'.[34] She acted secretly and
against his wishes, and once again this was considered acceptable
behaviour, because her primary allegiance was to God.

Another example of a woman whose faith was stronger than her
desire to be submissive was that of Mary Gore, who encountered
strong opposition to her faith from her husband. When she was 37,
around 1827, Primitive Methodist preachers came to Wildmoor, near
Birmingham, where she lived, and she was converted and joined
them. She was a member for 18 years, but her husband was opposed
to Methodism and sometimes turned her out of doors because she

had been to the chapel. She had to 'seek shelter elsewhere, or spend the nights in the open air'. Once he seized an axe and threatened to cut her legs off if she kept going to chapel, to which her response was 'Then I will go upon my stumps'.[35] Obituaries which give such insight into women's lives cannot simply be categorized as upholding the stereotype of the passive spiritual woman.

Another area of Nonconformist influence was the whole variety of activities outside the home, both in churches and in local communities. Admittedly these were in the role of what Helsinger calls 'Angel out of the house', an extension of women's recognized gifts and character in the wider environment.[36] Many obituaries show women teaching Sunday school classes, visiting the sick, collecting for missionary societies, and distributing tracts from door to door, sometimes stopping to discuss the gospel with people. In a few, women are seen in a teaching or even preaching role.

Many women were Sunday school teachers at some stage in their Christian lives. Out of the sample studied, 60 per cent of Congregationalist women were teachers, 33 per cent of Baptists and 22 per cent of Wesleyan Methodists. However, only 10 per cent of Primitive Methodists were recorded as being teachers.

The more conscientious teachers spent several hours a week in preparation. Mrs Colcroft, who was a Baptist, regularly spent six or seven hours a week preparing to teach.[37] Some held extra midweek classes, such as Maria Prudence Mayer who taught her class to sew and knit during the week.[38] Whilst this role clearly comes within the parameter of behaviour suitable for women, and could be seen as part of their conventional role, it was activity outside the home, and involved developing skills that would be useful in other contexts.

Other activities recorded in the obituaries included collecting for missionary societies, visiting the sick and poor, and the distribution of tracts. Bolder women tried to talk about the gospel when they made such visits: one Methodist woman, Mrs Harper, 'would go from house to house, inviting the people to attend the worship of God, and charging them to consider their latter end'.[39] There were many such active Nonconformists, taking their faith into society around them, always with the emphasis that nothing at home was being neglected, but definitely pushing out the boundaries of what was acceptable.

The obituaries also reveal that women were involved in more direct pastoral responsibility. They led Methodist classes, a role involving leading weekly meetings, teaching the class, and pastoral care of the members. In the Wesleyan Methodist obituaries, eight out of 60 women were fulfilling this function, whilst only five did from the Primitive sample. One Wesleyan woman, Margaret Darque, was believed by her obituarist to have been 'fitted to watch over, instruct, admonish and comfort the souls entrusted to her care'.[40] These women had the opportunity to lead and develop gifts within the context of their churches.

However, at least one Congregationalist woman in the sample fulfilled a similar function under a different name. Mrs Pitman taught a Bible class at her church in Bridgewater, and her lessons were apparently 'equal in practical acquaintance with religion, in clear views of the Gospel, in doctrinal knowledge, and in affection-ate application, to any sermons we ever heard'. The writer, who stressed that he was speaking from personal experience, com-mented that if she had been a Friend, she would have been a minister.[41] He comes close to suggesting that she should have been one in her own church.

Another Congregationalist woman is recorded as virtually start-ing a church on her own. Olive Holloway, later Mrs Helmore, started teaching some children on a Sunday, and soon found that their mothers and fathers also came to listen. As a direct result of her work, a dual-purpose building for a day-school and for worship was built, and it seems that she continued to teach people there, adults as well as children, although she was afraid 'lest she had vio-lated the apostolic prohibition'.[42] In both these instances, a natural extension of the ministry of the Angel to teach spiritual truths, came dangerously near to subverting the stereotype.

Methodism is more often thought of as giving women opportun-ities to preach. John Wesley's attitude to this had developed during his lifetime, and later in life he encouraged those whom he consid-ered had an 'extraordinary call', but after his death they were effect-ively banned by Conference, in a resolution of 1803. In her novel *Adam Bede*, George Eliot draws a portrait of the Methodist preacher Dinah Morris, based on her aunt, Elizabeth Evans. She was shown preaching from a cart on the village green to curious locals.[43] At the close of the book she is seen obeying the Methodist Conference edict that women should no longer preach.[44] Although a further resolution by Conference in 1836 was evidence that the first ban was not entirely successful, the mantle of women preachers passed largely to the Primitive Methodists and the Bible Christians, a smaller group originating in south-west England.[45]

Within Primitive Methodism such enterprise had official sanction. One of the founders, Hugh Bourne, was sympathetic to the practice and had even written a pamphlet on the subject.[46] Julia Werner estimates that in 1818 one in five Primitive Methodist preachers was a woman.[47] They became local and even itinerant preachers, a role that was clearly beyond the boundaries of even the Angel out of the House. Although the theology was never rejected, in this denomination, too, women faded from sight, their numbers declining as the church became more established. Swift traced 40 women itinerant preachers in the denomination, but all had started their ministry prior to 1844.[48] In the sample of 60 obituaries only Sarah Starbuck preached occasionally, whilst Mary Gilbert was an 'exhorter', able to speak but not give an exegesis of Scripture.[49] However, other obituaries give fascinating glimpses into this world of women preachers. For instance, Elizabeth Vernon was asked to become an itinerant preacher, and in the Louth circuit saw a small revival. 'For six months together she scarcely ever retired to rest till after midnight, being almost every night engaged till a late hour in praying with mourners [seekers after salvation].'[50] Another woman, Jane Foster, was ill with weak lungs – presumably tuberculosis – but she still continued to preach. Her obituary records that her preaching was 'clean, pointed and strictly Methodistical'. The 'unction' was apparently there when she preached, so even when she could hardly speak due to illness, 'suddenly the congregation has been bathed in tears and the place filled with the glory of God'.[51] The evangelical faith of these women led them beyond the conventions of their day, but the obituarists regarded their work as normal and to be commended, and within the parameters of womanly behaviour.

Being a minister's wife could also lead to wider opportunities, and was almost a career in itself.[52] Whilst it involved the conventional role of supporting and encouraging the husband, the obituaries show that some women took a much more active role. One Baptist minister's wife, Mrs Wigner, tried to be a 'fellow labourer' with her husband despite frequent illness, although the exact nature of her work is not made clear.[53] More unusual was Mary Emma Turquand, a Congregationalist who was described as being 'almost … the minister's co-pastor'. She was involved in many things, not only keeping church members away during his study times, but helping with pastoral visiting, suggesting people for suitable jobs, always choosing the hymns for services and often suggesting texts for sermons, because she knew 'full well the circumstances of the church and congregation'. The implication was that she was more familiar with the state of the church and people than was her husband. Even on her death-bed she was suggesting hymns and a text for a memorial service.[54] Yet there was no hint in her obituary that she was considered to have stepped beyond the bounds of acceptability in any of her activities.

In conclusion, therefore, it appears that the denominational obituaries demonstrate a less stereotypical view of women than appears at first sight. Although they often portray women in conventional roles, they also lift the curtain on another world, where women took initiative, worked in pastoral and evangelistic roles, and even preached – and in the case of one Congregationalist woman, pioneered a new church. It has to be remembered, however, that these women were often the 'spiritual cream' of their particular local churches, and as such maybe unrepresentative of the whole. Those who did not have fruitful lives and happy deaths were unlikely to have had their obituary published, though it is interesting to speculate what their stories would have been like, could we have read them. Despite their limitations, however, these obituaries do give us a fascinating insight into the variety of Nonconformist women's lives, especially when used alongside other sources such as biographies, autobiographies and hymns.

NOTES

1. I. Sellars, *Nineteenth Century Nonconformity* (London: Arnold, 1977), pp. vii–viii.
2. Ibid., p. 9. Whilst the population increased from 7,500,000 in 1780 to 18,000,000 in 1851, Old Dissent grew from 600,000 in 1800 to 1,500,000 in 1851, and Methodism mushroomed from 200,000 attenders in 1800 (Wesleyan and New Connexion only in 1800) to 2,000,000 in 1851, of which a quarter were Primitive Methodist.
3. L. Davidoff and C. Hall, *Family Fortunes* (London: Routledge, 1992), p. 131.
4. J. Obelkevich, *Religion and Rural Society* (Oxford: Clarendon Press, 1976), pp. 243–4.
5. J.S. Werner, *The Primitive Methodist Connexion. Its Background and Early History* (Madison: University of Wisconsin Press, 1984), pp. 155–6.
6. I am indebted to the Revd Margaret Jones for this observation.

7. S. Gill, *Women and the Church of England* (London: SPCK, 1994), p. 6.
8. J.A. James, *Female Piety* (1852), pp. 16–17 and 55.
9. C.H. Spurgeon, *Autobiography in four volumes compiled from his diary, letters and records by his wife and his private secretary* (London, 1899), Vol. 3, 1856–78, p. 186.
10. See for instance *Baptist Magazine* (1850) p. 745, and *Christian Witness* (1850), p. 60, which both stress the importance of the mother training up her children.
11. *Primitive Methodist Magazine* (1850), p. 250 (italics mine).
12. *Christian Witness* (1850), p. 207.
13. *Methodist Magazine* (1870), p. 573.
14. *Baptist Magazine* (1859), p. 637.
15. *Christian Witness* (1856), p. 350.
16. *Primitive Methodist Magazine* (1850), p. 250.
17. Obituary of Letitia McTurk in *Methodist Magazine* (1850), p. 429.
18. *Christian Witness* (1849), p. 347.
19. *Methodist Magazine* (1850), p. 542.
20. *Methodist Magazine* (1850), p. 544.
21. *Methodist Magazine* (1870), pp. 284–5.
22. *Christian Witness* (1850), pp. 206–7.
23. *Primitive Methodist Magazine* (1850), p. 265.
24. *Baptist Magazine* (1852), p. 772.
25. 'Activism' is suggested as one of four core attributes of evangelicalism in D. Bebbington, *Evangelicalism in Modern Britain* (London: Unwin Hyman, 1989), p. 10.
26. *Evangelical Magazine* (1846), p. 82.
27. *Christian Witness* (1849), p. 315.
28. *Primitive Methodist Magazine* (1850), p. 131.
29. *Baptist Magazine* (1849), p. 36.
30. *Methodist Magazine* (1852), p. 399.
31. S.S. Ellis, *Women of England, their social duties and domestic habits* (London: 1839), p. 44.
32. *Evangelical Magazine* (1860), p. 325.
33. *Methodist Magazine* (1852), p. 1052.
34. *Methodist Magazine* (1852), p. 112.
35. *Primitive Methodist Magazine* (1850), p. 62.
36. E.K. Helsinger, R.L. Sheets, W. Veeder, *The Woman Question*, Vol. 1 (Chicago: University of Chicago Press, 1983), Introduction, p. xv.
37. *Baptist Magazine* (1852), p. 772.
38. *Baptist Magazine* (1850), p. 436.
39. *Methodist Magazine* (1850), p. 645.
40. *Methodist Magazine* (1870), p. 478.
41. *Christian Witness* (1867), p. 536.
42. *Christian Witness* (1850), p. 164.
43. G. Eliot, *Adam Bede* (1859) (London Penguin, 1980), pp. 66–76.
44. Ibid., p. 583.
45. W.F. Swift, 'The Women Itinerant Preachers of Early Methodism', in *Proceedings of the Wesley Historical Society* 28/5 (March 1952), pp. 92f.

46. Bourne was influenced by Quaker Methodists. He published *Remarks on the Ministry of Women* in 1808. See Werner, p. 69.
47. Werner, p. 142.
48. W.F. Swift, 'The Women Itinerant Preachers of Early Methodism', in *Proceedings of the Wesley Historical Society*, Vol. 29, Part 4, pp. 79–80.
49. *Primitive Methodist Magazine* (1850), p. 189 and (1870), p. 306.
50. *Primitive Methodist Magazine* (1850), p. 259.
51. *Primitive Methodist Magazine* (1850), p. 385.
52. Leonard I. Sweet, *The Minister's Wife: Her Role in Nineteenth-Century American Evangelicalism* (Philadelphia, 1983) explores this subject in the American context.
53. *Baptist Magazine* (1851), p. 228.
54. *Christian Witness* (1860), p. 45.

11

The Paradigmatic Angel in the House: The Virgin Mary and Victorian Anglicans

Carol Marie Engelhardt

The figure of the Virgin Mary was symbolically charged and highly visible in Victorian England.[1] A marker of Roman Catholicism in England since the Henrician schism and the ensuing Protestantization of the Church of England, she became even more controversial in the middle decades of the nineteenth century, as members of the Oxford Movement revived and expanded the Marian devotion of the seventeenth-century divines.[2] Other Anglicans challenged this revival and accused the Tractarians of leaning towards Rome or even of being secret Roman Catholics. So pronounced was the anxiety aroused by the Virgin Mary that in 1845, the year that John Henry Newman and other prominent Anglicans converted to Roman Catholicism, John Keble, one of the leaders of the Oxford Movement, was persuaded by friends not to publish a Marian poem, 'Mother out of sight', for fear that it might signal a sympathy towards Roman Catholicism.[3]

The Virgin Mary was symbolically important during this period because she reflected social and cultural as well as religious concerns. Victorians' questions regarding the role, nature and characteristics of women – what was broadly referred to as The Woman Question – were reflected in their representations of the Virgin Mary.[4] Many of these concerns also found expression in Victorian representations of the ideal woman, popularly known as the Angel in the House. Thus the antipathy or at least ambivalence directed towards the Virgin Mary by many Victorian Anglicans is striking because of the resemblance she bears to the Angel in the House. Like the angelic woman, the Virgin Mary was defined by her role as mother; she was perceived by most Anglicans as either sinless, or at least as exceptionally good; and her work was assumed to be within the domestic sphere. Most importantly, the Virgin Mary was the only woman able to satisfy the contradictory demands of the angelic myth that woman be both virgin and mother. And yet Victorian Anglicans, with the exception of members of the Oxford Movement and Ritualists, remained uncomfortable with the figure of the Virgin Mary, and no Anglican upheld her as the feminine ideal.

The most obvious reason for the Anglican discomfort with Mary was the lengthy English tradition of anti-Roman Catholicism, of which anti-Marianism was always an important strand. Given this tradition, it was to some degree inconceivable to Anglicans that Mary could be imagined as an ideal woman. More importantly, however, the Virgin Mary posed fundamental challenges to the ideal of the Angel in the House. The Virgin Mary was understood by Catholics and Protestants alike as a powerful figure, whereas the Angel in the House, for all the influence that was attributed to her, embodied a limited view of female capability. The overt congruences between the Virgin Mary and the Angel in the House in those two pivotal areas – virginity and motherhood – show that it was because she challenged the paradigm of the Angel in the House that the Virgin Mary was not accepted by the mainstream of the Church of England.

As even a cursory reading of Victorian texts indicates, virginity was highly prized for marriageable females. Besides promising to ensure the legitimacy of heirs, virginity was also deemed expressive of innocence and naiveté, characteristics that Victorians prized in women. Most heroines of Victorian literature were virgins (although matrimony was ratified by their generally being married or engaged just before the novel ended), and the ideal male–female relationship was often represented as that of brother and sister, or father and daughter.[5] However, female virginity was often seen as ridiculous when carried on past the child-bearing years, as the scorn directed at 'redundant women' revealed. Virginity vowed for religious reasons, which the anti-Tractarian writer R.T. Hampson called 'a pure relic of heathenism',[6] was even less congruent with the dominant culture: Anglican nuns were regarded with suspicion and were forbidden to take permanent vows, and Roman Catholic convents were seen as little more than prisons.[7] Clearly, then, an essential part of the angelic myth – the extolling of female virginity – was problematic in the very culture that promulgated the image of the angelic woman.

In Christian belief, Mary's identity as a virgin was necessary to fulfil the prophecy of Isaiah 7:14[8] and to ensure that Jesus was the Son of God. Victorian Anglicans did not question the virgin birth of Christ, but they differed on whether or not Mary had maintained her virginity throughout her life. Tractarians and Ritualists believed, in the words of the Ritualist Frederick George Lee, that Mary had remained a 'pure and ever-virgin mother.'[9] Responding to a controversy in the late 1880s between the Bishop of Chichester and one of his clergymen over the eternal virginity of Mary, an anonymous pamphleteer argued that believing in Mary's eternal virginity was not only an expression of 'devout and reverent feeling' towards Mary, but also the tradition of the early Church and the Anglican divines.[10] Believing that Mary, as the Mother of God, was uniquely close to God, Tractarians and those they influenced tied their belief in her eternal virginity to the Incarnation. Her virginity before the birth of Christ was proof of his divinity; her virginity after the birth of Christ was necessary because any later intimate relationship would be unthinkable after she had borne the Son of God.

For Tractarians and Ritualists, the issue of Mary's virginity was part of the larger issue of how they understood virginity. Valuing virginity chosen for religious reasons, they were not among those whom the poet Lewis Morris characterized in a poem first published in 1880 as 'Rude souls and coarse, to whom virginity/ Seems a dead thing and cold.'[11] Unlike other Victorians, who saw virginity as something arid, many Tractarians believed it to be holy. Even as an Anglican, Newman believed that clergymen should be celibate, and E.B. Pusey (who encouraged his daughter in her desire to become an Anglican nun), John Mason Neale and Thomas Thelluson Carter all founded Anglican sisterhoods.

However, life-long virginity was at odds with the value Victorian culture placed on the family, and many Victorian Anglicans asserted that Mary and Joseph had a normal relationship after Jesus was born: 'It is evident from the last verse of the 1st chapter of Matthew, that Mary lived afterwards with her husband Joseph as his wife.'[12] The major objection to Mary's perpetual virginity was that it devalued matrimony. George Miller, an Anglican who identified himself as both 'protestant' and a member of the 'catholic church of Christ',[13] complained that Pusey's praise of virginity denigrated marriage and contradicted Scripture.[14]

In 1869, an anonymous Anglican writer devoted an entire pamphlet to the topic of *The Virgin Mary, a married woman*. The author asserted that God had not only commanded marriage, but had made it a more honourable state than celibacy,[15] and that there was no reason for Mary to remain a virgin after the birth of Jesus. 'No restriction whatever was placed either on Joseph or Mary when the mysterious incarnation of Christ was revealed to them, but rather the contrary: Fear not to take unto thee Mary thy wife, for that which is conceived in her is of the Holy Ghost.'[16] The writer's purpose was to exalt marriage over celibacy as well as to check Marian devotion, which he said was grounded in part on the belief that Mary was always a virgin. Thus the author understood Mary's maternity as limited to the actual childbearing: Jesus 'evidently regarded her simply as "the handmaid of the Lord" born to the high honour of becoming the Mother of the Saviour; but that purpose of her life ended, in no way different to other women of her time, nor bound to desist from carrying out the proposed marriage with Joseph.'[17] While in this particular instance virginity was troubling because it made Mary unique and led to the idolatrous worship of her, the writer's discomfort shows us that continued virginity was viewed with suspicion partly because it was empowering: the belief in Mary's eternal virginity was associated with the worship of her that the writer believed existed in the Roman Catholic Church.

As an eternal virgin, Mary repudiated Victorian family values. Her virginity opposed the family system, within which women were expected to marry and bear children. She also threatened the model of patriarchal control in the family, for although she had married and borne a child, her child had no human father. As Janice Capel Anderson has noted, divine intervention in Mary's womb meant that 'it is not the husband that ultimately controls the woman's reproductive powers.'[18] If Mary remained a virgin, then Joseph was a husband in name only, and her primary relationship was with the Trinity, to whom she was 'a Daughter born to God, Mother of Christ from stall to rood, and Wife unto the Holy Ghost'.[19] However, insisting that Mary had a sexual relationship with Joseph after the birth of Jesus returned her to the realm of ordinary female experience; it restored Joseph's control over her reproductive powers and separated her from her unique relationship with the Trinity.

In a culture that placed a high value on female virginity, it is ironic that most Anglicans could not assimilate the one woman who conformed to the angelic ideal by bearing a child while retaining her virginity. Even the Tractarians and Ritualists who asserted her virginity never held that virginity up as a model for women. As an eternal virgin, Mary showed that the logical extension of the Victorians' praise of female virginity could lead to female autonomy, whereas the Victorians valued virginity as a prelude to marriage and as a guarantee of female innocence and fidelity. In a culture and in a church that did not, in general, ratify women as independent actors, an eternally virgin Mary was an anomaly that threatened the dominant models of female behaviour.

Identified primarily as a mother, Mary exemplified the component of the angelic myth that having children was a woman's greatest duty and greatest happiness. However, Victorian representations of Mary and the infant Jesus further revealed problems with the angelic ideal, for they depicted motherhood as a source of some anxiety as well as of joy and comfort.

This ambivalence began with the reluctance to address the issue of pregnancy. While children were sentimentalized in Victorian England, pregnancy was virtually unacknowledged in popular discourse. Victorian novels tended not to depict the early years of marriage: they either ended with the marriage proposal[20] or they skipped from the acceptance of the proposal to a period several years later, allowing the heroine to re-emerge with children without the reader witnessing her transformation from virgin to mother.[21]

Because the Incarnation was one of the central facts of Christianity and had a long history of representation in the Western tradition, however, High Church Anglicans partly overcame their reticence regarding pregnancy. (Low and Broad Church Anglicans did not discuss the nine months before the Nativity much, if at all, in keeping with their view of Mary's role as a limited one.) However, they often avoided the physical reality of Mary's pregnancy by referring to her breast or bosom, rather than her womb, when speaking of the Incarnation. John Keble, for example, described the Annunciation as the event 'where the angel in the Thrice Great Name/ Hailed thee, and Jesus to thy bosom came.'[22] Archer Gurney, a High Church clergyman who was proud of his 'distinctly Anti-roman [*sic*] views',[23] hailed Mary as 'The Virgin Mother, highest raised of all,/ Who at her heart earth's Wondrous SAVIOUR bore ...[24] A.M. Allchin has suggested that this displacement emphasized Mary's faith 'as a greater calling even than that of bearing him in her womb'.[25] This interpretation was supported by the words of Charles Lindley Wood, president of the Anglo-Catholic English Church Union, who located the developing Jesus first in Mary's womb and then in her heart: 'The Blessed Virgin bore within herself for nine months God the Word, while he was taking to Himself of her substance, our nature from its very first beginning. The Deity contained in her bosom was recognised by St. John the Baptist, himself unborn.'[26]

However, in emphasizing Mary's faith, this displacement also elided the physical fact of her maternity.[27] In a culture that both asserted that women were naturally maternal and believed that Mary's pregnancy was one of the central facts of redemption, the silence surrounding Mary's pregnancy reminds us again that the physical realities of motherhood were often unacknowledged in Victorian public discourse. This reticence was in keeping with the Victorians' reluctance to discuss publicly other, related, topics, but it also suggests other concerns. A pregnant woman was creative in a way that men could not be. She was also both the antithesis and the embodiment of the angelic myth: her body acknowledged that she was no longer a virgin and proclaimed that she was becoming a mother. A woman pregnant with her first child was therefore in a liminal state: no longer a virgin, but not yet a mother.

This silence was also probably partly inspired by the specific situation: it was not just images of pregnant women that made Anglicans uncomfortable, but images of this particular pregnant woman. These images highlighted Mary's unique connection with the Trinity: she alone knew the Word made Flesh, and in a uniquely intimate way, before anyone else did. Given the ferocity of some Anglicans' attacks on representations of Mary and the baby Jesus, Mary's intimate knowledge of God might have been seen as excluding all others, who were relegated to the status of observers. A pregnant Mary stood between and mediated the relationship between Jesus and Christians.

Tractarians celebrated Mary's maternal role, although never to the extent that Roman Catholics did, with a proliferation of images of Mary and her infant.[28] Keble referred to Mary as the 'Mother blest,/ To whom, caressing and caress'd,/ Clings the Eternal Child.'[29] The Anglican Benedictine monk Fr Ignatius (Joseph Leicester Lyne) spoke of Christmas as a memorial of the time 'when Mary pressed her babe to her breast and wept over him'.[30] Archer Gurney described Mary as 'that Virgin Blest,/ Who cradled on her breast/ The Lord of all, and kissed His sleeping Eyes'.[31] These images celeb-rated the special intimacy between Mary and Jesus: Mary was the first to be caressed by Jesus, the first to weep over his death, the first to comfort him. Keble and Gurney represented motherhood as a blessing for Mary: she was blessed not only in being chosen to bear Jesus, but also in her closeness to him.

In contrast to the Tractarians' and Ritualists' celebration of the bond between Mary and Jesus, their opponents within the Church of England separated Mary from Jesus and argued that Mary's maternity had not conferred any special blessedness on her. They often interpreted Jesus' reply to the woman who praised his mother, 'Yea, rather blessed are they that hear the word of God, and keep it' (Luke 11.28), as denigrating Mary's maternity.[32] In an 1855 sermon against the recently declared dogma of the Immaculate Conception, W.T. Maudson declared that this incident demonstrated that 'He [Jesus] appears desirous, you see, to lessen the closeness, and destroy the distinction of that earthly relationship, which has been made the very ground of the especial reverence that is rendered to the Virgin.'[33]

These Anglicans especially objected to pictorial representations of the Madonna and Child as infantilizing Jesus and magnifying Mary's maternal power. One clergyman, residing in Italy because of his poor health, was horrified when he 'observed what numbers of persons fell down and worshipped before marble statues, pictures, or large *wax dolls*, which represent the Virgin Mary with the divine and omnipotent Saviour as a *feeble, helpless, babe* in her arms!'[34] Michael Hobart Seymour, an Anglican clergyman who was both anti-Roman Catholic and anti-Tractarian, argued that representations of Jesus 'as a little child in the arms of Mary' made Jesus 'subject to the will of Mary' when he was 'the King of kings, and Lord of lords'.[35]

These Anglicans also objected to Continental prayers to Mary that urged her to remind Jesus of her maternal role.[36] Seymour said that on his travels to the Continent he had seen a prayer that 'appeals to her [Mary] to shew her breasts to Christ, to remind Him of "the womb that bare thee, and the paps which thou hast sucked." And this appeal is made under peculiar circumstances. It supposes that Christ has sat in judgement upon the sinner, and condemned him; and that the sinner has had no satisfying plea to offer, so that the judge is inexorable. It then supposes that the Virgin Mary shews her breasts to Christ, and reminding Him by that act of her influence or authority as a Mother, she induces Him to forgive the sinner'.[37] The travesty of the mother showing her breasts to her grown son in order to make him do her will shocked Seymour (and no doubt his readers, as well) as it contrasted a son's reason with a mother's emotion. Reminding Jesus of her early nurturing of him in order to re-establish her early control over him, the Mary that Seymour described was a mother who would never allow her son to escape her control. Thus those early bonds, celebrated by the Tractarians and Ritualists in their joyful images of the Nativity, could ultimately be used to thwart a son's independence.

Seymour's complaint was representative of Anglican objections that depictions of the Madonna and Child infantilized Jesus and imposed maternal control over him at a time when he was ruling in heaven. Although the anti-Tractarians' objections to images of Mary and Jesus had religious grounds, their comments also reflected, and influenced, the larger Victorian culture. As such, these objections reflected broader concerns over the length of maternal influence. In a culture that exalted the maternal role, it was not surprising that there was some anxiety attached to the length and extent of a mother's influence over her son. Motherhood, praised for being unselfish, could become restrictive if prolonged beyond childhood. Mary's primary identity was as a mother; the fact that Victorian Anglicans were wary of that identity suggests that they were also wary of motherhood in general. Even those Tractarians and Ritualists who celebrated the mother–child relationship as a close, loving relationship never held Mary as a model mother or a model woman. Tractarians saw her as specially chosen and uniquely blessed in her motherhood, but never as a model mother.

When Mary did serve as a model for Victorian Anglicans, it was as an example of faith. However, making her a model of faith minimized both her sex and her motherhood. She was praised for doing God's will, a task that was open to anyone, not for having borne the Son of God, a task that could not be replicated. And yet, Mary was important to Christians precisely because she was a virgin and a mother. It is where the Virgin Mary's characteristics coincide with those of the Angel in the House that we can see most clearly why the Victorians rejected the Virgin Mary as an ideal woman.

Virginity was an important characteristic for both the Virgin Mary and the Angel in the House, but as I have tried to show, the topic of female virginity was a vexed question in Victorian England. Female virginity was highly valued, but only until marriage; most Anglicans rejected it as a life-long choice, and even Tractarians did not hold Mary up as a model of virginity. While the characteristics associated with virginity – innocence, naiveté, passivity – were praised in the angelic woman, virginity was not supposed to be sustained forever, for an equally important part of the angelic woman's identity was as a mother. Therefore, as a virgin, Mary was an imperfect model for Victorian women.

The rejection of Mary's virginity also showed a suspicion of female power. As a virgin, Mary was outside of male control, and thus was an uncomfortable anomaly in a society that, in its laws and customs, asserted a belief in male superiority. While the reality in the nineteenth century was that the single life was often a difficult one for women, the discussions of whether or not Mary was eternally a virgin revealed that virginity was seen as dangerous because it authorized female independence from male control.

Neither was Mary regarded as a model mother. The explanation for this lies partly in reasons not confined to Victorian culture. Christians believed that Jesus was sinless, and as the mother of a sinless child, Mary was not a realistic role model. Praising her motherhood might also have been seen by some as casting doubt on Jesus' sinlessness or even on his divinity. However, even when Victorian Anglicans argued that Mary had other children, they never represented her as an ideal mother of these other children; these children served only to return her to obscurity by making her ordinary.

Furthermore, the outrage directed at representations of Mary and the baby Jesus hints at broader concerns that prolonged maternal control would infantilize the child after he was grown. Although these attacks must be understood in the context of a religious culture that wanted to avoid 'Roman' devotion, their restrictions on the power of mothers in general shows their discomfort with maternal power, not just Marian devotion.

For all her resemblance to the Angel in the House, Mary was not accepted by Anglicans as an ideal woman because her identification with Roman Catholicism, her continued virginity, and the extent of her motherhood all were incongruent with the images of the ideal woman in Victorian public discourse. The most important distinction between her and the angelic woman, however, was that those traits that in the angelic woman ratified Victorian concepts about the nature of woman were in the Virgin Mary in opposition to those concepts.[38]

The Angel in the House myth certainly benefited women in some ways. It argued that they were morally superior to men; Victorian reformers, including Josephine Butler and Caroline Norton, used that image to argue for female rights or protection. But the angelic image fundamentally restricted women by confining them to the home, refusing them intellectual power and sexual equality, and making them subordinate to men. The Virgin Mary, however, had historically been seen as a strong woman, by virtue of her mother-hood and its attendant graces. This essential difference between the Virgin Mary and the Angel in the House explains to a large degree why many Victorian Anglicans were uncomfortable with her. Her virginity and her motherhood gave her independent power; it was this independence and power that prevented her from joining the Angel in the House as the ideal Victorian woman.

NOTES

1. For reading previous versions of this chapter and especially for their comments on the larger project out of which this piece comes, I would like to thank James Eli Adams, Frans Jozef van Beeck, S.J., Dyan Elliot, Shelley Grady, Gerry Magill, Andrew H. Miller, David Pace, Jeanne Peterson and Liann Tsoukas.
2. The resurgence of Roman Catholicism, which began with Catholic Emancipation in 1829 and continued with the wave of the conversions to Roman Catholicism by prominent Anglicans at mid-century and the re-establishment of the Roman Catholic hierarchy in 1850, also contributed to the Virgin Mary's prominence, for both the converts and the newly appointed Cardinal of Westminster, Nicholas Wiseman, emphasized Marian devotion. For more on Roman Catholicism and the Virgin Mary in Victorian England, see John Singleton, 'The Virgin Mary and Religious Conflict in Victorian Britain', *Journal of Ecclesiastical History*, 43, No. 1 (January 1992), 16–34.
3. J.T. Coleridge, *A memoir of the Rev. John Keble* 3rd edn. (Oxford and London: James Parker, 1870), p. 292.
4. The Virgin Mary was, of course, pre-eminently a religious figure. While not denying the theological and historical reasons for these representations or disagreements, in this chapter I want to understand these representations in the context of Victorian society and culture.
5. Deborah Gorham, *The Victorian Girl and the Feminine Ideal* (Bloomington: Indiana University Press, 1982), pp. 7, 44.
6. R.T. Hampson, *Religious Deceptions of the Church of Rome Exposed* (London: C. Mitchell, n. d.), p. 18.
7. For a study of Victorian attitudes towards Roman Catholic converts, see Walter Arnstein, *Protestant Versus Catholic in Mid-Victorian England: Mr Newdegate and the Nuns* (Columbia: University of Missouri Press, 1982). Catherine Sinclair's anti-Catholic novel *Beatrice: or, the unknown relatives* (London: Ward, Lock and Tyler, 1890; first

published 1852) depicts young Protestant women imprisoned in a Roman Catholic convent.

8. 'Behold, a virgin shall conceive, and bear a son, and shall call his name Immanuel.'

9. F.G. Lee, *The Truth as it is in Jesus: A sermon preached at the Church of S. Martin, Leicester, on Monday, March 2, 1868, at the opening of the Lent Assizes* (London: Joseph Masters, 1868), p. 3. See also, for example, E.B. Pusey, *Letter to the Right Rev. Father in God, Richard Lord Bishop of Oxford, on the tendency to Romanism imputed to doctrines held of old, as now, in the English Church* (Oxford: J.H. Parker, London: J.G. & F. Rivington, 1839), p. 199; R.J. Wilson, *Our Relation to the Saints: Some notes gathered from English divines* (privately printed, n.d. [1874?]), p. 3; 'The Virgin Birth', *The Church Eclectic* (October 1894), 637.

10. *The Views of Bishop Pearson and the Fathers of the English Reformation on the Subject of the Ever-Virginity of Saint Mary the Virgin* (London: J.H. Parker, Brighton: H. and C. Treacher, 1889), pp. 3–8. For a similar argument, see Alfred Lush, *A sermon, preached in the Church of Saint Mary, Greywell, on Good-Friday, 1853. Being also the Festival of the Annunciation of the Blessed Virgin Mary* (London: John and Charles Mozley, 1853), pp. 13–15. For an analysis of the treatment of Mary by the seventeenth-century divines, see A.M. Allchin, *The Joy of All Creation: an Anglican meditation on the Place of Mary* (revised edition, London: New City, 1993), chapters 2–6, and Hilda Graef, *Mary: a History of Doctrine and Devotion* (vol. 2, London and NY: Sheed and Ward, 1965), pp. 63–7.

11. Lewis Morris, 'Motherhood: an ode', in Orby Shipley, ed., *Carmina Mariana: an English Anthology in Verse in Honour of or in Relation to the Blessed Virgin Mary* (London: Spottiswoode, 1893), p. 250.

12. Catherine Sinclair, *Popish Legends of Bible Truths* (London: Longman, Brown, Green and Longmans, 1852), p. xxiii.

13. George Miller, *A Letter to the Rev. E.B. Pusey, D.D., in Reference to his Letter to the Lord Bishop of Oxford* (London: Duncan and Malcolm, 1840), pp. 4–5.

14. Ibid., p. 64.

15. *The Virgin Mary: A Married Woman* (London: William Macintosh, n. d. [1869]), p. 6.

16. Ibid., p. 7.

17. Ibid., pp. 12–13.

18. Janice Capel Anderson, 'Mary's Difference: Gender and Patriarchy in the Birth Narratives', *Journal of Religion*, 67, No. 2 (April 1987), 195–6.

19. Dante Gabriel Rossetti, 'Ave', in Shipley, p. 334.

20. As Joan Bellamy has noted, 'The destiny of the true heroine [of the Victorian novel] was to marry and it is with a declaration of love, or the proposal that the nineteenth-century novel generally ends'; Bellamy, 'Barriers of Silence: women in Victorian fiction', in Eric Sigsworth, ed., *In Search of Victorian Values: Aspects of Nineteenth-century Thought and Society* (New York: Manchester University Press, 1988), p. 134.

21. This tactic is used in novels as diverse as George Eliot's *Adam Bede*, Charles Dickens' *David Copperfield*, Wilkie Collins' *The Woman in White* and Bram Stoker's *Dracula* (in which the marriage occurs early in the novel, but the consummation is apparently delayed until after the death of Dracula in the novel's penultimate entry).

22. John Keble, 'Mother out of Sight', in Coleridge, p. 316.

23. Archer Gurney, letter to W.E. Gladstone, Tuesday, 27 October 1857. British Library, Gladstone papers, vol. 303, 215v.

24. Archer Gurney, 'The Communion of the Saints', in Orby Shipley, ed., *Lyra Mystica: Hymns and Verses on Sacred Subjects, Ancient and Modern* (London: Longman, Green, Longman, Roberts and Green, 1865), p. 21.

25. Allchin, p. 128.

26. Earl of Redesdale and Charles L. Wood, *The Doctrine of the Real Presence* (London: John Murray, 1879), p. 23.

27. Extreme High Churchmen occasionally acknowledged the physical realities of Mary's pregnancy: see Robert Stephen Hawker, 'Aishah Shechinah', in Shipley, *Carmina Mariana*, p. 160, and Lee, p. 3.

28. Tractarians also emphasized the figure of the Mother and Child because they emphasized, and somewhat idealized, childhood. Cf. Allchin, pp. 151–3.

29. John Keble, 'The Annunciation', *The Christian Year* (New York: Thomas Cromwell, 1890, first published 1827), p. 232.

30. Fr Ignatius, *The Catholic Church of England and What she Teaches: A Lecture by Father Ignatius (Monk of the Order of Saint benedict), Delivered in the Corn Exchange, Manchester, Tuesday, September 27, 1864*, p. 38.

31. Archer Gurney, 'The Holy Sacrifice', in Shipley, *Lyra Mystica*, p. 299.

32. Tractarians interpreted this passage not as denigrating Mary's motherhood but as blessing Mary more for her belief than for her maternity. See, for example, Keble, 'The Annunciation', in *The Christian Year*, p. 232.

33. W.T. Maudson, 'The Dogma of the Virgin Mary's Immaculate Conception: A Sermon', (*The Pulpit*, 67, No. 1, 784 (8 March 1855), 239. See also John E. Armstrong, *Armstrong's Reply to Wiseman's Pastoral Letter on the Immaculate Conception* (London: Wertheim and Macintosh, 1855), p. 9; William Ford Vance, *On the Invocation of Angels, Saints, and the Virgin Mary* (London: James Nisbet, 1828), p. 41; Catherine Sinclair, *Popish Legends, or Bible Truths*, p. xxiii; J. Endell Tyler, *Primitive Christian Worship: or, the Evidence of Holy Scripture and the Church, Concerning the Invocation of Saints and Angels, and the Blessed Virgin Mary* (London: J.G.F. & J. Rivington, 1840), p. 284; J. Endell Tyler, *The Worship of the Blessed Virgin Mary in the Church of Rome Contrary to Holy Scripture, and to the Faith and Practice of the Church of Christ though the First Five Centuries* (London: Richard Bentley, 1844), pp. 87–8, 273; M. Hobart Seymour, *A Pilgrimage to Rome* (London: Seeleys, 1848), p. 508; *An Address to the Parishioners of Leominster upon the Worship of the Virgin Mary* (London: John F. Shaw, 1866), p. 15.

34. *An Address to the Parishioners of Leominster …*, p. 5, emphasis original.

35. Seymour, p. 552.

36. That many of the Marian prayers and devotions to which the Anglicans objected were Continental (usually Italian) indicates the strong current of nationalism that was also part of this debate.
37. Seymour, p. 508.
38. For a serialized novel that rejected the Virgin Mary as a model for female behaviour at the same time that it incorporated the figure of the angelic woman, see Mrs. Oliphant's 'Madonna Mary' *Good Words* 7 (1866): 1–17, 72–88, 145–60, 217–31, 289–303, 361–77, 433–46, 505–22, 577–91, 649–62, 721–36, 793–806.

12

Heroines of Missionary Adventure: The Portrayal of Victorian Women Missionaries in Popular Fiction and Biography

Sean Gill

Charlotte Brontë's Jane Eyre is the best-known anti-heroine of the Victorian missionary movement. Yet her refusal to marry the zealous St John Rivers and to be his fellow-missionary to India stems not from any serious questioning of missionary aims and methods, but rather from a deep unease about the demands placed upon women by patriarchal Christianity in one of its most imperious nineteenth-century manifestations.[1] For the cold, stern and self-possessed Rivers, modelled it is said upon the real-life missionary hero to India Henry Martyn, Jane has all the feminine qualities required of the exemplary Christian helpmeet. As he tells her, he has studied her character carefully and found her to be 'docile, diligent, disinterested, faithful, constant, and courageous; very gentle and very heroic'.[2] Above all, she is endowed in abundance with that most prized of female Christian virtues: self-sacrifice. In his plans for Jane's future this capacity for self-immolation is to be tested to the full, as he urges her to simplify her 'complicated interests, feelings, thoughts, wishes, aims' and to pursue only one goal: that of fulfilling 'the mission of your great Master'.[3] The ambivalence of just who is the master whom Jane is called upon to obey is evident from River's androcentric identification of his own ambitions for the future with the will of God himself, and it was a feature of many Victorian Christian appeals to women. As the epitome of right-thinking Christian femininity, the novelist Charlotte Yonge urged, women ought to regard themselves 'as the help-meet of man; not necessarily of any individual man, but of the whole Body whom Christ our Lord has left to be waited on as Himself'.[4] From such a patriarchal theological perspective Rivers sees nothing wrong in pressing Jane to marry him out of a sense of Christian duty, even though she admits to being unable to love him.

This she indignantly refuses to do, accusing him of killing her inner life, an assertion of selfhood so at variance with the ideal of Christian womanhood that Rivers accuses Jane of being 'violent, unfeminine, and untrue'.[5] Charlotte Brontë's questioning of orthodox constructions of gender was not lost on one of the novel's sternest early critics, Elizabeth Rigby, who complained in *The Quarterly Review* of December 1848 that in her heroine no Christian grace was perceptible since 'It is by her own talents, virtues, and courage that she is made to attain the summit of human happiness, and, as far as Jane Eyre's own statement is concerned, no one would think that she owed anything either to God above or to man below.'[6]

Charlotte Brontë's sense that women's involvement in the nineteenth-century missionary movement raised problematic questions about gender and power was far removed from the idealised way in which women missionaries were portrayed in a series of popular accounts of their work, mostly written by male clergy intent on gaining recruits and funds for their cause. Books of this kind combined a sense of romance and adventure with an unshakeable belief in the religious and cultural superiority of the missionary enterprise. The tone of the genre is perhaps best captured by the title of a work by Canon E.C. Dawson: *Heroines of Missionary Adventure: true stories of the intrepid endurance of missionaries in their encounters with uncivilized man, wild beasts and the forces of nature in all parts of the world.*[7] Most of the copies of works of this type which I have acquired contain plates indicating that they were awarded to girls as school or Sunday school prizes, and not surprisingly women missionaries are portrayed in their pages as Christian exemplars whose lives are an arduous but intellectually and emotionally untroubled triumph over adversity.

Accounts of this kind are partly the product of a process of selection and censorship by the missionary societies themselves in the interest of presenting a positive image of their work for home consumption. While the societies did not shy away from stressing the physical hardships of the missionary life, they were much more reticent about revealing other tensions and frustrations which women encountered. For example Miss Johnson, a young woman sent out to Delhi by the Anglican Society for the Propagation of the Gospel in 1869, had to contend not only with the trials of ill-health and a fearsome climate, but also the bitter opposition of the formidable Mrs Winter, the wife of the clergyman responsible for the station to which she was posted. Mrs Winter regarded all single women as a threat to the authority of missionary wives, which led to a bitter and revealing series of letters being sent home by the two women, but Mrs Winter urged the SPG's secretary to ensure that Miss Johnson's letters 'may not be read at working parties as if she writes all that she says she will I fear many at home may be discouraged'.[8]

Apart from stereotypical popular lives, there are however also a series of much more detailed biographies of women missionaries which usually contain selected extracts from their own letters and diaries. Because the authors of these works were mostly women they were often more aware of the pressures upon other women who attempted to lead public lives within a Christian context. As with the more sensationalized accounts, the standpoint is invariably sympathetic to missionary work and attempts to portray their subjects in the best possible light. But what I want to suggest is that such writings do not simply reveal the gulf which existed between the representation of women missionaries and the reality of their lives, but that the ambiguities and closures within the texts can reveal a great deal about the ideological contradictions experienced by Victorian Christian women missionaries as they sought to negotiate the constraints of gender, class, and race within their chosen calling.[9]

There is no doubt that for many women part of the appeal of the mission field lay in the opportunities which it offered to use their abilities freed from some of the crushing limitations of Victorian society. As one candidate told the women's committee of the SPG in 1876, she was seeking 'a wider field for her talent than that which she found in England'.[10] This was particularly true for single women who, despite early opposition to the idea, had been increasingly employed by the missionary societies in the second half of the century, and who had in the case of the Anglican Church Missionary Society come to form the largest group of overseas missionary workers by the end of the nineteenth century.[11] Regarded in W.R. Greg's notorious phrase as 'redundant' unless married or caring for parents or young relatives, the mission field held out the prospect of far greater autonomy and self-fulfilment for unmarried middle-class women than was possible at home.[12] Such women found overseas opportunities to preach, to assume authority over native helpers, and to run schools and hospitals on a scale which would not have been possible within the mainstream churches in England.[13]

Yet it was precisely this degree of freedom that created difficulties for the depictors of women as missionary heroines. Such work demanded bravery, toughness, organizational skills and independence of thought and action – qualities that in a society based upon sharply polarized gender identities were held to be masculine not feminine attributes. The Bishop of Grahamstown, Allan Beecher Webb, who had experience of the workings of an Anglican missionary sisterhood in South Africa, was one churchman who was uneasily aware of the problem posed by overseas missionary work in this respect. The position in which missionary women found themselves was, he conceded, an unusual one and for that very reason there were particular dangers that had to guarded against in their training:

> It cannot be too much impressed upon us, that the education and mental discipline which help most to build up the typical character of Woman are also the best for those called to any unusual work. For in whatever measure a woman becomes unwomanly, so far exactly is her usefulness as well as her charm impaired. She can lose no grace naturally belonging to her, without losing at the same time power, influence, and capacity for the work for which she was formed. We all know what that work was: to be a 'help-meet' for Man.[14]

It was true, he went on, that missionary work did involve a kind of 'womanly strength', but he was at pains to stress 'how far this ideal of the valiant woman ... is from any approach to what is commonly called a "strong-minded" woman'.[15] Appropriate feminine behaviour was partly to be guaranteed by strict organizational control of the sisterhood designed to ensure that there should be no danger of what he called 'arbitrary government by a woman', as well as a clear recognition on their part that the sisters were not to impinge upon the quite separate work of the clergy; and partly by fostering in the women a sense of their own weakness for, he enthused, 'in her feebleness, Love shall be the secret of Women's strength'. Bishop Webb was writing at a time in which, he lamented, a good deal was being heard about 'Women's Rights', and it is significant that it was this challenge to conservative constructions of femininity that also exercised another champion of women's missionary work, the Archbishop of Dublin, William Conyngham, when he preached the annual sermon to the Church of England Zenana Missionary Society in 1885. Such claims, he cautioned, could only be accepted by the church in so far as they lay 'within the limits of true Womanhood', limits which involved a recognition of the different but complementary components of masculinity and femininity. For the Christian, he argued, this immutable truth was first fully revealed in Christ whose character exhibited 'a mysterious union of those distinctive qualities of manly and womanly excellence', a union exemplified by the heroism of Christ's voluntary suffering on Calvary, and the 'woman-like sympathy' of his tears shed at the death of Lazarus.[16] Of course, quite how such a hypostatic union of gendered opposites applied to the actual relationships of men and women in Victorian society was not altogether clear, and the most usual Christian recourse was to the ideal of Christ as the model of chivalry, that interplay of masculine strength and feminine weakness which served to reinforce both ideals.[17]

In a number of ways portrayals of women missionaries attempted to reassure their readers that this delicate balance of appropriate gendered behaviour was maintained. Most, for example, go out of their way to stress that women, and particularly single women, never answered the call to work overseas until they had met all possible family obligations at home. Thus Irene Petrie, the daughter of a colonel who was himself a keen supporter of the Anglican Church Missionary Society, was nevertheless not allowed to serve with the CMS in Lahore and Srinigar until his death in 1892.[18] Christina Forsyth's biographer was similarly at pains to stress that his heroine did not offer herself for service in South Africa with the United Presbyterian Church until her clerical brother married, and he wrote approvingly that 'Christina saw that this was the pattern of duty for her and cheerfully subordinated her own ambition to his interests'.[19] Yet a number of biographies hint that such deference to the demands of family life was not so easily given. Christina Coillard was the daughter of a Scottish Baptist minister who at the age of 13 was inspired to work overseas after hearing a talk by the South African missionary hero Robert Moffat. Yet when she grew older it was some time before 'her widowed mother had become reconciled to the step' and she was forced to defer an offer of missionary service for two years because of family opposition.[20] Compared to another missionary, Charlotte Tucker, Christina Coillard might have regarded herself as relatively lucky, and some sense of the frustrations and impatience experienced by would-be missionary women is apparent in her biography. Held up by its author as a paragon of Christian self-abnegation who was content to regard her father's prohibition on her undertaking missionary work 'as in itself sufficient indication of the Divine Will', Charlotte and her sister gave their 'time, talents and energies to successive generations of juveniles, without a murmur'.[21] Even after her father's death, and despite what her biographer admits to have been her dislike of housework and nursing, she devoted her life to looking after her mother and then a bachelor brother, only beginning to work with the Indian Female Instruction Society in the Punjab in 1875 at the age of 54. By then she could write far from submissively to her sister that she was not prepared to end her life 'a third or fourth lady in – perhaps – a Curate's dear little home'.[22]

Missionary work by women was also justified as suitably feminine on the grounds that it was quite distinctive from the work done by men since only women could reach their sisters imprisoned in the zenanas and harems of Asia. It was also held to be an extension of the philanthropic work undertaken by women at home, an application of their maternal qualities of care and compassion to those in need. The importance of this sanction for women's work is evident in the biography of Christina Forsyth where even though she had been married for less than a year and had never had children, it is emphasized that 'her homely motherliness made her the idol of the people'.[23]

Yet the contradiction between the self-abnegation expected of women and the self-assertiveness needed to succeed in a missionary calling remained. Christina Coillard's biographer commented that 'Her brothers and sisters called her the Heroine, so early did she manifest not only the longing but the power to do something and be something'.[24] In a sense religious belief could empower women like this by providing a divine sanction for their own ambitions, but this often sat uneasily with the Christian norm of self-denial which girls internalised at an early age.[25] The sense of conflict to which this could give rise is evident in the life of Fanny Woodman who served with the China Inland Mission in 1895, and

who died of cholera within her first year of service. Brought up in
an evangelical family in Lichfield, she undertook the normal round
of parish visiting and Sunday school teaching expected of any
devout middle-class young woman. Inspired by attending a
Keswick holiness meeting in 1888, she felt called to greater evangelistic efforts but recorded in her diary that she was brought up short
by doubts about the propriety of adopting such a public role:

> I have had a wave of ambition sweeping over me, perhaps just a
> learning of the lesson 'Contented not to do, at last, at last.' I think
> I have been wanting to convert half the world, forgetting it's
> none of my work at all. Then came the chance question, 'Should
> a woman speak publicly in face of 1 Timothy ii 12 and 1
> Corinthians xiv 34'? Of course we may deliver a message, but it
> seems to touch some of my doings a little closely. I feel inclined to
> say, 'Oh, that I were a man' for the minute, only the Master did
> not wish it, that is very clear, and then there flashed through my
> mind Who are God's great ones?[26]

The answer she felt was those who undertake 'the things nobody
cares about doing, and nobody ever notices are done' and she up-
braided herself for having admitted to such ambitious thoughts,
adding ruefully that 'ones's writing tongue, as well as one's speaking tongue, is a most unruly member, unless He has complete
control'. Yet only three years later she was busy addressing large
gatherings of men in barracks and prisons and had resolved to
become a missionary, justifying her actions not as acts of self-will
but as the working out of the biblical truth 'Not I but Christ'.[27]

Once in the field far more was demanded of women than eulo-
gies on the power of feminine gentleness and sympathy might
suggest. In his own account of their missionary work in central
Africa, François Coillard paints a picture of Christina as the dutiful
missionary wife whose life and aspirations were totally subordinated to his aims and wishes: 'If God had clearly called me to the
ends of the earth she would joyfully have followed me thither,
without consulting her tastes or her ease.'[28] This was not untrue,
but in the description of their work published by Christina's niece a
very different picture emerges. Coillard, she noted, lacked self-
confidence and 'hated, almost dreaded, having to assert himself',
while his wife's character 'was a very powerful one'. On the long
arduous journey across the western part of what is now Zambia

undertaken by the Coillards in 1877–8, it was Christina who was the dominant personality not only organizing domestic matters, but bargaining successfully with hostile natives to obtain the provisions on which the survival of the expedition depended.[29] Confronted with such an obvious contradiction to the ideal of missionary femininity, her niece was at pains to explain that such a situation was unusual, concluding of Coillard that 'more than most men, he was dependent upon such companionship'.

Charlotte Tucker was another woman who presented a challenge to Victorian Christian expectations about gender. Not that this was evident from one of the most successful of the popularizing accounts of women missionaries, John Telford's *Women in the Mission Field: Glimpses of Christian Women among the Heathen* published in 1895. Telford's account is a panegyric upon the power of Charlotte Tucker's femininity, triumphantly concluding that '"The New Apostolate of Women", by whom the Church's victories are being spread in many lands, has scarcely had any more attractive figure than the gentle English lady whom we shall long and lovingly remember as ALOE'.[30]

However, from Agnes Giberne's much fuller biography published in the same year a very different picture emerges. Charlotte Tucker was the daughter of a Bengal civil servant who rose to become Chairman of the East India Company. According to her biographer she was an ambitious woman, and scarcely conformed to the conventional stereotype of the gentle missionary heroine. The family motto was *nil desperandum* and this seems to have been Charlotte's guiding principle in her missionary career. The work, she wrote, required 'a great deal of steel', and she once expressed doubts about the fitness of an acquaintance to embark upon it on the grounds that 'Anyone who in England suffers from headache, liver, back, and uneven spirits, I would rather entreat to avoid the Punjab … she would be one of the choice delicate palfreys, yoked to artillery, who break down and give extra work to the already fully-taxed horses'.[31] Certainly she herself could be accused of no such weakness in her own methods of confronting non-Christian women, pointing out on one occasion that 'one's manner must be gentle and conciliating, even when meeting the question, "Do you think that Muhammad told lies?" with a simple straightforward, "Yes"'. She could, though, on occasion go too far in her enthusiasm even for her fellow workers, as when she formed a daring plan to kidnap a Christian convert from her Muslim family and was, in the words of her biographer, 'with difficulty dissuaded from a scheme which others of longer experience knew too well might lead to serious complications'.[32] As Agnes Giberne was aware, such a forceful personality could hardly be accommodated within the limits of Christian norms of feminine behaviour, and she summed up her character somewhat warily: 'with all her exceeding kindness, hers could hardly be described as the true sympathetic temperament.'[33] The overseas Angel in the House might well encapsulate the ideal of the Victorian missionary heroine, and Charlotte Tucker did indeed describe one of her colleagues as 'an angel without wings', but quite how the epithet could be applied to herself is far from clear.

Another dominant theme in the representation of women missionaries was also problematic. Most biographies describe their motivations and methods in terms of Christian ideals of love and service for women less fortunate than themselves. Typical of this approach is Frank Mundell's account of the work of Mary Whately in Cairo in his *Heroines of the Cross* published by the Sunday School Union. The daughter of an archbishop of Dublin, she first visited Cairo in 1856 in an effort to improve her health, and decided, in her biographer's words, to 'try and do something for her poor sisters of that land'.[34] This led to the setting up of a girls' school in the face of considerable parental opposition, and later the founding of a small hospital which provided simple but effective surgery for eye complaints which would otherwise have led to blindness. It was enterprises such as these that Baroness Burdett-Coutts had in mind when she proudly wrote in one of a series of papers on women's work prepared for the Chicago World fair in 1893, that overseas philanthropy was one of the great facts of the age, and one that was 'helping to break down those barriers of race, colour, and creed, which are opposed to the progress of true civilisation'. Such efforts, she concluded, were 'elevating womanhood, and making all countries, but especially ours, proud of their women'.[35] Nor were such claims without foundation: in their provision of schools and medical care, in their campaigns against child marriage in India and footbinding in China, missionary women could point to tangible successes in the emancipation of women in other societies.[36]

But whereas gender could form a link across cultures, issues of class and race created significant barriers and often these obstacles to understanding were mutually self-reinforcing. As we have seen, one of the most powerful justifications for female missionary work was the need to transform non-western societies by making use of women's maternal qualities. This meant transplanting what were regarded as uniquely Christian models of family life to other cultures. Thus in her account of Persian society in 1899, Mary Bird, a CMS worker in Julfa, could claim 'I had almost written home-life, but this does not exist; there is no word for home in the Persian language, because it has not been required; the Moslems have none of the associations and tender memories which that word awakens in us.'[37] As the biographies of women missionaries make clear, nearly all had gained their first experience of philanthropic Christian service amongst the poor in England, and attitudes which cut them off from understanding working-class culture at home could have the same effect overseas. Work among the lower classes in Victorian cities conjured up powerful images of dirt, disorder and moral darkness, which were both a challenge to the compassion, and a threat to the sexual innocence, of Christian women philanthropists. Similar anxieties prevailed in the mission field, and one important aim in recreating English family life abroad was to put a *cordon sanitaire* around the mission and its converts. As Mina Gollock wrote of the CMS mission in Cairo, 'the children have a most important part to play in a Mission, these bonnie little English children, brought up in purity and in love, an object-lesson to all around who know nothing of such sheltering relationships between parent and child'. The purity of the Christian mission was for her as much spatial as moral, for it was only when the first-floor of the building was attained that 'the region of order and method is reached also'.[38]

The way in which the constraints of both class and race combined to isolate the missionaries from the women whom they sought to serve could not be more starkly visible than in Ruth Fisher's accounts of her work in Africa with the CMS. For her the continent was a Conradian heart of darkness where even the African convert was not to be trusted since he had, in her view 'no natural weapons to wield – no self-respect, self-control, public opinion, healthful instincts, and inherent virtue, but a heritage of corruption, a weak physique, and an inertia born of the tropics to handicap him'.[39] Yet amongst the children some progress was possible, and they proved to make such excellent house servants that she 'sometimes wondered whether the problem of the over-taxed English market could not be solved by exporting some of these small people'.[40]

This was no doubt an extreme example, but most missionary biographies of the period uneasily combine a representation of their subjects as the embodiment of universal Christian ideals of love and service, with a sense of the necessary distance which the missionaries felt it imperative to maintain between themselves and those whom they sought to help. The ambiguities of this situation are evident, for example, in Canon Dawson's account of Irene Petrie's work in Kashmir:

One sign of Miss Petrie's deeply-seated missionary feeling at this time appears in her innate shrinking from the exaggerated homage which the subject race pays to the conqueror … She had none of the feeling of the Anglo-Indian who goes out merely to rule. She had gone out to associate herself with the people, and to raise them if possible to the level of children of God. From this point of view all men were equal, as they are in the sight of the Heavenly Father. She began, however, at once to understand how difficult the task would be, and how wide a gulf must be crossed before the teacher can hope to enter into the inner life of the taught. There is no doubt that she managed to bridge this gulf to a very remarkable extent, but she had the rare gift of combining simplicity and accessibility with a personal dignity which effectually warned the trespasser. Later on, the Kashmiri boys at Srinigar discovered this, and idolized her as friend and queen.[41]

In a passage which purports to describe the missionary's commitment to the Christian ideal of human equality, Dawson's readers could nevertheless be reassured that the proper boundaries of class and race had been safely maintained. What Irene Petrie shrank from, Dawson suggests, was only the exaggerated homage owed by the conquered not the deference which he implies was her due, while her upper-class upbringing as the daughter of an army officer allowed her to keep at arm's length any who dared to overstep these limits. The concluding image of his heroine as both the 'friend and queen' of those to whom she ministered identified the missionary in the minds of his readers with the Victorian monarchy, the most obvious symbol of paternalistic imperial power.

It would be wrong, though, to conclude with any one transparent image of the Victorian female missionary, for it has been the purpose of this chapter to suggest that the nature of such work exposed women to an unusual degree to all the pressures of Victorian ideologies of gender, class and race, and that as a result the representations of their lives were often ambiguous and contradictory. While it remains true that nineteenth-century missionary societies were firmly under male control, and overseas work by women could plausibly be seen as an extension of their maternal qualities of love and self-sacrifice, the depiction of the reality of their lives constantly threatened to destabilize socially and theologically constructed ideals of what constituted true femininity. Similarly missionary women's symbolic status as the carriers of western Christian values which had emancipated women in ways unknown elsewhere, sat uneasily beside their own experiences of confronting female working-class poverty, prostitution and disease in a supposedly Christian England, a society from whose stifling restrictions upon middle-class women's lives they were often thankful to have escaped. None of this is to denigrate the achievement of the many thousands of women who gave their lives in the missionary cause, but rather to suggest that no representation of their work and aspirations could be more than partially true. Perhaps Charlotte Brontë recognised this too. It is, after all, St John Rivers and not Jane the missionary manquée who has the last word.[42]

NOTES

1. This is not to imply that Charlotte Brontë herself had no such doubts. As Tom Winifrith has shown, Helen Burns' rejection of the doctrine of eternal damnation in the novel, which was a fundamental tenet of nearly all Victorian missionaries, was shared by her creator. See T. Winifrith, *The Brontës and their Background* (London: Macmillan, 1973), p. 52.
2. J. Jack and M. Smith, eds, *Jane Eyre* (Oxford: Clarendon Press, 1969) p. 515. This is a reprint of the first edition of 1847.
3. Ibid., p. 518.
4. C. Yonge, *Womankind*, 2nd edn (London: Walter Smith & Innes, 1889), p. 2.
5. Jack, p. 527.
6. Quoted in R.J. Dunn, ed., *Jane Eyre: Authoritative Text Background Criticisms*, 2nd edn (New York: W.W. Norton & Co., 1987), p. 442.
7. E.C. Dawson, *Heroines of Missionary Adventure* (London: Seeley & Co., 1909).
8. USPG Archives, Rhodes House, Oxford, Copies of Letters Received, India, CWW231/3.
9. In formulating this approach I have drawn upon M.J. Corbett, *Representing Femininity: Middle-Class Subjectivity in Victorian and Edwardian Autobiographies* (Oxford: Oxford University Press, 1992).

10. USPG Archives, Rhodes House, Oxford, Women Candidates' Sub-Committee Book 1874–1885, CWW27/1.

11. In 1909 out of a total staff of 1390 overseas workers in the CMS, 438 were single women. For a discussion of the significance of the rise in the numbers of single women missionaries, see S. Gill, *Women and the Church of England From the Eighteenth Century to the Present* (London: SPCK, 1994), pp. 173–81.

12. Greg's article 'Why Are Women Redundant?' appeared in the *National Review* 14 (1862), 434–60.

13. The same point has been made with regard to Canadian women missionaries in R.R. Gagan, *A Sensitive Independence: Canadian Methodist Missionaries in Canada and the Orient, 1881–1925* (Montreal: McGill-Queen's University Press, 1992).

14. A.B. Webb, *Sisterhood Life and Woman's Work in the Mission Field of the Church* (London: Skeffington & Sons, 1883), p. 10.

15. Ibid.

16. *Fifth Annual Report of the Church of England Zenana Missionary Society* (London: CEZMS, 1885), p. 15.

17. For a fuller discussion of this theme, see Gill, pp. 83–7.

18. Mrs Ashley Carus-Wilson, *Irene Petrie, Missionary to Kashmir* (London: Hodder & Stoughton, 1900), pp. 49–50.

19. W.P. Livingstone, *Christina Forsyth of Fingoland: The Story of the Loneliest Woman in Africa* (London: Hodder & Stoughton, 1918), p. 13.

20. C.W. Mackintosh, *Coillard of the Zambesi. The Lives of Franÿois and Christina Coillard of the Paris Missionary Society in South and Central Africa*, 2nd edn (London: T. Fisher Unwin, 1907), pp. 96–7.

21. A. Giberne, *A Lady of England: The Life and Letters of Charlotte Maria Tucker* (London: Hodder & Stoughton, 1895), pp. 83, 114.

22. Ibid., p. 176.

23. Livingstone, p. 175.

24. Mackintosh, p. 91.

25. This theme is explored in J. Rowbotham, *Good Girls Make Good Wives: Guidance for Girls in Victorian Fiction* (Oxford: Basil Blackwell, 1989).

26. A. Hodges, ed., *Love's Victory: Memoirs of Fanny Woodman* (London: Marshall Brothers, 1899), pp. 13–14.

27. Ibid., p. 46.

28. F. Coillard, *On the Threshold of Central Africa. A Record of Twenty Years Pioneering among the Barotsi of the Upper Zambesi* (London: Hodder & Stoughton, 1897), p. 433.

29. Mackintosh, pp. 237, 287.

30. J. Telford, *Women in the Mission Field: Glimpses of Christian Women among the Heathen* (London: Charles H. Kelly, 1895) p. 192. ALOE (a lady of England) was Charlotte Tucker's *nom de plume* as a writer of uplifting stories for children.

31. Giberne, p. 315.

32. Ibid., p. 292.

33. Ibid., p. 161.

34. F. Mundell, *Heroines of the Cross* (London: Sunday School Union, no date) p. 49. My copy has a book plate showing that it was given as a prize by the Newport School Board for good attendance in 1900.

35. Baroness Burdett-Coutts, ed., *Woman's Mission. A Series of Congress Papers on the Philanthropic Work of Women by Eminent Writers* (London: Sampson Low, Marston & Co., 1893), p. 360.

36. There is a growing literature on the impact of women missionaries on non-western societies. This includes F. Bowie, D. Kirkwood and S. Ardener, eds, *Women and Missions: Past and Present* (Oxford: Berg, 1993); N. Chaudhuri and M. Strobel, eds, *Western Women and Imperialism: Complicity and Resistance* (Bloomington: Indiana University Press, 1992); *Women's Studies International Forum*, 13 (1990).

37. M. Bird, *Persian Women and their Creed* (London: Church Missionary Society, 1899), p. 25.

38. M.C. Gollock, *River, Sand and Sun being Sketches of the CMS Egypt Mission* (London: CMS, 1906), pp. 50–75.

39. R. Fisher, *Twilight Tales of the Black Buganda*, 2nd edn (London: Frank Cass, 1970), p. 198. The work was first published in 1911.

40. R. Fisher, *On the Borders of Pigmy Land* (London: Marshall Brothers, 1905), p. 82.

41. Dawson, pp. 73–4.

42. The significance of the ending, and in particular its bearing upon a feminist reading of the novel has been much debated. For one attempt to sustain such an interpretation within the context of the history of nineteenth-century missions, see V. Cunningham, '"God and Nature intended you for a missionary's wife": Mary Hill, Jane Eyre and Other Missionary Women in the 1840s', in Bowie et al., pp. 85–105.

13

The Victorian Lady's Domestic Threat: The Good, the Bad and the Indifferent Female Adversary in Contemporary Art

Susan P. Casteras

The Victorian woman of religious faith and commitment was challenged by both real and fictional 'adversaries' in life, literature and art, among them the formidable foes of the aesthetic female and the decadent modern or New Woman during the last quarter of the century. In the realm of art, all three simultaneously coexisted, although it was the Victorian lady who triumphed in typology, popularity and sheer numbers. The apex of this ideal female was the 'modern Madonna', who reigned supreme in the iconology of Victorian womanhood in narrative or genre paintings such as Charles West Cope's 'Prayer Time' (Fig. 1) of c.1860, also a portrait of the artist's wife and daughter Florence. Cope chooses as his subject – and interestingly casts his own spouse as – the perfect wife, shown here as the 'guardian of the hearth' in a microcosm of domesticity and socially endorsed femininity. Isolated in a handsome room, she and her surroundings personify the Victorian home, the primary seat of power where female spirituality and moral superiority both resided.[1] The art on the wall, the furnishings, the flowers on the mantel and the bourgeois decor are all aesthetically pleasing and attractive, without any extremes of fashion. Similarly, the inhabitants' dresses and accessories are likewise tastefully appointed, conventional rather than bohemian. The sitter and her daughter are

186

Figure 1   Charles West Cope, Prayer Time, *ca.* 1860. Oil on canvas, 28″ × 21 ³/₄″. Reproduced by permission of Harris Art Gallery, Preston.

portrayed in an intimate moment of evening prayer; the mother does not merely listen, she too joins in prayer with folded hands. All the details are seemingly perfectly orchestrated: from the Bible on the table to the statue of holy motherhood above, to the faithful dog

at the lady's feet. As a role model, she is an iconic embodiment of
the cult of Victorian womanhood and perfect Christianity, and her
total absorption in a prayerful attitude emphasizes her purity,
innocence and humility. She does not tend to flowers or gaze at
objects: all her energies are focused upon her child and the act of
prayer. This 'Angel of the House' is, in fact, almost Christlike as she
listens to the outpourings of her kneeling daughter, in whose pose
is arguably a visual reminder of the fallen woman and Christ's
acceptance of human repentance. The message conveyed is that this
Victorian woman is watchful, attentive and angelic, mindful of her
duties in a way that is didactic, if not blatantly propagandistic. In
Cope's visual homily, the construction of womanhood is total, and
her moral virtues are all subtly and not so subtly conveyed in a
vignette of contemporary female quasi-divinity.

Yet such images of unblemished wifehood were, partly due to a
decline in the popularity of such sentimental pictures, on the wane
by the 1860s, when other kinds of art, social trends and reforms
emerged and challenged the porcelain perfection of such painted,
doll-like heroines with their covertly sacred missions and messages
for the public. While individual images of saints, annunciation
scenes and the Virgin Mary continued to be created by artists –
especially for specific religious paintings, commissions, and contexts
– the prayerful Christian wife (unless in the form of charitable
Dorcas) was less in evidence in the realm of art. In addition to this
tamer strand of gendered imagery, an iconology of dissatisfied and
disaffected females surfaced, notably of the female aesthete, the dis-
content wife and the 'strong-minded' New Woman. All these types
reflected, on various levels, the revolt from the status quo being
enacted by women who essentially sought escape from the tedium
of everyday life, the restrictions placed upon their sex by social
codes and the toll of industrialism. Their anomalous behaviour,
however, in obvious contrast to Cope's beatific heroine, was typically viewed as dangerous to the entire female sex and to society at
large, a bias also mirrored in the art of the period, which tended to
laugh at or deride these atypical gender roles.

In the case of Aestheticism, a rejection of a supposedly philistine
or bourgeois lifestyle, a worship of beauty instead of religion, and a
craving for new stimulation or sensations were signs of rebellious
female behaviour, and all were thought to result in dire effects
upon women and their families. The Pateresque notion of passion-
ately enjoying beauty for its own sake, for example, similarly under-

mined established values and religion, leaving women who 'worshipped' beauty, flowers and art not only idolatrous but also – and more importantly – intensely narcissistic and neglectful of their prescribed roles and duties. Dedication to making one's home beautiful was one thing; dedicating one's life to the altar of beauty was another and was deemed artificial, eccentric and unacceptably hedonistic. Thus, while the 'Angel of the House' was a commanding figure in Victorian art particularly in the 1850s, her more rebellious 'sisters' – the aesthetic female and especially the New Woman – were quite elusive in paintings. A brief examination of several salient images in the typology of such anomalous femininity offers compelling commentary on gender, class tensions, social discourse and other factors affecting the period's representation of women.

The Aesthetic Movement was the cause of much furore, influenced partly by the sensuous poems of Algernon Swinburne and paintings of Dante Gabriel Rossetti in the 1860s and beyond to the full-blown art for art's sake of the 1870s and 1880s. At its zenith the Aesthetic Movement was in the latter decades susceptible to a great deal of censure and lampooning from contemporary critics, especially for its literature, physical affectations, credo and taste in art, fashion and interior decoration. It was in the realm of popular culture, notably in the prescient pages of *Punch*, that the aesthetic female and the New Woman both found themselves reflected – or more accurately, problematized – and continually ridiculed.[2] While George Du Maurier produced cartoons on the general subject from 1873 to 1882, it was in 1877 (the year that the highly aesthetic Grosvenor Gallery opened) that he introduced the Cimabue Browns, a brilliant satire on a privileged family preoccupied with Chinamania and other elite aesthetic traits. Mrs Cimabue Brown was in many ways a complete foil to Cope's madonna: she was an amusing, if extreme, example of the Victorian lady afflicted with Aestheticism, adopting every fad with ease – from the vogue for china and oriental objects to peacock feathers, aesthetic dress and an intense absorption with beautiful flowers and the concept of beauty itself. Even her Italianate name reflected an unhealthy adulation of and affectation for the foreign. In modern culture, her 'defection' from culturally defined norms of womanhood and propriety might be likened to the disapproval registered when a twentieth-century woman embraced beat, hippy or Generation X cultures and affected its key styles – wearing black, taking drugs and wearing long hair, or adorning herself with pierced body parts, tattoos and certain trendy attitudes like nihilism. Of course, looking at *Punch* cartoons was merely entertaining to readers, while in real life the behaviour and look of aesthetic women were often more seriously criticized.

One pithy yet acid description of 'A Female Aesthete' by an anonymous detractor offers a concise list of the main affectations that were often lampooned:

> Maiden of thy sallow brow,
> Listen whilst my love I vow!
> By thy kisses which consume;
> By thy spikenard-like perfume;
> By thy hollow, parboiled eyes;
> By thy heart-devouring sighs;
> By thy sodden, past cheek;
> By thy poses, from the Greek;
> By thy tongue, like asp which stings;
> By thy zither's twangy strings;
> By thy dress of stewed-sage green;
> By thy idiotic mien.[3]

Among these traits are several which contrast with those which the 'ideal woman' or wife might possess: consuming or passionate kisses, listless eyes or expression; melancholic moods and Greek poses; a sharp tongue, idiotic mien and eccentric attire of Aesthetic hues such as 'stewed-sage green'. The author obviously disdains this languid creature, whose unhealthy pallor and limp demeanour and posture offended many. The aesthetic female was physically as well as temperamentally the antithesis of the Victorian lady, standing in a slouch and displaying a degree of narcissism that was both blatant and sinful – or, as another *Punch* poet stated, she possessed 'hopeless languor' and was 'satiated of all delight beneath the sun …'[4] Besides her general morbidity, this new aesthetic creature was very different from the coy coquette of the drawing room; the former's powers were siren-like, possessing a powerful sexual drive which blended melancholy with a seemingly terminal ennui and enervation that were implicitly the result of sexual fatigue and satiation of the senses with beauty as well as passion. This fatal languor, which is simultaneously both sexually threatening as well as outwardly curiously neutral in appearance, underscores a central paradox manifested in many of the period's representations of the female aesthete (as well as the New Woman): her middle- and upper-class rank made her a lady, but her behaviour – while socially acceptable among the avant-garde – was not lady-like or entirely respectable. Aestheticism in the highest social circles was a sign of taste and refinement, yet the practitioner paid a certain price: for, as another poet satirized, to belong to the ranks of the 'sallow, sick, and spare', she must '… shun mirth,/ Have suffered, fruitlessly desired,/ And wear no flush by hope inspired.'[5]

A few cartoons establish some of the aberrations of this aesthetic being, which at one extreme were labelled by Du Maurier himself as 'nincompoopiana'. An 1881 cartoon, for instance, pits an aesthetic lady at right – haggard, oddly dressed and with her hair coiffed *à la* Pre-Raphaelite – against a more conventionally adorned 'rival' in a parlour. The aesthetic lady says to her companion, the Professor, 'Is that not Mrs Brabazon, whose Photograph is in all the Shop Windows?' He replies, 'It is. She is Handsome, is she not?', to which the Aesthetic Lady grumbles: 'Well, yaas, – but – a – *essentially a woman of the Nineteenth Century!*' Such remarks suggest a polar tension and dichotomy between the old-fashioned Victorian lady and the avant-garde aesthetic rebel, whose intense state of being often resulted in application of current slang such as 'consummately quite', 'distinctiously precious', or 'quite utterly' and 'too too'.[6] There were even music covers adorned with these words, one entitled 'My Aesthetic Love' and subtitled 'Utterly utter and Consummate too too', both featuring male and female aesthetes who had succumbed to the 'malady' of Aestheticism.

The limp qualities of the aesthetic woman reached their apogee in fine art in the plethora of sleeping women who predominated in many paintings of the period.[7] Albert Moore was one of the important contributors to the Grosvenor Gallery exhibitions, and his study entitled 'Two Women on a Sofa' (Fig. 2, Yale Center for British Art) offers a classic visual interpretation of both aesthetic values and the connections between femininity and a state of eternal slumber and lassitude. When this powerful state of dreamy withdrawal extended the cultivation of 'the sallow sick and spare' into the domain of high art, responses were often strong. This quasi-trance and sense of collapse were not merely annoying; they were morally repugnant to some viewers and readers. Indeed, the aesthetic female's vulnerable state of total abandon and escape from reality into fantasy was linked with feminine indolence and insatiable sexual desires in poems such as 'Faustine', 'Hesperia' and

192

Figure 2 Albert Moore, Two Women on a Sofa, 1870s. Oil on canvas, 11 3/4″ × 19 1/4″. Reproduced by permission of Yale Center for British Art, Paul Mellon Collection.

'Dolores' by Algernon Swinburne. It is not the innocuous reverie or yearning found in most 'mainstream' images of women deep in thought or in retrospection over love; instead, it suggests an almost drug-induced state triggered by an excessive stimulation from sex, beauty or art. In Vernon Lee's (Violet Paget's) sensation novel of 1884 entitled *Miss Brown*, for example, a young female character described gatherings of aesthetic society in which 'ladies went to sleep, or pretended to do so, over the descriptions of the kisses of the cruel, blossom-mouthed women, who sucked their lovers' hearts out their lips, and strewed their apartments with coral-like drops of blood'.[8] Such a vision of feminine evil, morbidity and menace reveals just how threatening such somnolence might be in its mixture of listless lolling with sensuality and sadism. It has even been suggested that these inscrutable females, in their pale lethargy, convey a sense of unhealthy libidinous and aesthetic appetite that stem from exhaustion due to masturbation.[9] Thus, while frail in appearance, these females are not ordinary invalids or women in confinement (during pregnancy): they are debilitated by sexual passion and destructive – in Swinburne's poems and otherwise – to themselves and to the men they have seduced.

Another excellent example of this admixture of languid sleep, sexuality, Aestheticism and danger is found in Edward Burne-Jones' 'Laus Veneris' (Laing Art Gallery) of 1873–5, on display at the Grosvenor Gallery (nicknamed 'the palace of the aesthetes') in 1878.[10] As in Moore's paintings, the ambiguity, fecundity and vulnerability of slumbering young females are contained in a static world, where any latent threat to males is masked by a seemingly idyllic order of picturesque indolence and the contemplation of beautiful forms. Both the physically weak, hollow-cheeked aesthetic female and her sleeping counterpart are kindred souls, and both are paradoxically sexually strong, provoking anxiety on several fronts as an emblem of both the spiritual and aesthetic malaise of the period. Moreover, the unconscious metaphor of a woman somehow satiated by sleep, beauty and art but not by sexual desires served as an important precursor to the *femme fatale* and her more malevolent materialization in the 1890s, as well as the 'abnormal' behaviour of the New Woman.

As these few images indicate, there was a decided aura of cultural enigma and menace generated by Aestheticism, which was clearly at odds with the traditional role ascribed to the Victorian lady and wife. Enervated maidens asleep in bowers or presiding over bohemian Aesthetic environments conveyed a mood of inertia, illness, dissatisfaction and escapism which ran counter to the norm. Yet while perceived as physically weak in poems and paintings, the aesthetic female was passionate, if not downright intimidating. Asleep, anorexic, enervated or communing with a flower or piece of exquisite china, she still projected libidinal anxiety, transforming her passive gloom and unhealthiness into an active source of threat, especially sexual. Like the Victorian lady, she might be devoid of expression or recumbent; but her idleness was lethal – instead of arranging flowers, for example, she was intensely absorbed with them and with her private thoughts, and was thus egregiously narcissistic.

While most of the aesthetic females and New Women in *Punch* were depicted as young and unmarried, there was also a strand of imagery which suggested that a perversion or jeopardizing of traditional marital roles was being conveyed by Aestheticism. For example, in 'The six-mark teapot' from *Punch* in 1881, for example, Du Maurier presents an 'aesthetic bridegroom and his intense bride'. A decidedly Jane Burden Morris-like woman and her Oscar Wildeish husband admire a teapot amid a clutter of fashionable *orientaliste objets*. He pronounces the teapot 'quite consummate', and she hopes the pair 'lives up to it!' On one level, this dialogue includes a covert pun on 'consummate', and an additional irony that the newlyweds focus on lavishing attention more on an object than on one another – a sarcastic aside of neglect on both sides because of their total preoccupation with Aestheticism.

In other examples, an underlying cultural anxiety about contemporary masculinity as imperilled by Aestheticism is revealed in cartoons such as Du Maurier's 1880 'Nincompoopiana: Mutual Admiration Society' (Fig. 3), which explicitly scrutinizes the effeteness of another Wildeish figure. The text posits a colonel asking Mrs Cimabue Brown, 'And who's this young hero they're all swarming over now?' She replies, 'Jellaby Postlethwaite, the great poet ... who sat for Maudle's "Dead Narcissus" ... Is he not beautiful?' The colonel asks her to explain, and the lady answers, 'Look at his grand head and poetic face, with those flowers like eyes, and that exquisite sad smile. Look at his slender, willow frame, as yielding and fragile as a woman's!' Mrs Brown's description of the poet is entirely phrased in terms of womanly qualities and anatomy: soft, flowerlike eyes, sad smile, slender frame. Indeed, Postlethwaite resembles the other aesthetic, androgynous, Burne-Jonesian (and

Figure 3   George Du Maurier, 'Nincompoopiana: Mutual Admiration Society', wood engraving for *Punch* cartoon, 1880.

Jane Morris-like) women in the room in terms of body type, posture, hair and neurasthenic, haggard face. With his male companion (or lover) the artist Maudle, Postlethwaite is shown as the centre of attention of a female mutual admiration society of sorts. Slightly bent over, emaciated and unkempt, the droopy weakling male poet arguably looks rather like a 'sister' image to the women, thus making both sexes androgynous. As this and other examples attest, the underlying weakness with Aesthetic art was perceived at least partly in terms of its supposedly feminized qualities – its emphasis on droopy posing, decorativeness, androgyny, retrospection and reclusiveness. In his own time, it was said of Du Maurier's visual productions that they not only reeked of his own favoured status among the world of salons, the titled and the society of the Upper Ten Thousand, but also that his satires on Aestheticism were feminized. Accordingly, one critic preferred the 'manly style and fresh breezy humor of John Leech, bold, vigorous, and thoroughly English, whose girls were real, merry, healthy, laughing, jolly girls, not the sickly, namby-pamby, over-dressed, all-alike-at-the-price, young ladies of Mr Du Maurier ...'[11] While some saw the aesthetic female as a foolish acolyte or fanatic addicted to peacock feathers and bizarre poetry, there were others, such as Walter Hamilton, who defended the Aesthetic Movement and its achievements in distinctly feminized terms: 'the cultured taste which appears in their homes, from a kitchen utensil to a carpet and wall-paper and a lady's dress, and which contrasts so marvellously with the barbaric horrors of the early Victorian era ... were the work of theses so-called ridiculous people.'[12]

Perhaps the most scathing indictment of the Aesthetic woman occurred in images in which her maternal instincts are shown as compromised and neglectful, as in 'Acute Chinamania' (Fig. 4) from *Punch* in 1875. Here a Victorian lady and mother is shown as deficient in her responsibilities, for example, appearing dishevelled and slumped (thus having abandoned proper standards of appearance and posture). Moreover, she grieves excessively – not over a lost child, but instead over a broken teacup. In the accompanying text, her young daughter begs her mother to stop weeping: 'Mamma! Mamma! don't go on like this, pray!', to which her parent replies, 'What have I got left to live for?' The girl answers, 'Haven't you got ME, Mamma?', but her mother complains, 'You, child! You're not Unique! There are six of you [indicating the rest of the family] – a complete set!' The irony of her child consoling her is

Figure 4 George Du Maurier, 'Acute Chinamania', wood engraving for Punch cartoon, 1875.

acute, yet still the aesthetically obsessed mother laments that while she has other children, she can never again possess a matched pair of sextuplet teacups! Surely this is not only the stuff of humour, but also of heresy, revealing to readers the danger of aesthetic excess to susceptible women beguiled by the worship of beauty and the vogue for lovely things. Consumerism, yoked with selfishness, thus rendered women victims of Aestheticism; yet the female aesthete also victimized society by disregarding her maternal and wifely duties, embarrassing her family and succumbing to dilettantism in the worst ways. Another contemporary example from *Punch* is entitled 'The Passion for Old China' of 1874, which places an aesthetic husband and wife amid their precious collection. In the dialogue, the man says with a scowl to his seated spouse, 'I think you might let *me* nurse that teapot a little *now*, Margery! You've had it to yourself all the *morning*, you know!' The woman interestingly holds the teapot (with its dual male and female forms) close to her chest, in a position near her breast where a baby – not a culinary object – might rest and nurse. In contrast to Cope's heroine, this couple, like the mother who is a chinamaniac, nurtures not a child or children but a seemingly beautiful thing. The teapot, like the teacup, thus functions as yet another surrogate child, making both 'parents' seem rather selfish, uncaring and 'unnatural' from the viewpoint of most readers. And in a different way from 'Nincompoopiana', this image also emasculates the male protagonist, who expresses a feminized desire to 'nurse' their mutually beloved possession.

In her devotion to high culture over religion, the aesthetic female also found a responsive ally in the New Woman, whose more strident ambitions, iconoclastic behaviour and attire often dominated the pages of *Punch* after the heights of Aestheticism faded. Like her predecessor, the New Woman was a quintessentially middle- and upper-class phenomenon even more daring in her free-spirited desires and actions – she wanted not to loll and imbibe beauty but to pursue a career, attend college or live an unbourgeois existence. Yet as with her forerunner, the New Woman was also anomalous being who – due to an even greater dearth of images in paintings – must be judged on a rather superficial, external set of schematized traits (namely, how she dresses or acts in society).[13]

While virtuous ladies in parlours or gardens were recurrent motifs, as in Cope's painting, there was countless imagery in which women were portrayed in seemingly innocuous activities like perusing books. Most interpretations of women at leisure reading (generally untitled) books were not culturally overloaded with meaning,

but after the 1880s there were some representations that, as cultural
emblems, suggest more sinister implications about the identification
of women with certain 'forbidden' publications. These iconoclastic
images include, for example, Aubrey Beardsley's early 1890s design
(not used) for a cover of *The Yellow Book* (Fig. 5), in which a woman
prepares to fill her shelves with modern works of a questionable or
even taboo nature for consumption by ladies: *The Yellow Book* itself,

Figure 5   Aubrey Beardsley, cover design for *The Yellow Book, ca.* 1892.
Private collection.

Beardsley's own *Story of Venus and Tannhäuser* and *Discords* by George Egerton (the pen name of a notorious feminist). Unlike Cope's protagonist, this daring, independent reader owns not the proverbial 'Good Book' but mostly controversial ones. She blasphemously 'worships' certain contemporary literature, and her tomes form a jumble on a table held aloft by grotesques. In other images too, Beardsley created decadent or avant-garde images of the New Woman linking her with radicalized books and periodicals.[14]

Both the aesthetic female and the New Woman were social realities as well as literary fictions, yet they were exploited by journalistic hyperbole partly in response to rapidly changing legal, social, and cultural events and reforms.[15] While there were individual portraits of actual women who endorsed aesthetic and/or feminist beliefs, there were few genre paintings or subject pictures of these types. This absence is explicable mostly due to the conservatism both of the public whose tastes helped to define what was popular on Royal Academy walls, and by the artists themselves, who although rarely writing about their attitudes towards women, in the majority probably shared conventional beliefs towards them. Eliza Lynn Linton, for example, spoke of this innate preference when she expressed her own misgivings about the so-called Girl of the Period:

Men are afraid of her; and with reason ... It cannot be plainly told to the modern English girl that the net result of her present manner of life is to assimilate her as nearly as possible to a class of women whom we must not call by their proper – or improper – name ... [The Girl of the Period] thinks she is piquante and exciting when she thus makes herself the bad copy of a worse original; and she will not see that though men laugh with her they do not respect her; she will not believe that she is not the kind of thing they want, and that she is acting against nature and her own interests when she disregards their advice and offends their taste.[16]

The kind of self-expression and awareness of her feelings, sexuality and conflicts communicated by the female aesthete and the New Woman were unnerving to middle-class viewers and readers. Whether overly aesthetic of overly modern, the late Victorian women was – in literature at least – often allowed to work out her own moral and other problems: to err, to suffer and sometimes to achieve heroic stature (or, conversely to be punished) for her mistakes and tribulations. One dimension of the male–female relationship and its changing dynamic was mirrored in certain strands of marital imagery in art, notably in portrayals of a couple's tiff or more serious disagreement. One of the few artists to deal with such issues was William Quiller Orchardson, who without outwardly condemning or sanctioning a woman's actions in his paintings, nonetheless captures her misery, boredom and dissatisfaction (often of her spouse as well) with the seeming stranglehold of nuptial ties. His 'First Cloud' (Tate Gallery) of 1887, for example, shows a modern woman striding out of the parlour presumably after a heated discussion of some sort with her husband. He glowers and sulks to one side in a rather slumping pose, and a gap of opinion and intimacy is suggested by the physical distance between the two and their lack of communication or even eye contact. Both are clearly disenchanted, and while the bored wife is not a new subject (William Hogarth dissected it brilliantly in 'Marriage à la Mode'), the Victorian parallel often wears an overt expression of dissatisfaction and seems to wield real power in the relationship. An even more emotion-charged canvas by Orchardson is 'Trouble' (private collection) of 1896, in which there is again no resolution provided in this open-ended 'problem picture' with its dramatic dénouement. Here yet another disgruntled Victorian lady turns her back on her husband and leaves the room, yet in this case the husband crumples into a chair and buries his face in his arm. Who wronged whom is once again unclear, yet in both examples the woman is not a vapid mannequin passively accepting her fate or the dictates of her spouse or turning to the Bible for help. For a moment – the one created by the artist – she takes some degree of charge of her life and walks away from cultural assumptions of feminine submissiveness. If marriage is not a prison in such images, it is at least a velvet cage in which the woman is now envisaged as possessing some power, as well as the courage to externalize her doubts about the relationship. Her independence may seem of a minor key, but even considering leaving a spouse, home, and family – much less wanting a more fulfilling life was a bold step for a Victorian lady to contemplate.

In contrast to the many images of the ideal Victorian wife – and even of the lower-class woman worker (both with varying capacities to provoke sympathetic responses) – there were few paintings of women shown involved in professional vocations. Once again, it was *Punch* that proved a key source, although attitudinally it dismissed as ridiculous the notion of women aspiring to careers. In an 1887 cartoon of two ladies passing by a group of medical students, for example, one woman says to the other, 'Do you know Eva, I feel I should very much like to be a hospital nurse!' Eva replies, 'How strange! Why the very same idea has just occurred to me!' With just a few words, *Punch* thus brands these females as brainless ninnies, considering careers only to meet potential mates.

Just as there were few painted portrayals of women engaged in serious professions, there was only a visual smattering of women intellectuals (apart from portraits of talented society matrons who belonged to elite salons or circles such as The Souls). Once again, it was caricature that filled the void. In 'Our Decadents (Female)' (Fig. 6), of 1894, for example, a severely dressed, bespectacled

OUR DECADENTS (FEMALE).

Figure 6   George Du Maurier, 'Our Decadents (Female)', wood engraving for *Punch* cartoon, 1894.

woman inquires of her male companion: 'Tell me, Monsieur Dubosc, of course you've read that shocking case of "Smith v. Smith, Brown, Jones, Robison and others"?' He replies, 'I confess I 'ave, Miss Vilkies. I am a lawyer, you know'. Her rejoinder is: 'Well, now, what do you think of it as a subject for dramatic treatment?', to which he fumblingly answers, 'I-I-I do not know vat it may be as a subject for dramatic treatment, Mademoiselle. I-I-I- find it very – a-a- *embarrasant* subject for conversation with a young lady!' While the woman seems nonplussed by his discomfiture, both her appearance (masculinized and untidy) and demeanour convey her unladylike tendencies and make her into a visual joke. Here, as in many cases, she is depicted with a foil with whom she might contrast, argue or commiserate. This female–male exchange crystallizes the clear social discomfort that the presence of an intellectual woman made, with foreigners as well as everyday Britons. She looked demonstrably different, acted differently, and was even able to embarrass and perplex a Frenchman with her 'unfeminine' inquiry into allegedly male areas of knowledge, particularly a law case which might involve divorce as well as adultery. Rather than being situated in the parlour, many cartoons located the New Woman outdoors, invading allegedly male turf or activities by bicycling, playing sports or hunting. Sometimes she is shown wearing masculinized attire, and very often she is endowed with an imposing stature that blurs gender boundaries and visually serves to overpower her rather effete male companions. Even on the dance floor, the New Woman was a towering presence, turning etiquette on its head by suggesting that women take the lead, so to speak. Some New Women were depicted as handsome in appearance (they were, after all, members of the elite), but they were nonetheless deemed to be rebels. Occasionally, the novelty of the intellectualized female was visualized: for example, university 'girl graduates' merited sporadic attention, but they were usually shown as freakish curiosities who sacrificed their eyesight, health, beauty and marital prospects to achieve their goals. *Punch* had a heyday with the female intellectual, frequently depicting her as homely, strident and bespectacled, from Du Maurier's 1874 'Extremes That Meet' to his 1881 'Inverted Maxims'. In the latter a man who has 'lately married one of the Strong-minded Sisterhood' admires a friend's fiancée, who is beautiful, timid and undemanding. Not surprisingly, brains and strong character – particularly in a member of the 'Shrieking Sisterhood' – did not triumph in *Punch* over 'weak-minded' pulchritude and mild-mannered femininity.

In contrast to the dull-eyed, passive aesthetic female, the New Woman was often shown as vigorous, enterprising and passionate (in different ways, however, that is, by espousing feminist beliefs); she was also visibly more robust and aggressive than her predecessor.[17] Overall, in her frankness, zeal and even her eccentricity, the New Woman was more fully realized in the pages of *Punch*, in posters and in avant-garde periodicals like *The Yellow Book* than she ever was in contemporary painting, where her Amazonian stature was seemingly grafted onto that of the goddess figure in particular. The athletic 'superwoman' who appeared in *Punch* cartoons of female bicyclists and sportswomen thus found her equal towards the end of the century in the plethora of superhuman females, mythological beings, and personifications that proliferated in English art. Just at the same time that some women were trying to get off their pedestals, so to speak, many artists either kept their heroines firmly ensconced in the parlour or elevated them to almost godlike status for viewers' contemplation and adoration, as in various paintings by Thomas Gotch and in Frederic Leighton's larger-than-life goddesses and allegorical female figures such as his commanding image of dormant female sensuality and narcissism in 'Flaming June' (Museo de Ponce, Puerto Rico) of 1895.

A related threat to the modest Victorian Englishwoman during this period was the seeming 'invasion' of affluent American women who became social rivals in the 'marriage market'. Numerous social commentators remarked upon this phenomenon, and some young English girls deliberately trained with American nannies so that they could 'masquerade' as American and thus more easily marry a duke or other titled male.[18] The New Woman in *Punch*, when allowed to be attractive, was quite young and pretty indeed, and this was also true of her American parallel, the Gibson Girl. However, the latter often treated male suitors rather callously, and her pretty face, half-closed eyes, bee-stung lips and nipped-in waist all projected a decided sex appeal. She was often rather exquisitely condescending, far more arrogant than her English 'sister'; overall, she had the aloofness and cruel, cool stare of a *femme fatale*, yet she was ultimately innocent, fresh and American.[19] The more strident and intimidating qualities of the American modern woman are apparent, for example, in a 1900 Gibson illustration entitled 'Warning to Noblemen: Treat your American Wife with Kindness' (Fig. 7), an allusion to the increas-

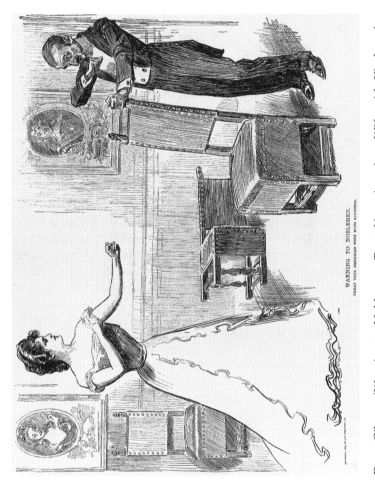

Figure 7 Charles Dana Gibson, 'Warning to Noblemen: Treat Your American Wife with Kindness', engraving, 1900. Author's collection.

ingly common intermarriages between wealthy American heiresses and titled Englishmen. Here Gibson portrays a pugilistic encounter between an Amazonian American wife and her puny English husband, who cowers in a corner. Such ambitious or aggressive female conduct was rare in English art, for while the modern British matriarch may have *de facto* wielded much power in the household, canvases for public display and consumption preserved the status quo and kept the lady's secret. That this is more than a mock-war in this image is suggested by the overturned chair; the female portrait on the wall on the lady's side smiles at what transpires, while the male ancestor with the trappings of war in the portrait seems equally bemused at his male descendant's cowardice. The female here is, like many a New Woman in art, much larger than the male, and she does what *Punch* counterparts did not openly do – namely, fight with a man and thus physically intimidate him while simultaneously poking fun at the institution of marriage and the equality of the sexes.

Ultimately, the swooning female aesthete and the confident New Woman were both attacked in the pages of *Punch* for their peculiarity and aberration from the norm of ladylike conduct. They were visual jokes and sometimes even punchlines, and fine art paid them little heed, preferring instead to lavish pictorial attention on their retardataire, virtuous counterpart (or, ironically, on their wayward – yet potentially rescuable – moral opposite, the fallen woman). While on canvas, the tamer aspects of the personas of the aesthetic female and the New Woman appeared – for example, as protagonists gazing at flowers or playing sports, respectively – the more militant or intimidating attributes were ignored, 'airbrushed' and trivialized. As this brief iconological survey has indicated, both types were seen as emancipated to some degree as well as shockingly dangerous, with their radical assertions allegedly imperiling the innocence of other women and contaminating the reputation of 'fair womanhood' in general. In the end, the ongoing tension between old and new, traditional and modern, moral and immoral, remained constant, leaving English high art with no fully-fledged or very satisfactory pictorial reply to the so-called 'Woman Question' that refused to disappear from the nineteenth-century social, political and personal consciousness of artists, writers, critics and audiences.

NOTES

1. For more analysis of the model Victorian lady and wife in paintings, see S. Casteras, *Images of Victorian Womanhood in English Art* (London and Toronto: Associated University Presses, 1987), pp. 50–60.
2. On the subject of the readership of *Punch*, see D.J. Gray, 'A List of Comic Periodicals Published in Great Britain, 1800–1900, with a Prefatory Essay', *Victorian Periodicals Newsletter* (March 1972), 3–9.
3. As quoted in W. Hamilton, *The Aesthetic Movement in England* (London: Reeves and Turner, 1882), p. 25.
4. 'The Two Ideals', *Punch*, 77 (13 September 1879), 120.
5. 'The Aesthete to the Rose', *Punch*, 81 (1 October 1881), 154.
6. On the oddities of aesthetic language, see A. Adburgham, *A Punch History of Manners and Modes* (London: Hutchinson & Co., 1961), pp. 124–5.
7. On the near-epidemic of somnolent women, see Casteras, pp. 171–5.
8. V. Lee, *Miss Brown* (London: Routledge & Co., 1884), Book IV, chapter 6, p. 19.
9. An interesting chapter on autoeroticism entitled 'The Collapsing Woman: Solitary Vice and Restful Tumescence' is found in B. Dijkstra, *Idols of Perversity: Fantasies of Evil in Fin-de-siècle Culture* (Oxford and New York: Oxford University Press, 1986), pp. 64–82, especially 76–7 on English art.
10. For further discussion of critical reaction to the eroticism of this painting, see S. Casteras, 'Burne-Jones and the Pre-Raphaelite Circle at the Palace of the Aesthetes', in S. Casteras and C. Denney, eds, *The Grosvenor Gallery: A Palace of Art in Victorian England* (London and New Haven: Yale University Press, 1998), pp. 84–5.
11. Hamilton, p. 83.
12. From an article quoted in Hamilton, p. 111.
13. On the subject of the emancipated female, see e.g. J. Beckett and D. Cherry, eds, *The Edwardian Era* (London: Phaidon Press, 1987); L. Tickner, *The Spectacle of Women: Images of the Suffrage Campaign 1907–1914* (Chicago: University of Chicago Press, 1988); and C. Rover, *The 'Punch' Book of Women's Rights* (South Brunswick, N.J.: A.S. Barnes & Co., 1967).
14. On this subject see, e.g. B.J. Elliot, 'Covent Garden Follies: Beardsley's Masquerader Images of Poseurs and Voyeurs', *Oxford Art Journal*, 9 (1986), 38–48.
15. On the origin of the term 'New Woman' see e.g. E. Jordan, 'The Christening of the New Woman: May 1894', *The Victorian Newsletter* (May 1983), 19.
16. E. Linton, *The Girl of the Period and Other Social Essays* (London: Richard Bentley, 1883), pp. 2–9 passim.
17. This opinion is offered, e.g., by a contemporary such as Mrs Humphry Ward, *Manners for Women* (London: James Bowden, 1897), pp. 4–5: 'The girl of today, with her fine physical development ... is an improvement ... Her mind and character are strung up to a

firmness of which a sentimental heroine of fifty years since would have been thoroughly ashamed.'

18. Adburgham, p. 132.
19. A good source on this subject is A. Gengarelly, *Images of Women in the Mauve Decades: Edward Penfield and his Contemporaries* (Williamstown, Mass: Sterling and Francine Clark Art Institute, 1985), n.p. brochure.

14

The Power of Womanhood – Religion and Sexual Politics in the Writings of Ellice Hopkins

Sue Morgan

INTRODUCTION

Throughout the autumn of 1894, *The Daily Telegraph* documented the activities of a group of middle-class Christian women intent on seeking out and expelling prostitutes from London music halls notorious for their promotion of morally dubious entertainment. Entitled 'Prudes on the Prowl', the series was a hostile parody of the sexual prurience of the evangelical campaign for social purity – an organization which, according to the satirical *Punch*, was dominated by the interfering, self-righteous prudery of 'Mrs Prowlina Prys'.[1] Social purity reformers had come to public prominence during the latter decades of the nineteenth century, that period described by George Gissing as one of 'sexual anarchy'. Against a backdrop of increasing sexual scandal and 'white slavery' media scares, these pious women committed themselves to the moral purification of society through an elimination of prostitution and other forms of vice.[2]

As the orchestrator and leading exponent of purity politics, Ellice Hopkins epitomized the sense of elevated moral duty and social accountability that characterized much late Victorian evangelicalism. Sacrificing a promising literary career she had entered rescue work in 1866 after the death of her father William Hopkins, inspired by a commonality of suffering to 'devote herself to the cause of lost womanhood'.[3] Hannah More's phrase that 'action is the life of virtue' could have found no truer disciple. Hopkins' capacity for work was phenomenal, even by the standards of that indefatigable Dickensian philanthropist, Mrs Jellyby. Ten years of active campaigning for the greater legal protection of the young and sexually vulnerable was brought to an abrupt end by chronic ill-health, but she maintained an international profile within reform circles until her death in 1904, publishing almost 40 separate titles relating to social purity.

A lifelong spinster, Hopkins was an obvious target for the lampoons of the secular, libertinist press. She also earned herself a not insignificant degree of opprobrium from feminist colleagues, who viewed with alarm the preparedness of her vigilance committees to utilize coercive, interventionist methods of vice control such as enlarged powers of police surveillance and the forcible suppression of brothels. Josephine Butler, celebrated leader of the campaign to repeal the Contagious Diseases Acts, eventually disassociated herself from social purity tactics, disturbed at the new direction in feminist sexual politics and declaring herself convinced of 'the folly, and even wickedness, of all systems of *outward repression* of private immorality'.[4]

Repelled by the religious obscurantism and puritanical severity with which female social purists articulated their rigorous sexual code, contemporary critics easily and frequently conflated repressive forms of anti-vice agitation with the greater anti-sensualism of its perpetrators. However, a closer examination of Hopkins' sexual theory, best summarized in her penultimate book *The Power of Womanhood* published in 1899, reveals certain aspects that demand a serious re-reading of this evangelical prudish archetype. First, Hopkins' sexual Puritanism was driven not simply by the demands of religious tradition but by a powerful sense of gender-identification, incorporating a savage critique of the dominant moral double standard which acknowledged sexual activity in men as 'natural' and healthy, whilst pathologizing it in women.

Secondly, her discourse of anti-sensualism was also reconciled with a very pro-sensualist account of marital sexuality as will be seen. This shift resulted from her clear differentiation between sacred and profane forms of sexual activity. It was also related to the eclecticism of her religious milieu, for whilst a devout Anglican churchwoman, Hopkins' personal faith was considerably broader. An adolescent influenced by mid-century evangelical revivalism, she was an avid student of medieval mysticism and the High Churchmanship of John Henry Newman – a complex alliance of spiritual influences combining evangelical Puritanism with Anglo-Catholic sacramentalism that informed her understanding of human sexuality in unexpected and contradictory ways.

INTERPRETING THE BODY

A defining feature of the social purity movement was its attempt to infuse society with a level of sexual respectability through the mass dissemination of prescriptive moral literature. Early purity efforts at sex education were frequently excessive, harmful and plagued by class limitations and have subsequently been assessed by historians in wholly negative terms as explicitly concerned with the control and regulation of working class sexuality.[5] Viewed on its own terms, however, the desire to speak out openly on sexual matters at a time when this was still considered highly problematic at authoritative levels was radical indeed.

Hopkins' sincere belief that 'one could not expect virtue without knowledge'[6] brought her into direct confrontation with ecclesiastical positions that claimed sexual immorality as beyond the parameters of civilized Christian discourse. In July 1879 she submitted a paper to a Committee of Convocation entitled *A Plea for the Wider Action of the Church of England in the Prevention of the Degradation of Women* .... The *Plea* was an unprecedented attack by a woman upon the Church's continuing toleration of the sexual double standard and concomitant apathy towards the plight of the prostitute. Hopkins declared the Anglican Church a major contributor to the present lascivious climate through its 'utter want of all teaching or training on the all-important subject of purity'. Referring to the thousands of obscene prints, photographs and catalogues retrieved by the Vice Society over the previous 50 years, she was to remark with customary acidity, 'it does seem sardonic in this flood of foul speech to talk about keeping silence on this subject, which can only mean the Church enforcing silence that the Devil may be the better heard'.[7]

At the root of this conflict lay a fundamental discrepancy in the spiritual interpretation of social purity. Hopkins' understanding of the concept was informed by two main factors – her great love of science inherited from her father, a prominent Cambridge geologist and a highly incarnational theology. The centrality of the incarnation to her religious framework produced a surprisingly positive reading of the body and, by implication, sexual identity. She believed that the fullest and most complete expression of Christianity lay 'in the consecration of our bodies as well as our souls',[8] and that the attainment of purity constituted the very apex of the divine possibilities of human existence.

Hopkins consequently opposed those prelates who presented a reductionist account of purity as a purely negative suppression of vice and repudiated traditional Christian doctrines which taught the inherent depravity of human corporeality. 'This matter which we have been accustomed to call 'brute', gross, dead is … a glory and a wonder,' she wrote. 'We need to recognize the material part of us as a far more vital factor in the divine life … to teach with far more emphasis that the body is the temple of the Holy … its functions … sacramental.'[9]

This affirmative portrayal of social purity was tactically expedient in that it diffused the alarmist rhetoric of those who regarded purity as improper for female discussion. 'The purity which is unfit for a woman's eye is to me a very suspicious thing to begin with,' wrote Hopkins. She defended vigorously the right of women to enter public debates on sexuality, touching as it did on all the traditional trusts of womanhood: 'the sanctity of the family, the purity of the home, the loftiness of love and the sacredness of marriage'.[10] Her polemic on the collective moralizing power of female purity reformers appealed typically to an extension of the domestic spiritual custodianship of Victorian womanhood into the public sphere. 'Just as God gave up his only Son, so we must be prepared to give up our daughters sending them into the world to pour out their life-blood for its redemption,'[11] she wrote during a recruitment campaign for rescue workers. Women were called to be the moral saviours of the nation and, more particularly it would seem, of their less fortunate sisters.

RESCUING PROSTITUTES

By the end of the century, the original ideological impulse of the mid-Victorian boom in rescue societies within High Church and evangelical circles had begun to falter. Hopkins' efforts to revitalize the flagging movement comprised a series of exhausting lecturing tours resulting in the establishment of over 200 vigilance and rescue committees nationwide. Her vision was for a permanent and preventive approach to the problem of prostitution in contrast to the merely curative, 'bread, dripping and prayer' mentality of existing penitentiaries. 'We need to fence the cliff at the top, rather than provide ambulances at the bottom,'[12] she declared on frequent occasions. Her own rescue organization, the Ladies' Association for the Care of Friendless Girls, accordingly reflected a more personally involved, less punitive regime of rehabilitation, with smaller, homelier refuges and less emphasis on continuous penitence.

Hopkins has been described as 'one of the most rhapsodically magdalenist voices'[13] of the period. Her sentimental discourse on prostitution deployed with consummate skill that essentially Victorian narrative of female seduction which, from the publication of Mrs Gaskell's *Ruth* in 1853, had earned increasing sympathy for the prostitute as tragic social victim. Hopkins' seduction melodramas, whilst they denied the prostitute any powers of active agency, succeeded in absolving her from blame entirely. Through the overtly religious metaphors of temptation, fall, guilt and repentance, Hopkins traced the apotheosis of a poverty-stricken 'damaged pearl', culpable only of yielding to innocent love and betrayed by aristocratic male lust, into an inspirational figure of abject remorse and passionate discipleship.

According to this model of sexual redemption, the unrepentant or recalcitrant prostitute was to pose something of an insurmountable problem for rescue workers. More significantly, however, the subtext of Hopkins' rhetoric reveals that female sexual proclivity was no impediment to the salvation of the prostitute, rather it was male depravity that required spiritual and moral reorientation. One of the strongest feminist currents in her writing is in the portrayal of a sexual system where men are constantly depicted as the sexual aggressors and perpetrators of the moral destitution of women. In her 1883 pamphlet *The Ride of Death*, an apocalyptic scene is depicted in which a great multitude of women stand at the brink of the river of death into which they are being pushed and hastened. 'And who has driven them into that position,' she challenges, 'Men; men who ought to have protected them instead of degrading them; men who have taken advantage of a woman's weakness to gratify their own selfish pleasure.'[14]

As Judith Walkowitz has demonstrated, little resemblance to social reality occurs in such accounts.[15] Yet these 'narratives of sexual danger' evinced clear political objectives as, through the creation of a climate of intense guilt and moral inferiority, Hopkins sought to discredit male sexual power in the minds of her readership. She ultimately mistrusted the merit of a system of female penitentiaries which 'only touch women, and leave the really vital factor, the man, untouched'.[16] In order to get to the root cause of the problem, therefore, she instigated a network of male purity leagues in 1883 entitled the White Cross Army (WCA) under the sponsorship of Bishop Lightfoot.[17]

MALE CHASTITY

Hopkins remained singularly unimpressed by traditional religious and medical arguments that posited the male sexual urge as a biologically given imperative. Her appropriation of moral Darwinism suggested the profound malleability of male sexual identity, open to influence by social context and cultural expectation. 'Men are by nature just as modest and full of personal self-respect ... as women,' she asserted, 'had not all their natural and finer instincts been trodden down ... by the dictates of the world and the low tone of social opinion'.[18] Her aim was to sweep the country in a network of male societies committed to social purity, convinced that sexual self-control was a mark of superior spiritual development and that what might at first require a supreme effort of will would eventually become a 'natural' disposition itself.

Aware of the limited appeal that a message of sexual chastity might have for men, she popularized the concept by projecting a flattering construction of masculinity combining romantic images of the chivalrous knight with current notions of 'muscular Christianity'. 'Treat all women with respect and ... endeavour to defend them from wrong',[19] was the first obligation of the WCA, its members wooed with stories of medieval heroism in a compelling yet extremely ambivalent appeal to male protectionism.

It was the evangelical language of moral outrage, however, that most characterized Hopkins' anti-sensualist passages on the perceived 'bestiality' of male sexual behaviour – 'for this ye know,' she quoted, 'that no whoremonger nor unclean person hath any inheritance in the kingdom of Christ and God'.[20] In the minds of purity reformers, the spectre of prostitution, illegitimate births and the increasing occurrence of public divorce suits formed nothing less than 'a moral sewer laid on to the whole nation, poisoning the deepest springs of its life'.[21] Against this the institution of marriage presented an increasingly significant metaphor for the fortification of personal and national stability.

HOPKINS AND THE NEW WOMAN

Throughout the 1880s an extraordinarily high level of public disputation ensued as feminists and progressive thinkers alike proffered alternative strategies for marriage. The debate was stimulated by the immensely popular 'New Woman' fiction, whose outspoken defiance of sexual norms evoked a response of deep anxiety amongst many religious commentators. Like her Anglican colleagues, Hopkins reiterated the indissolubility of the sacrament of holy matrimony on the grounds that Christ himself used marriage as a symbol for his eternal and imperishable relationship with the church. Marriage for Hopkins, as for the poet Coventry Patmore, was no mere contract, but a sacred and permanent bond, a 'sacramental union of love and life'.[22]

In a chapter from *The Power of Womanhood* entitled 'The Modern Woman and her Future', Hopkins responds in a particularly hostile fashion to Mona Caird's article 'A Defence of the So-Called Wild Women'. Caird's profound misgivings on the iniquitous state of marital relations had initiated much of the early controversy on marriage. In this essay she decries the morality of large families, an insight on marital sexual restraint with which Hopkins would not necessarily have disagreed. 'The rights of the existing race are at least as great as those of the coming one ...' exclaimed Caird, 'there is something pathetically absurd in this sacrifice to their children of generation after generation of grown people.' Nevertheless Hopkins ignores the explicit neo-Malthusianism which was the basis of Caird's argument and instead construes it as a simple advocacy of laissez-faire sexual ethics, retorting, 'I suggest that it would be still more pathetically absurd to see the ... whole noble future of the human race, sacrificed to their unruly wills and affections, their passions and desires.'[23]

Hopkins' conflation of decadentism with the *modus vivendi* of the New Woman was not an uncommon one, highlighting the privileged class position of many 'advanced women' by contrasting the psychological, economic and emotional vulnerability of the ordinary wife and mother:

5

the burthened mother of a family ... cannot compete in companionship with the highly-cultured young unmarried lady, with the leisure to post herself up in the latest book or the newest political movement ... . It is therefore on the woman that any loosening of the permanence of the marriage tie will chiefly fall in untold suffering.[24]

Whilst inspired by Christian marital values of permanency and loyalty, Hopkins' defence of the sanctity of family life is refined by a gender-based pragmatism that recognizes only too well the economic and legal fragility of many women's situation. A common critique of Victorian religious reform sentiment has been its preparedness merely to tamper with superficialities rather than address any fundamental transformation of the social structure.[25] Yet in her account of marriage, Hopkins presents a controversial critique of the social decadentism not just of the New Woman, but the entire upper echelons of society. Explicit connections are made between inflated living standards, delayed marriages and levels of prostitution as Hopkins advocates a radical simplification of lifestyle. 'If we are to prevent or even lessen, the degradation of women ...' she announced, 'we must be content to revolutionize much in the order of our own life, and adopt a lower and simpler standard of living.'[26]

Hopkins' revisioning of marriage left no room for the idle, ornamental Victorian woman whose social respectability had been brought at the cost of her unfortunate sister. Forefronting the Puritan values of simplicity, frugality and earnest labour, her conservative moral pragmatism placed her on the offensive against what she perceived as the overly intellectualized, non-practical and sexually promiscuous lifestyle of the New Woman. In one of her more cutting jibes, she depicted these women as damagingly akin to the tadpole – 'all head, no hands and much active and frivolous tail.'[27]

Purity writings on marriage endeavoured to expose the disorder, chaos and detriment to women emerging from 'advanced', progressive interpretations of voluntary sexual liaisons. Fiercely intolerant of any transient form of physical relations that threatened to undermine the sacred state of marriage, women social purists fulminated against the growing presence of sexual unruliness with puritanical zeal. But to what extent was such censoriousness replicated when considering sex within marriage?

MARITAL SEXUALITY

Throughout the nineteenth century, conservative religious thought continued to stress the primarily prophylactic function of marriage, adhering to orthodox Christian prescriptions of procreation and the conjugal debt. Alongside the propagation of this dominant doctrine of sexual containment, however, was the burgeoning Miltonic view of marriage as a site of sensual delight rather than a mere remedy for concupiscence.[28]

Many purity reformers, whilst unavowedly Augustinian in their belief that lust represented the enslavement of the higher moral senses,were anxious to point out that in the relation of social purity to marriage, 'Christians do not hold the manichaean doctrine that passion is absolutely evil'.[29] Hopkins herself declared an indebtedness to Milton on frequent occasions. Repudiating the traditional Augustinian correlation of Edenic sexuality with sinful lust she described the joy of spousal intimacy in typically Miltonic terms as a glimpse into the 'paradise of the ideal' – as 'that last bit of Eden that is left us in this poor, sinful, sorrowful world'.[30] In what amounted to a radical reversal of dominant theological scruples on human sexuality, the pre-Fall perfection of the garden was contemplated as a model of passionate matrimonial love where wife and husband gave 'without stint or limit' in their physical and spiritual devotion to each other. Only by aspiring to such a relationship she suggested, could humanity regain its paradise lost.

Hopkins' exaltation of marital love was a direct consequence of her sacralizing of human reproductive abilities. Her sacramentalist understanding of sexual relations, meant that for her, as for Patmore, sex was heavily symbolic of God's relationship with humanity. It was, she argued, in the moment of marital union that wife and husband approximated most closely the life-giving powers of the divine. The procreative impulse was the pinnacle of God's gifts and the sexual organs the 'inner sanctum' of the temple of the body.

Hopkins' representation of the sexual act as primary analogy of the divine-human encounter meant that her discourse of physical passion was frequently endowed with semi-mystical qualities. In her pamphlet *The Secret and Method of Purity* (1883) she wrote of the sanctifying purpose of procreation as an elevation of fleshly bodies 'where the material ... is taken up and transfused into the divine, and gives rise to a union deeper and purer even than the communion of saints'.[31] Sex was also rationalized as a temporal prefiguration of the blissful spiritual delights of the hereafter as, in an undisguised metaphor for marital eroticism, she remarked upon 'the purity of the Alpine peak, "Rosy and rapt with lovely lights of heaven" that can be found within the loving Christian home'.[32]

This pro-sensual stance, in marked contrast to her condemnatory attitude towards other forms of sexual activity, was a logical extension of the distinction between profane and sacred forms of sexual behaviour, that is, between lust and love. Marriage constituted the definitive boundary between these two states of sexual ardour, circumscribing and sacralizing fulfilling sexual experience. The pure affection of conjugal love was for Hopkins sexuality in its most holy form – 'the most sacred thing on earth'.[33]

Her effusive tenor was not limited to an uncritical advocacy of the biblical injunction to 'be fruitful and multiply', however, for she maintained a vehement opposition to coercive forms of marital sexuality. This attitude complemented a parallel mainstream feminist debate surrounding greater awareness of the sexual dangers within marriage for women. Experiences of non-consensual sex and perpetual involuntary childbirth had led feminist campaigners such as Elizabeth Wolstenholme Elmy to an outright condemnation of this unjust situation.[34] Unlike Elmy, who was an ardent individual rights activist, Hopkins never referred to marriage in such derogatory terms as 'legalised prostitution'. Nevertheless, she did invoke the moral law of purity to warn that those who had indulged in premarital promiscuity or licentiousness would find it far harder to exercise their duty of self-control as husbands, believing that the perils of enforced motherhood were nothing less than a blatant disregard of the fundamental Christian principle of chivalrous, self-sacrificing masculinity. She cautions her male readership:

> If you are married then remember the Christian ideal, that the husband is to love the wife and give himself for her ... all that you have and all that you are you will hold for the good of the woman you love. And there will be one woman the less in England to fill an early grave or have her constitution broken for life by having her children faster than her strength can bear.[35]

Sexual non-reciprocity within marriage was an anathema to Hopkins, both as an abhorrent continuation of male physical abuse of women and as a violation of the sacramental status of the marital bond. Whether configured through the moral suasion of evangelical purity rhetoric or as an issue of civil libertarianism, feminist and social purity discourse coalesces at this point with recommendation of male sexual restraint borne out of a common concern for the physical well-being of the married woman. But when contemplating the extent to which certain secular feminists like Elmy were prepared to develop their critique of sexual abuse within marriage, the pro-sensualism of Hopkins' purity feminism becomes more apparent still.

PROMOTING FEMALE SEXUAL DESIRE

In her study of nineteenth-century feminist theories of sexual continence Sheila Jeffreys explains how one solution to the problem of female sexual oppression was to infer a virtual eradication of the marital union except in cases of absolute procreative necessity.[36] Alternative systems of substitute, non-genital 'psychic love' were proffered by Elmy and others, illustrating the ultimate sensual encounter as a sort of ecstatic mental fantasy. Physical sex was conversely depicted as innately degrading, animalistic and evidence of a lower form of evolutionary existence. The sexual austerity of this particular stance, which aimed to transcend or deny the body in preference to the intellectual stimulation of love, was constructed in terms of a rigid body/spirit dualism, where, in an unavoidable anti-corporeal cast, 'sex and the delights of the flesh' were regarded as inherently defiling and 'most deadly to spirit life'.[37] This is a subtle, but all-important shift of emphasis from that of purity feminism's theory of marital sexuality. As has been noted, Hopkins stressed the absolute proximity of the physical and the spiritual within marriage effecting a far closer integration of the traditional binary oppositions of mind and body. Through the oft-cited Pauline ethic of mutual consideration and spousal self-surrender, her Christian ideal of marriage viewed physical sex as the direct route to a heightened experience of ultimate creativity, whereas for feminists like Elmy, sensual satisfaction was only possible through a complete circumvention of the bodily act. Hopkins' positive sacramental reading of the body, constructed over and against the dominant anti-carnal, misogynist mindset of the Anglican hierarchy, led her to view with suspicion any denigration of the physical aspect of matrimony. A fascinating constellation of attitudes is present here in which the desire to advance the value and spiritual worth of human corporeality prompted Hopkins to castigate an articulate group of radical feminists in language not dissimilar to that used against the religious asceticism of her conservative fellow churchmen:

> One most undesirable, and may I add unnatural result noticeable among the more advanced section [of women] is a certain distaste for marriage, a tendency to look upon it as something low and animal, which strikes me as simply a fatal attitude for women to take up.[38]

At this historical juncture then, Hopkins' brand of social purity feminism, so long considered the epitome of sexual prurience, inadvertently formed a nascent discourse of active female desire. In earlier attacks against the double standard, mid-century feminist sexual politics had simply consolidated the passionless, chaste ideal of Victorian womanhood in order to claim a higher moral ground. Whilst Hopkins employed this tactic in her appraisal of the plight of the prostitute, social purity's additional focus on marital relations represented a perceptible shift in the defining of female sexuality. Because sex was rationalized as a spiritual act and sanctioned by an authoritative religious tradition, it provided a socially acceptable way for women to engage in sexual pleasure, albeit heavily circumscribed within heterosexual, matrimonial and class-based limitations.

Even those historians sharply critical of the conservatising and repressive impact of the movement for social purity have acknowledged its achievement in successfully converting the sexual culture of the middle classes to one of consensual and mutual marital sex. As Ellen DuBois and Linda Gordon have admitted, 'Inasmuch as they believed that sexual drive and initiative were primarily male, they understood this as women's right to say no.'[39] Vigorous campaigns surrounding sex education for women meant that purity feminism at least 'opened up new heterosexual expectations for middle-class women'.[40]

Whether Hopkins' celebration of marital sex was anything more than a straightforward equation of female sexuality with motherhood is difficult to assess, as the texts themselves fail to distinguish between sex for the purposes of procreation and sex for pleasure only. As Michael Mason has argued, medical acknowledgement of any female sexual drive was generally allied with the maternal instinct at this time, with theories of the 'utero-orgasm' reiterating the extent to which the possession of ovaries and womb influenced the entire physical and psychological status of women. A sexuality that is never disconnected from the womb may appear a rather ambiguous advance of course, yet as Mason also observes, procreation was the most significant dignifier of female eroticism in the nineteenth century.[41]

CONCLUSION

The received Foucauldian insight that the Victorians did not so much repress sex, as positively produce, multiply and disperse it is nowhere better illustrated than during the late nineteenth-century campaign for social purity. As the movement's major spokeswoman, Ellice Hopkins was responsible for not only naming female sexuality but placing it firmly within the orbit of ecclesiastical discourse. Many of the strands of her argument were irreconcilable. Her sympathetic approach to the prostitute, for example, was countermanded by her accession to more interventionist, coercive legal policies; her castigation of male sexual behaviour interspersed by pleas for male protection. Hopkins' sexual politics manifestly depended less upon theoretical analysis and more upon the power of emotive persuasion, yet her success as a religious and political mobiliser was unquestionable in so far as she was single-handedly responsible for the incorporation of thousands of Christian women and men onto rescue or vigilance committees. Lacking the sensual charisma of a Josephine Butler or a Christabel Pankhurst, she utilized her physical frailness, diminutive size and celibate status to great effect as tangible, visible reinforcements of her message of purity.[42]

Her contribution to the Anglican clergy's volte-face towards the topic of purity cannot be overestimated. Successful precisely because it appealed to conservative notions of femininity and masculinity whilst simultaneously subverting them, Hopkins' rhetoric illustrated the many ambiguities of women's sexual discourse at this time, yet clearly demonstrated the display of female agency and power through religious and devotional language. Her own paradigm of womanhood reflected her reluctant realization that sexual innocence was no longer an adequate protection for young women. A new moral order had arrived, signalling the demise of Ruskinian

222 *Sue Morgan*

notions of a sheltered queen or indeed, Patmore's innocent but
sexually anaesthetized angel:

> May ... [God] not be leading us to form a wider, deeper, stronger
> ideal; to aim for our girls not so much at Innocence, with her
> fading wreath of flowers – fading, as, alas! they must ever fade in
> a world like this – but to aim at Virtue, with her victor's crown of
> gold, tried in the fire? May it not be that His Divine providence is
> constraining us to take as our ideal for our womanhood, not the
> old sheltered garden, but a strong city of God, having founda-
> tions, whose very gates are made of pearl, through which
> nothing that defileth is suffered to enter, and whose common
> ways are paved with gold?[43]

Hopkins' concern to transform the sexual morality of the present
order, articulated in an unashamed vocabulary of anti-sensualism,
was borne out of an overwhelming desire to eradicate all forms of
female sexual abuse. She achieved this through the demarcation of
marriage as sole location of the right ordering of sexuality, investing
it with sacred proportions and producing a distinctly pro-sensualist
account in the process. Whilst it is unlikely that she envisaged
marital sexual pleasure outside of the reproductive role, she did
much to construct a domestic aura of male self-control, mutual
concern and sympathetic sexual rapport that was extremely conducive to the anticipation of female sexual pleasure. Hopkins, like
many female purity reformers,was the quarry of her contemporaries' simplistic associations of religiosity and sexual prurience, yet
it is evident from the above that accusations that pious prudery
belied the radical implications of her sexual agenda.

NOTES

1. See *Punch* (27 October 1894) for a description of social purist Laura
    Ormiston Chant as 'Mrs Prowlina Pry' and Lucy Bland, 'Purifying
    the Public Sphere: Feminist Vigilantes in late Victorian England',
    Women's History Review, Vol. 1, No. 3 (1992), 397–441, for a recent
    examination of the feminist implications of this particular feature of
    the social purity campaign.
2. The panic surrounding the so-called 'white slave trade', the
    trafficking in young girls across to Europe, was prompted in 1885 by
    the journalist W.T. Stead in his celebrated *Pall Mall Gazette* series 'The
    Maiden Tribute of Babylon'.

3. R. Barrett, *Ellice Hopkins: A Memoir* (London: Wells, Gardner, Darton & Co., 1907), p. 6.
4. J. Butler, *Personal Reminiscences of a Great Crusade* (London: Marshall, 1896), p. 174.
5. See, for example, E. Bristow, *Vice and Vigilance: Purity Movements in Britain since 1700* (Dublin: Gill and MacMillan, 1977), and J. Walkowitz, *Prostitution and Victorian Society* (Cambridge: Cambridge University Press, 1980).
6. E. Hopkins, *Per Angusta ad Augusta* (London: Hatchards, 1883), p. 4.
7. E. Hopkins, *The Present Moral Crisis* (1886), p. 6.
8. E. Hopkins, *The Standard of the White Cross* (London: Hatchards, 1885), p. 14.
9. E. Hopkins, *A Plea for the Wider Action of the Church of England* (London: Hatchards, 1879), p. 13.
10. Hopkins, *The Standard of the White Cross*, p. 3.
11. Cited in R. Barrett, *Ellice Hopkins: A Memoir* (London: Wells, Gardner, Darton & Co., 1907), p. 47.
12. Ibid., p. 10.
13. M. Mason, *The Making of Victorian Sexual Attitudes* (Oxford: Oxford University Press, 1994) p. 105. See J. Walkowitz, *City of Dreadful Delight: Narratives of Sexual Danger in Late-Victorian London* (London: Virago, 1992), pp. 87–92 for the impact of literary melodrama upon Josephine Butler's narratives of prostitution.
14. E. Hopkins, *The Ride of Death* (London: Hatchards, 1883), p. 4.
15. Rescue workers and reformers frequently failed to acknowledge the large working-class sector of the prostitute's business, the financial benefits and the complex structure of their often supportive culture; see J. Walkowitz, *Prostitution and Victorian Society* (Cambridge: Cambridge University Press, 1980).
16. Hopkins, *A Plea for the Wider Action of the Church of England*, p. 9.
17. The White Cross Army was formed in 1883 when Hopkins was asked by Bishop Lightfoot to address the Young Men's Institute in Bishop Auckland, Durham. Prior to the meeting Hopkins and Lightfoot drew up a scheme of five obligations including of the promotion of male purity and the protection of all women from degradation. Over half the male audience pledged their immediate support to the organization. The White Cross Society, as it was eventually known, became an international Anglican movement for moral education.
18. E. Hopkins, *Is it Natural?* (London: Hatchards, 1883), p. 9.
19. E. Hopkins, *Damaged Pearls. An Appeal to Working Men* (London: Hatchards, 1884), p. 3.
20. I Cor. 6. 9, 10.
21. E. Hopkins, *The Power of Womanhood, or Mothers and Sons* (London: Wells Gardner, 1899), p. 148.
22. Ibid., p. 147.
23. M. Caird, 'A Defence of the So-Called Wild Women', *Nineteenth Century* (May 1892), cited in E. Hopkins, *The Power of Womanhood*, p. 150.
24. Hopkins, *The Power of Womanhood*, p. 151. See L. Dowling, 'The Decadent and the New Woman', *Nineteenth-Century Fiction*, 33 (1979), 434–53.

25. See, for example, D. Gorham, '"The Maiden Tribute of Modern Babylon" Re-Examined: Child Prostitution and the Idea of Childhood in late-Victorian England', *Victorian Studies*, Spring (1978), 353–79.
26. Hopkins, *The Power of Womanhood*, p. 153.
27. Ibid., p. 156.
28. See J. Maynard, *Victorian Discourses in Sexuality and Religion* (Cambridge, Cambridge University Press, 1993) for a helpful discussion of this.
29. Rev. A.T. Lyttleton, *The Vanguard*, April (1887), 25.
30. Hopkins, *Damaged Pearls*, p. 11.
31. E. Hopkins, *The Secret and Method of Purity* (London: Hatchards, 1886), p. 11.
32. Ibid., p. 11. It is remarkable, not to say a little ironic, that Hopkins felt able to speak so confidently about marital passion in the light of her own spinsterhood. She was, as far as we can know from available sources, a confirmed celibate throughout her life. As should be evident from this chapter, however, interpreting her discourses in terms of a simple model of sublimated sexuality denies the complexity of this intriguing situation.
33. Hopkins, *The Power of Womanhood*, p. 151.
34. See S. Jeffreys, *The Spinster and Her Enemies: Feminism and Sexuality 1880–1920* (London: Pandora Press, 1987) for a useful discussion of Elmy's strategy.
35. E. Hopkins, *Man and Woman: the Christian Ideal* (1883), p. 14.
36. See Jeffreys, *The Spinster and Her Enemies*, pp. 27–53.
37. Margaret Sibthorp, cited in Jeffreys, *The Spinster and her Enemies*, p. 40.
38. Hopkins, *The Power of Womanhood*, p. 142.
39. Ellen DuBois and Linda Gordon, 'Seeking Ecstasy on the Battlefield: Danger and Pleasure in Nineteenth Century Sexual Thought', *Feminist Studies*, vol. 9, no. 1, Spring (1983), 13.
40. Walkowitz, *City of Dreadful Delight*, p. 7.
41. M. Mason, *The Making of Victorian Sexual Attitudes* p. 199. See pp. 195–205 for a fuller discussion of women's sexuality.
42. See Frank Mort, *Dangerous Sexualities: Medico-Moral Politics in England Since 1830* (London & New York: Routledge & Kegan Paul, 1987), p. 121.
43. Hopkins, *The Power of Womanhood*, p. 143.

Index

Good Words, 143, 171 n.38
Goethe, J.W. von, 125
Goffe, Eliza Fanny, 129
Gollock, Mina, 181
Gordon, Linda, 220
Gotch, Thomas, 204
Graham, Dorothy, 145
Greenwell, Dora, 137–141
Greenwell, William, 137, 138
Greg, W.R., 174, 184 n.12
Gubar, Susan M., 129
Guido, 53–5
Gurney, Archer, 163, 164–5

Hamilton, Walter, 196
Hampson, R.T., 160
Hardy, Thomas, 98, 128
Havergal, Frances Ridley, 3, 129, 141–3
Hegel, G.F.W., 108, 109
Helsinger, E.K., 153
Hildegard of Bingen, 66, 77 n.10
Hogarth, William, 201
Holbrook, David, 118
Hopkins, Ellice, 5, 209–24 passim
Hopkins, Gerard Manley, 51–2, 65
Hopkins, William, 209
Howitt, Mary, 7, 26 n.6
Humphreys, Cecil Frances, see Alexander, C.F.
Hurwitz, Siegmund, 117
hymns, collections of
A Child's Christian Year (Yonge), 130, 136
Hymns and Meditations (Waring), 130
Hymns for Infant Minds (Taylor & Taylor), 130
Hymns for Little Children (Alexander), 130, 132, 136
The Invalid's Hymn Book (Elliott), 129

Ibsen, Henry, 46
Immaculate Conception, 165
Infant Custody Bill (1839), 9, 27 n.15
Ingelow, Jean, 138, 140
Islam; Moslems, 179, 181

James, John Angel, 147
Jeffreys, Sheila, 219
Jerrold, Douglas William 16, 23
Jesuits, 93, 94, 96
Jesus Christ, 67, 68, 70, 71, 72, 73, 74, 86, 131, 132, 133, 134, 135, 138, 140, 142, 143, 148, 150, 161–7, 173, 176, 178, 188
Jews, Judaism, 82, 86, 121
Jewsbury, Geraldine, 23, 27 n.13
Joan of Arc, 58, 59
John the Baptist, 164
Joseph (husband of Mary), 161–2
Judaism, see Jews
Julian of Norwich, 66
Jung, Carl Gustav, 117

Kant, Immanuel, 108, 109
Keble, John, 159, 163, 164–5
Kempe, Margery, 73
Kingsford, Anna (Annie Bonus), 2, 48–62 passim
Kingsley, Charles, 51
Koltuv, Barbara, 117, 118
Kristeva, Julia, 106, 110, 113, 115, 118, 121, 125

Lacan, 68, 74
Ladies Association for the Care of Friendless Girls, 213
Leapor, Mary, 128
Lee, Frederick George, 161
Lee, Vernon (Violet Paget), 193
Leech, John, 196
Leeson, Jane, 130
Leighton, Frederic, 204
Lewes, George Henry, 79
Lightfoot, J.B., 214, 223 n.17
Lilith, 117–27 passim
Linton, Eliza Lynn, 200
Locke, John, 108
Luke, Jemima, 130
Luther, Martin, 140
Lyne, Joseph Leicester (Fr Ignatius), 164

MacDonald, George, 3, 117–27 passim
madonna figure, 81, 89, 189